DIANA
DORS

DIANA
DORS

Hurricane in Mink

DAVID BRET

BOOKS

N'oublie pas...
La vie sans amis c'est comme
un jardin sans fleurs

This book is dedicated to my friend, *la grande chanteuse* Barbara (1930–97) who would have been eighty this year....and to Amália Rodrigues (1920–99) who would have been ninety. My greatest inspirations!

First published in Great Britain in 2010 by
JR Books, 10 Greenland Street, London NW1 0ND
www.jrbooks.com

ISBN 978-1-907532-10-8

1 3 5 7 9 10 8 6 4 2

Typeset by Saxon Graphics Ltd, Derby
Printed by MPG Books Ltd, Bodmin, Cornwall

Acknowledgements

Writing this book would not have been possible had it not been for the inspiration, criticisms and love of that select group of individuals who, whether they be in this world or the next, I will always regard as my true family and *autre coeur*:

Barbara, Irene Bevan, Marlene Dietrich, René Chevalier, Axel Dotti, Dorothy Squires and Roger Normand, *que vous dormez en paix*. Lucette Chevalier, Jacqueline Danno, Héléne Delavault, Tony Griffin, Betty and Gérard Garmain, Annick Roux, John and Anne Taylor, Terry Sanderson, Charley Marouani, David and Sally Bolt. Also a very special mention for Amália Rodrigues, Joey Stefano, those *hiboux, fadistas* and *amis de foutre* who happened along the way, and *mes enfants perdus*. Thanks too to Chris Rogers and Theo Morgan.

And where would I be without Jeremy Robson and the munificent team at JR Books? Likewise my agent Guy Rose and his lovely wife, Alex? Also to my wife, Jeanne, for putting up with my bad moods and for still being the keeper of my soul. And finally a *grand chapeau bas* to Diana, for having lived it.

David Bret

Contents

Introduction

'When I first embarked on my acting career, a piece of advice I repeatedly heard was that one must develop the skin of a rhinoceros in order to survive the terrible notices which inevitably come from the critics, and the dreadful backbiting from other contemporaries in the business.'

Diana Dors suffered more than her share of both, not least the indignity of being touted as 'The British Marilyn Monroe', or 'The English Bardot' – unfairly so, because she was no less original than the tragic American beauty, equally charismatic, certainly more down to earth than the French sex-kitten, and many would agree as good an actress as both when given the appropriate material. In *Yield to the Night*, one of the finest of all the *films noir*, she proved outstanding as the condemned murderess, a self-effacing performance that went some way towards the abolition of the death sentence in Britain.

When her controversial lifestyle looked like putting paid to her film career, Diana added another string to her bow – that of a surprisingly versatile cabaret entertainer and an accomplished jazz singer, though sadly she only got around to recording one album of the genre. Then, as her figure became a little fuller, she developed into an equally gifted character actress. The emphasis was still on sex, though by now she had become adept at self-parody, another facet of her seemingly limitless talent which saw her penning several witty and insightful volumes of memoirs. Diana Dors pulled no fewer punches criticising others than she always had herself: there were no prisoners!

It is of course for her blonde-bombshell image that Diana will be best remembered, and the trappings which went with it: the flashy cars and mansions, the Darnell gowns, the glitzy no-expense-spared all-night shindigs, the sex parties with two-way mirrors through which even her children were permitted to watch the goings-on in the room below...and a trio of abortions.

Then, of course, there were the men. Her first lovers, when she was just 14, were American GIs stationed in her native Swindon during World War II. These early relationships were just for fun, but when fame beckoned, love took on a different meaning. Like her rivals – one also thinks of Jayne Mansfield – Diana had the unfortunate knack of always choosing the wrong kind of man. After each failed affair, she invariably declared herself the injured party, when almost always she had been the orchestrator of whatever catastrophe had taken place. It was as if the highlight of the romance had been that anticipation of mental and physical suffering. One of her three husbands was a psychopath and serial cheat who beat her black and blue, used her earnings to finance his nefarious activities, and finally succumbed to syphilis, aged just 34. Her celebrity lovers included method actor Rod Steiger and Tommy Yeardye, the co-founder of the Vidal Sassoon empire who accompanied her on location, and promptly went off and had a fling with Rock Hudson. Then there were the pop stars, invariably married, whose lives she turned upside down but who nevertheless enjoyed every moment of the hedonistic lifestyle which continued almost until the very end.

It was only in her later years that she found the happiness for which she had searched her whole life: three sons and a doting husband who, when she died of cancer, mourned her for just five months before taking his own life.

Diana Dors was a national institution. This is her story.

Chapter One

The Swindon Years: Darling of the GIs

Her parentage remains enshrouded in mystery. She was born Diana Mary Fluck on 23 October 1931, at the Haven Nursing Home in Swindon, Wiltshire. The father whose name appears on her birth certificate is Albert Edward Sidney Fluck – Bert – a former World War I veteran, though in her memoirs, for reasons known only to herself, Diana refers to him as Peter. Bert had served with the Royal Warwickshire Regiment in India, suffered a bout of malaria that had left him with a weak heart, and had been posted to France – where he almost lost an eye when an enemy grenade had been tossed into the trench where he was billeted. In peacetime, when not working in the accounts department of Great Western Railways, Bert could be found at his Masonic Lodge – where he held the position of Worshipful Master – or playing the piano at the local working men's club, or the one at the Swindon Empire. Diana was a so-called 'black baby', on account of near-suffocation during delivery. Delivered after a 72-hour labour, she had been pronounced dead and removed to an anteroom while doctors had fought to save the life of her 42-year-old mother who, after 13 years of marriage, had long since given up hope of ever having a child. Fortunately, one of the nurses had observed that Diana had still been breathing, and she too had been saved. Bert had been witness to none of this: in his opinion, having babies was a woman's job – his friends at the Masonic Lodge needed him far more than his wife did.

Diana's mother, Mary (Winifred Maud Mary), had been born

in Somerset. Her mother, Georgina Dors, one of eight children of a Somerset farmer, had married Elijah Payne at 16 and by the age of 20 had four children by him, including Mary, before running off to Wales with her brother-in-law, James. Here they had lived as a common-law couple, while telling everyone they were married, and Georgina had five more children – after each one doing a 'moonlight flit' to another part of the country to avoid having each baby baptised and the truth coming out. In the days before the Welfare State they had supported their brood as best they could – Payne working on the farms, Georgina taking in washing.

Mary herself was no stranger to scandal. In her late teens, while working as a lady's maid for a wealthy local family, she had fallen for the son of the household, who was subsequently 'deported' to Australia from bringing the family name into disrepute. Why they had not taken the easier option of firing the maid, Diana never explained. In 1914, Mary married a local man, William Padget, and soon afterwards they relocated to Swindon to look for work. Mary took a job as a postwoman – one of the first in the district – but that same month war was declared, and Padget enlisted for military service. So too had one of Mary's brothers, leaving his young fiancée to be looked after by Georgina Dors and James Payne – who promptly eloped with her!

William Padget was an early casualty of the war, and his death coincided with Albert Fluck's discharge – he and Padget's widow met at a Swindon dancehall, and married on 9 March 1918 – Mary was 28 and Bert four years younger. Their honeymoon took place at Osborne House, Queen Victoria's former residence on the Isle of Wight, then a convalescent home to which Bert had been sent to recover following a relapse after his wartime ordeal. Home for the Flucks was a respectable semi at 210 Marlborough Road. Their marriage appears to have been a contented but complicated one because, until Diana's arrival, it had openly involved three people. Gerald Lack was a young bachelor who lodged with the Flucks for much of the time: the trio shared a car and did everything together – sometimes even sharing the same room when they went on holiday. If Bert was preoccupied with one of his club functions, Lack would escort Mary to the theatre or cinema, or take her dancing. This free and easy *ménage à trois* came to an abrupt halt, however, when Mary learned that she was pregnant and the two men in her life began arguing over which of them was the child's father. Lack stormed out of their lives for good – returning briefly to attend Diana's christening on 13 December, when Mary insisted that he be registered as one of the godparents, just in case anything happened to her husband. In view of his wartime afflictions, Bert's doctors had given him 10 years to live at the most (though he would survive much longer than this). Today, of course, the child's paternity might have been scientifically determined, but in those days there was no such thing as DNA tests and it is quite likely that Diana Dors – or her mother – never really knew which man was her father.

Diana's childhood appears to have been happy and privileged. She would lovingly recall the seaside summer holidays with her parents, always at the same guesthouse in Weston-super-Mare, where she had genuinely believed the 'Aunt Bessie' who ran the establishment to have been an actual relative. There were the harvest festivals, the picnics in the bluebell woods, the trips to Wales, the outings to the theatre with her parents. Throughout her life she would remain closer to her mother than her father, who she dismissed as cold and remote: 'I was never a Daddy's girl. As far as I can make out, I had not one single point of which he approved. My love and affection went completely to my mother – but I adored every other male in sight and grew up with a desire to captivate the opposite sex.' The reason for Bert's indifference, of course, had much to do with his having had Mary and Gerry Lack to himself for the first 13 years of his marriage – now, one was gone for good, and the other had someone she regarded as more important than either of them to devote her life to. Equally, it could have stemmed from him never being quite sure that he was Diana's natural father.

Needless to say, Mary spoiled her child rotten. Diana was always the best-dressed child at school, and her parties were the talk of the neighbourhood. Weekends were usually spent visiting relatives, most of whom belonged to the farming community. 'This no doubt explains my love of the country, and the attraction of earthy men,' she declared. She loathed her paternal grandmother, Catherine Carter – the second-youngest of 25 children of a Gloucestershire farmer – and Catherine's second husband, Albert Fluck, a widower with five children whom she had wed after her first husband's death, when Bert had been around six. Catherine was an insufferable snob: in her youth she had boasted an 18-inch waist and worked as a seamstress's model. On account of her preoccupation with collecting expensive porcelain, Diana scathingly referred to her as 'Grandma With The Teapots'. These dreary sojourns at her house, where everyone sat around saying and doing nothing, left her with a hatred of the Sabbath. 'To this day I cannot hear church bells on a Sunday without being reminded of that time of my life,' she recalled.

Mary's mother, she claimed to have adored – claimed, for as Georgina died in 1937 when Diana was only six years old, she cannot have known her all that well. The old lady lived in a pink-walled cottage in Llantrithyd, with a smallholding that housed a coterie of animals, including an antisocial cat named Deedles. Diana nicknamed her 'Grandma With The Chick-Chicks', and subsequently described her as 'a perfect target for Cupid's arrows when a dark man appeared', adding that she had obviously passed this trait down to her. Randiness, it appears, ran in the family. In her memoirs, Diana recounts an incident that took place at the property when she was 10, after her grandmother's death. This involved Georgina's perpetually sozzled brother, Arthur. 'He tried to make it with me in the stables,' she recalled, suggesting that she was probably a flirt even at that tender age. 'However, I got away from his cider-soaked clutches and remained happily *virgo intacta*!'

The Depression of the 1930s did not affect parts of southern England quite so much as the North, and Bert Fluck's promotion to sub-head of the Great Western Railway's accounts department enabled him to enrol Diana at the prestigious Selwood House private school, in Swindon's Bath Road. Here, young women were taught French, algebra and geometry, tennis and badminton, needlepoint, and the fine art of being a lady in preparation for becoming genteel society housewives or secretaries. Diana was only really interested in learning English and elocution, which suited Mary, who did not want her daughter to grow up speaking with a West Country accent – and Diana would never regard herself as genteel! She would subsequently win first prize for reciting poetry and prose in the children's section of the 1943 and 1944 Cheltenham Arts Festival, and have her photograph in the

Swindon Advertiser. Otherwise, in class she spent much of her time daydreaming, scribbling the names of her favourite movie stars in the margin of her exercise book. In later years she remembered an important essay she had written back then, entitled, 'What I Would Like To Be When I Grow Up' – revealing her ambition to become a famous film star herself, living in a big house with a cream telephone and a swimming pool. This was her way of coping with the snobbish establishment run by Daisy and Ruth Cockey, two well-connected (to the Admiralty) spinster sisters who considered most of their 40 or so pupils beneath them. 'I loathed them and their stuffy little school,' she recalled, 'vowing that when I grew up I really would become that famous film star I'd written about.' Needless to say, Diana's school reports were far from satisfactory, yet when Bert tore a strip off her for not trying hard enough, Mary defended her with, 'What does it matter, just so long as she knows how to count up the few pounds she'll earn at the end of the week?'

Of course, Mary had never really wanted her daughter to end up with some nine-to-five job. Like many show-business parents who had failed to make the grade themselves, not through lack of talent but because luck and timing had never been on their side – one instinctively thinks of the mothers of Judy Garland, Montgomery Clift, and Maria Callas – Mary Fluck yearned to achieve for Diana what she had never achieved for herself. A great beauty in her younger days and possessed of a pleasing light soprano voice, Mary had entertained soldiers at the local barracks and clubs during the early years of the Great War, and had occasionally performed since with Bert at the piano. Marriage and the expectations of a middle-class household in those days – one where the husband provided, while the wife looked after the family – had put paid to this career, since which time Mary had developed a passion for the movies. She and Diana visited their local cinema at least three times each week – including matinee shows, which saw Diana frequently wagging school. A favourite star was Shirley Temple, who with Mary's help Diana emulated – at seven, she was taken to the hairdressers and her then mousy-brown hair given a bubble perm that she retained for several years. The new hairdo coincided with her developing a 'lazy' eye, courtesy of a punch she received from the school bully, which for several months necessitated her wearing not just glasses, but a black patch over the right lens, her good eye, to strengthen the other one. Later in life, Diana would cringe at how she looked back then.

When war broke out in September 1939, Diana began maturing far more quickly than her parents would have preferred. Her passion for men in uniform was kick-started by Bert, who took her to the local army base where he was engaged to play for the troops. A quip from Bert that her mother saw her as the next Shirley Temple resulted in Diana being asked to take to the stage, where she tap-danced and piped the latest Temple ditty. News of her 'fame' spread locally, and she was invited to perform – always with Bert at the piano – at social and working men's clubs, and the odd church function. Her favourite song was 'Ma, I Miss Your Apple Pie'. By the age of 10, the Shirley Temple routine had become old hat: Diana got it into her head that she was going to be Britain's answer to Lana Turner, the 'Sweater Girl' who at 15 had been discovered sipping soda at a drugstore counter by a movie mogul who had with little effort persuaded her to hop on to the casting couch. As there was no drugstore in the vicinity, Diana devised her own way of hopefully getting noticed: she left her 'CV' by way of a note attached to the dustbin lid, in expectation of the refuse collectors passing on her details to some movie mogul! 'It did not occur to me, in the optimistic fantasy world of childhood, that the dustbin men did not have a private line to Louis B. Mayer,' she later mused.

Diana's love of soldiers continued when, in April 1944 in the run-up towards D-Day, Swindon and the neighbouring Army and Air Force camps were invaded by American GIs and the slogan was invented: 'Over-paid, over-sexed and over here!' Until now, her 'love life' had begun and ended with a 12-year-old boy named Michael Wheeler, who sang in the local church choir. He and Diana took long walks in the countryside, and discussed their individual plans for the future, carving their initials in the trunk of their favourite tree. Diana became so obsessed by him that she began attending church just to be near him. Then her bubble was burst when Mary threw a party for her 12th birthday – when Michael was the only boy to turn up in short trousers.

And now, Diana found herself being chatted up by real men: loquacious hunks, some of whom strode around the town as if they owned it. Because there were so many GIs, once the barracks were filled to overflowing the surplus lodged with local families, who were rewarded handsomely for taking them in. One young soldier – in her memoirs she calls him Joe – stayed with the Flucks on Marlborough Road. When Diana learned that he was from California, she readily assumed that he would know all of her favourite movie stars personally – only to be disappointed that he hailed from Orange County and had never been to Hollywood! By this time Diana had grown her hair long, and begun adding peroxide to the shampoo she used. Though it was not yet as blonde as it would be, Joe told her that when her fringe flopped coquettishly over one eye, she was the spitting image of 'peek-a-boo' actress Veronica Lake!

Joe's intentions may have been honourable, but Bert Fluck was having no nonsense under his roof, and the young soldier was quickly found another place to stay – the next American to occupy the spare room was a young female nurse. The 'Veronica' tag stuck, though, and Diana – still only 12 but when wearing make-up, nylons, high heels and a borrowed flouncy skirt, able to pass herself off as 17 – became a mascot for the GIs. They invited her to their weekend dances at Swindon's Bradford Hall, where she displayed her prowess with the jitterbug. At first she was chaperoned by Mary, who had formed a friendship with the camp cook, one which saw her leaving the venue with a bagful of 'goodies' – extra food for the family in those tough days of rationing. Then Diana began dating one of the GIs, and started smoking, emulating the way Bette Davis dragged at her cigarettes on the screen. From her point of view her behaviour was pretty innocuous, though one of the teachers at Selwood House – an unattractive woman named Miss Knight, who also attended the dances but found herself snubbed once too often by the handsome soldiers who crowded around Diana – was not of the same opinion. When a few sharp words to Mary Fluck failed to convince her that her daughter was rapidly turning into a 'little tart', the matter was brought to the attention of the Misses Cockey – who had been informed that this particular pupil had also been seen staggering through the streets of Swindon under the influence of drink, and with a cigarette dangling from the corner of her mouth! Diana's excuse that her pineapple juice had been spiked with gin was ignored and she was promptly expelled from Selwood House. To protect the Cockeys' reputation, however, the other parents were told that her parents had removed her from the school because, on account of various illnesses (actually, truancy!) she had been falling behind with her lessons.

Within the week, and with no intention of curtailing her weekend visits to the Army camp – the Flucks believed that whatever their daughter did in her own time was nobody else's business – Diana had enrolled with another school. This coincided with an amorous but platonic liaison with a boy from a neighbouring school. Desmond Morris, a 17-year-old from Purton, Wiltshire, lived with his wealthy parents at their tobacconist's shop on Victoria Road. Their house had a large garden with a lake, in the middle of which was a small island where Desmond had set up his den. Diana recalled how they would paddle across to this in his boat – to engage in activities no more adventurous than listening to gramophone records and dancing the jitterbug. When Desmond's parents bought him his first car, he began driving Diana out into the country, a sojourn that ended abruptly when he turned 18 and was conscripted into the war. Barring an exchange of semi-romantic letters and a few chance meetings later in life, usually on television chat shows, that was that. Some years later, Desmond Morris would achieve fame as a zoologist, anthropologist and ethologist. 'I would be Britain's top sex symbol and he would be the author of *The Naked Ape*,' she recalled, adding with a chuckle, 'I hope he did not base his scientific findings on me!'

With Morris gone, Diana – headstrong as ever and not yet past her 14th birthday – dwelled on her future career. In her mind, there was never any question of this never happening: it was merely a matter of sooner rather than later. The fact that she was a minor was immaterial, to her or to Mary. She was pretty, she was already voluptuous. Men found her irresistible, while other girls envied her 'pulling power', and she had every intention of using her assets to get what she wanted. In the summer of 1945, during the Fluck's annual trip to Weston-super-Mare, Diana entered a Pin-Up Girl contest sponsored by *Soldier* magazine. The official in-house publication for the British Army had recently been launched on the advice of General Montgomery: intended as a fortnightly magazine for issue during wartime only, such was its popularity that it continued (monthly) in peacetime, and is still going strong today. The competition rules stipulated a minimum age of 17, so Diana lied on the entry form, which Mary countersigned. Wearing a scarlet and white bathing suit with matching stilettos, Diana won third prize and was presented with a rosette by Jack Watson, a well-known comic at that time.

Soldier published Diana's catwalk photograph in its next issue, as did the *Swindon Advertiser* – who, while making comparisons with the young Betty Grable, also reported that she was 17, not as easy a fib to get away with in a town where everyone knew her. A photographer from the paper, Percy Evans, also talked her into visiting his seedy back-street studio where, after posing for a series of regular shots, she was asked to pose for a series of 'French postcards' – semi-nude studies which Evans hoped would be mass-produced and sold from under counters up and down the country. Diana was snapped as Scheherazade, reclining in a sequinned top and tiny shorts – and sitting on a chair, topless and turning slightly towards the photographer exposing one breast. This, though, was as far as she was willing to go. For the time being, she was prepared to heed her mother's theory that sex was a necessary evil women endured for the sake of pleasing their husbands in order to bear their children.

Diana's father may have been urged by other members of his family, who had witnessed enough scandals of their own, to exercise a firm hand and bring his daughter into line. Bert, however, had long since given up the struggle to fight Mary over which of them wore the trousers in the Fluck household. When Diana was contacted by the arts department of the Shrivenham American University and invited to pose for the students, aware that whatever decision he made would only be overruled, he merely told her to go ahead and please herself. Formerly a British training barracks, this had recently been refounded as an education centre for GIs 'sweating out' between periods of overseas deployment, or those awaiting repatriation. At Shrivenham, the regime was more relaxed than soldiers were used to – aside from reveille, there were no drills or exterior manoeuvres. Diana had no qualms about live modelling – whether she posed entirely nude is not known, but unlikely. The campus drama department also hired her for some of their stage productions, including one of the leads in Alberto Casella's avant-garde play, *Death Takes a Holiday*. She also sang with the college band on their home radio station.

For a while, Diana dated an (unnamed) 18-year-old Texan who wooed her with make-up parcels sent over by his mother: such luxuries were hard to come by in wartime Britain. Their relationship ended abruptly when Diana received a response from a letter she had sent to the London Academy of Music and Dramatic Art, on the off chance that she might be offered an audition. This trip to the city put paid to her smoking. 'Armed with a cigarette case,' she recalled, 'it seemed the right thing to do until I encountered on the 5am workman's train carriage-loads of dirty old workmen sucking away at their non-filtered cigarettes. The sight of them made me feel so ill that suddenly smoking was no longer the grown-up, sophisticated thing I had watched my mother's friends doing when I was a child.' LAMDA provisionally accepted her on a one-day-a-week basis. By now, the war was all but over and most of her beloved Americans had gone home, so there was little to keep Diana in Swindon. Therefore a compromise was reached: as her father had virtually washed his hands of her, she would be permitted to live in London during the week, but only providing she enrolled on a teaching course. Then, once the acting bug was out of her system, she would be able to return to Swindon and teach elocution at a well-paid private establishment similar to Selwood House.

Accompanied by her mother, Diana travelled to London in November 1945. In her portmanteau was a letter of introduction, given to her by a GI photographer from Shrivenham – this was for Alf Keating, the assistant director who had worked on several George Formby films and who was currently (under director Marcel Varnel) shooting *This Man Is Mine*, with Glynis Johns. Formby, the archetypal Northern comic legend, had always been given leading ladies with clipped Colonial accents, such as Phyllis Calvert and Pat Kirkwood, neither of whom he had liked. Keating, it was hoped, would recognise similar potential in the posh-speaking Diana. The first thing he objected to was her name. Several names were suggested. She liked Diana Carroll, while Keating favoured Diana Scarlett, after the heroine in *Gone with the Wind*. Diana hated this, and a telephone call home saw her father hitting the roof. In his opinion, if she changed her name this would mean she was ashamed of her family. Diana herself, like Keating, saw problems arising from using her birth name, as she later quipped, 'What would happen if my name was in neon lights, and the 'L' went out?' Eventually, it was Mary who came up with the situation: if she became Diana Dors, she would not be letting her family down, for this had been her grandmother's name!

What Keating had in mind for her, while she was studying at LAMDA, was a small part in George Formby's movie swansong, *George in Civvy Street.* This was until he insisted on seeing her birth certificate for studio insurance purposes, and realised that she was barely 15. He was however suitably impressed to pass her on to Weston Drury Jr, one of the city's leading casting directors. It was probably he who pulled the strings to get her into LAMDA full-time, and make arrangements for her to lodge at the YWCA in Kensington, where over the next three years she would share a dormitory with three other girls. Though she would be returning home each weekend, her mother was heartbroken to be losing her anchor, her excuse for having had a life of her own extant of her stuffy, boring husband for the last 15 years. 'Her life was ending,' Diana recalled. 'The void I left would never be filled again.'

Chapter Two

The Rank Years: Muse of the Chelsea Set

Diana was confident that she would not fail. So many people – including the pupils and staff at Selwood House – had drilled it into her that she *would* end up flat on her face, that she was determined to prove them wrong at whatever cost. Her confidence was given a boost when she embarked at Paddington Station and observed a poster of Margaret Lockwood promoting Drene shampoo. In her first letter home she promised her parents that one day they would be seeing *her* face up there on a hoarding.

She lost no time getting to know the boys at LAMDA, particularly the good-looking ones. During her first acting class she clicked with a young student named George Raistrick (1931–95), who later became a popular television character actor. That same evening they went to see Charles Laughton in *Captain Kidd*, and afterwards went drinking in Earl's Court. Diana had never been in a pub before: wearing make-up and clothes given to her by her mother, no one asked her age. Pub visits became a regular occurrence after this, though she had to be careful: the YWCA imposed a 10pm curfew, and it was not beyond the manageress to wait up to collar stragglers as they crept by her door and smell their breath for telltale signs of alcohol.

The romance with Raistrick was short-lived. During her first year at LAMDA, and as their youngest ever pupil (though most of the people there did not know this), Diana was more interested in knuckling down to work. She studied Shakespeare, Ibsen, the Romantic poets, elocution, mime, and even took fencing lessons:

she attended self-expression classes, which appear to have been another form of Method where she was taught how to show every kind of emotion, and how to die eloquently. To supplement the 10-shillings weekly allowance from her father, she hired herself out as a model for student photographers at the London Camera Club – for the then astronomical fee of 21 shillings an hour. This time, she did pose nude but for a strategically placed piece of gauze or feather, but only after writing to her mother and asking her permission. Mary agreed, and even Bert did not put up much of a fight – the more Diana earned (just so long as it was on a 'look but don't touch' basis) the less he would have to fork out for extra expenses such as her clothes. Another student who posed for the club was the starlet Susan Shaw, with whom she would soon work.

Diana passed her first exams – gaining a bronze and silver medal for elocution, and a bronze for acting, which required her to perform solo scenes from *As You Like It* and *Wuthering Heights*. Such was her parents' delight that they placed an announcement in the *Swindon Advertiser*. Unbeknown to them, Diana had endeared herself to one of the examiners, the British casting director for Warner Bros., Eric L'Epine Smith. He was currently casting for the film adaptation of former Conservative MP Edward Percy's crime thriller, *The Shop at Sly Corner*, which had enjoyed a successful run in the West End, and on Broadway with horror star Boris Karloff playing one of the leads. The director was George King (1899–1966), feted for his Tod Slaughter melodramas such as *The Demon Barber of Fleet Street* (1936). King had also directed Laurence Olivier in his first major film. When L'Epine Smith found out how old Diana really was, rather than admonish her he advised her to keep on lying, otherwise she would never get the kind of parts which he believed would suit her brassy, forthright character. Little did she know then that for her entire career she would find herself almost always typecast in such roles!

The storyline, which unfolds against an eerie soundtrack by George Melachrino, centres around French convict Desius Heiss (Oscar Homolka) who escapes from Devil's Island and heads for London, where he opens an antique shop. The tagline for the film read, 'When A Man Has A Secret Like This, He'll Do Anything To Keep It!' In Percy's screenplay, this alludes to the gay subplot and creepy shop assistant Archie's (Kenneth Griffith) fondness for wearing silk undies. This of course was wholly unacceptable for the big screen, where attitudes towards homosexuality were not as relaxed as they were in the theatre. Therefore in King's film, the secret that Heiss is keeping from his daughter (Muriel Pavlow) is that his shop is a front for fencing stolen goods, and that Archie is blackmailing him and must be silenced. Diana, looking considerably older than 15 and on a far from modest salary of eight pounds a day, played Archie's rough-edged girlfriend, Mildred. She handles the part well, though in early prints of the film her name does not appear on the credits.

In Swindon, this did not matter. The mayor was so proud of this local girl made good that when *The Shop at Sly Corner* opened there in May 1947, he had playbills printed displaying her photograph beneath the title as if she were its only star, and had these posted all over town. The cinema manager bought her a sequinned gown, and her mother a beaver-lamb wrap, which with her Woolworths paste jewellery caused a flurry of excitement as her father escorted her into the building. Each time she appeared on the screen, a huge cheer went up in the auditorium.

A few weeks earlier, Diana had acquired her first manager of sorts, agent and playwright Gordon Harbord. It was he, having seen the rushes for the film, who sent her to Adele Raymond, then casting for Michael Powell and Emeric Pressburger's *Black Narcissus*, a tale of passion, intrigue and adventure set in a convent in a Himalayan valley. The very idea of Diana playing a nun would have been enough to give any producer palpitations, so Raymond tested her for the part of the Nepalese girl, Kanchi. This fell through when Raymond learned that she was only 15, and when Diana refused to strap down her ample bosom. The part went to the genuinely 17-year-old Jean Simmons and, to pacify her, Diana was given a minuscule part in *Holiday Camp*, the first of the phenomenally successful Huggett-family films starring Jack Warner, Kathleen Harrison and Flora Robson. Precursors to the *Darling Buds of May* series, these depicted life as enjoyed (and sometimes not!) by the post-war working classes: in this instance a slightly risqué scenario involving crooked poker players, an unmarried couple about to have a baby, and a man-eating spinster in search of a husband. Diana, uncredited once more and as yet still a brunette, spent just one day on the set playing a flighty distant relative with a passion for dancing the jitterbug.

Diana's third film was historically more important than her Huggetts outing, though not because she happened to be in it. *Dancing with Crime*, directed by John Paddy Carstairs – he later made *The Saint* television series – was the first (along with *Brighton Rock*, released at around the same time) to feature Richard Attenborough in a prominent role. He played a former soldier, now a London cab driver, who becomes involved with a criminal cartel. Playing his love interest was Sheila Sim, Attenborough's real-life wife. Dirk Bogarde, then virtually unknown, had an unbilled cameo role as a policeman. Like his predecessors, Carstairs admired Diana, but did not see fit to add her name to the credits. She played Annette, the sluttish hostess in a sleazy dancehall where a murder takes place, and one exchange between her and the camp investigating detective, played by Garry Marsh, became the rage of the closeted gay bars around Piccadilly. This was when Annette swanned across the empty dance floor and purred, 'Are you dancing?' – to which he responded, 'No, it's just the way I walk!'

There was also a new man in Diana's life. Geoffrey Roach was a 19-year-old aspiring actor from Nottingham who, like George Raistrick, could not venture anywhere – even on a date – without his own best friend tagging along. Diana described him as 'dark and strikingly handsome, with an irrepressible sense of humour', adding that he had sworn like a trooper, and that he had been the first man to seriously touch her emotions. He was also the first of her lovers to take their affair seriously and give her a ring. She was, of course, what would today be called a 'prick tease', deliberately making herself look more mature to taunt these young men into wanting to have sex with her, giving them the impression that she *wanted* to go all the way, before backing off abruptly and sometimes with great fuss. Little wonder, then, that some of these anticipated sex, only to have her dismiss them as 'lechers' (when *she* was invariably partly to blame for their frustrated actions). Many was the time, she recalled, when Geoffrey had walked her through Hyde Park late at night, hoping to have his way with her while she, the siren, endlessly protested that she did not wish to end up with a reputation as 'easy meat'. And yet, this was exactly the kind of reputation she *was* getting. Needless to say, the confused young man ended their relationship and asked for his ring back.

In June 1947, Gainsborough Pictures' writer-producer Sydney Box, who had scripted *Holiday Camp*, suggested Diana for *Streets Paved with Water*, a melodrama by Joe Mendoza and Anthony Skene, who were also to direct the film. For the leads, the pair had contracted the dashing Maxwell Reed (who later became Joan Collins' first husband) and Jane Hylton. On Box's recommendation, Diana was inducted into the Rank Organisation's Company of Youth on a starting salary of £10 a week, and offered the role of Hylton's brassy sister. The location shooting began around the Grand Union Canal, and immediately hit a snag when the directors, dissatisfied with the early rushes, wanted to dismiss Box's cameraman, Stephen Dade – who had photographed *The Brothers* – and hire someone else. Box refused to compromise, and took the unusual step of cancelling the production.

The Rank Organisation had been formed in 1937 by Hull-born flour tycoon and devout Methodist, J. Arthur Rank – its films would all be introduced with the legendary sequence of the muscle-bound Bombardier Billy Wells striking a gong. The enterprise had moved forward in leaps and bounds. In 1938, Rank had acquired the Odeon cinema chain, and the following year had merged the Denham Film Studios with those at Pinewood and Borehamwood – not long afterwards he had taken over the ones at Ealing and Islington, and he rounded off his operation in 1942 by purchasing the Paramount cinema chain. His Company of Youth, subsequently baptised 'The Charm School' by a sarcastic press well aware that some of those running it were anything *but* charming, had been formed in 1945. The Charm School launched the careers of Petula Clark, Anthony Steele, Christopher Lee, Donald Sinden, Dirk Bogarde, Shirley Eaton and many others. Their recruitment policy, though, differed from that of their rivals, as head of employment Olive Dodds explained in *J. Arthur Rank & The British Film Industry*: 'We weren't so much concerned with acting talent. It was a fact that in as far as you needed it for film work, it could be acquired. We looked first of all for faces, personalities, figures and so on. They had to be the typical heroines and heroes.'

In overall charge of the operation was American film producer

Earl St John, an autocratic tyrant (in the stamp of MGM's Louis B. Mayer) who most of the Rank hierarchy could not stand – but who was tolerated by those at the top because he got the job done, and never allowed any production to run over budget. The Company of Youth operated from a disused church hall in Highbury. Running the show was David Henley, a former chorus member of the D'Oyly Carte Opera Company who had co-founded Equity and gone on to manage Robert Donat and Vivien Leigh. Henley, however, was content to delegate to Olive Dodds, ex-secretary to John Davis, who ran Rank's accounts department.

Like Earl St John, Dodds took absolutely no prisoners. Her alumni were taught how to dress, how to speak, how to conduct themselves in public – though in the latter respect she failed with Diana Dors. If a recruit adhered to the rules, he or she would be granted more or less the same privileges and protection as their American counterparts working under the studio-system regime. If they did not, they were fired and stood little chance of working elsewhere. Diana's acting teacher was no less pleasant than Dodds. Molly Terraine had started out as a silent-movie actress and failed to make the grade, since which time she had held a grudge against the world. In a 1982 interview with film critic Barry Norman, Diana denounced her as 'a dreadful harridan of a woman who struck fear and terror into everyone'. Heading promotions was Theo Cowan, who was almost as bad, though with Diana he had his work cut out. It was not beyond her to be seen strutting through the streets of London wearing shorts and a revealing bikini top, even if the weather was inclement, simply to ensure that she was noticed.

Diana was offered a 10-year contract with Rank, but with an unusual proviso: she would start on £10 a week, and this would be doubled annually, though the studio would be permitted to fire her should they deem her to be not up to scratch, or at a moment's notice should she step out of line and provoke a scandal. Shortly before signing her contract she had graduated from LAMDA and received the prestigious Alexander Korda Diploma, though this had cut no ice with J. Arthur Rank and his executives. At LAMDA she had represented their very finest, the cream of the crop. Here at Rank she was but one of scores of young 'starlets' hoping to make it to the top in an environment where comparatively few succeeded.

Rank put Diana into four films during the latter half of 1947: these were released the following year, and not in the order they had been made. In *Good Time Girl*, the first to include her name in the credits, she played runaway teenager Lyla Lawrence, who is hauled before sympathetic juvenile-court magistrate Flora Robson, who dissuades her from a life of crime by recounting the harrowing, cautionary tale of Gwen Rawlings – played by 27-year-old Jean Kent – whose wild ways saw her end up in an approved school. Because of the subject matter, rarely discussed in those days, it took Rank almost two years to acquire a certificate for the film to be released. In *My Sister and I*, scripted by comic actor Michael Medwin and starring Sally Ann Howes and Dermot Walsh, Diana was unbilled. Arguably her ablest performance was in *Penny and the Pownall Case* – not a film, as such, but a 47-minute supporting feature. Based on the famous *Jane* cartoon strip, this centred around cartoon model Penny (Peggy Evans) who turns amateur detective to help Scotland Yard track down a gang aiding Nazi war criminals to escape from Europe. Diana played Penny's cocky flatmate Molly, though today the production is best remembered as being the first to feature future horror star Christopher Lee in a prominent role.

While shooting this film, Diana unsuccessfully tested for the part of the street-walker in *Precious Bane*, a Scotland Yard drama to be directed by Robert Siodmak (the movie was never made). Testing for the lead role (and equally unsuccessfully) was Guy Rolfe (1911–2003), the six-foot-four saturnine but sardonically handsome actor who had a small part in Sydney Box's *Easy Money*, shooting on an adjacent lot. Later in his career, Rolfe would carve a niche for himself playing sinister roles, from the dastardly Prince John in *Ivanhoe* (1952) to the insane André Toulan in the gory *Puppet Master* movies. Rolfe was married to actress Jane Aird, and 20 years Diana's senior, but this did not prevent them from having a fling – platonic, though not by choice so far as he was concerned. Initially, their trysts took place in the studio canteen, or maybe they would call in at a local pub, after which Rolfe would drive 'Agatha', as he called her, back to the YWCA before curfew. Then he started getting a little more adventurous, inviting her to his home – when his wife was out, naturally – and taking her out to dinner, eating rarely himself because he had booked the same table for later in the evening, to dine with his wife once Diana was safely tucked up in bed. She recalled that he was always polite, but a man with a dark side, a control freak who instructed her what to wear, what make-up to use, how to conduct herself in public, often tearing a strip off her in front of the technicians to the extent that she developed an inferiority complex. 'My life revolved so much around him that I dared not venture a step without his instruction or advice,' she said. His constant demands for sex also made her feel cheap, she added, though in this respect she only had herself to blame by flaunting herself at him, and then resisting the advances he assumed she *wanted* him to make.

Diana was not the only young woman Rolfe was seeing behind his wife's back, and Jane Aird hired a private detective who informed her not just of her name, but that her husband was also 'intimately involved' with a 15-year-old starlet – an imprisonable offence if he had had actual sex with Diana, which with her reputation would have been difficult to disprove. It also emerged that Sydney Box, the man generally credited with discovering her, had given her the secret nickname 'Jailbait', and that Rolfe and every other man who had come into contact with her had been warned about going too far with her. Diana may have been the Lorelei wooing these hapless men towards the rocks, but *they* would have been prosecuted had any one of them relieved her of the virginity she now professed to hating. Therefore on the eve of what he thought was her 18th birthday – but which was actually her 16th, which would have made having sex with her no longer against the law – Guy Rolfe dumped her.

Meanwhile, Diana's fourth and final film this year was *The Calendar*, a horseracing melodrama based on an Edgar Wallace play. Directed by Arthur Crabtree, it starred Greta Gynt, the glamorous Norwegian actress who Rank had hoped to market as Britain's answer to Jean Harlow, who had died of uremic poisoning in June 1937 just as Gynt had been coming into her own. This never quite worked: though very popular with cinemagoers during the war years, Gynt's star was already starting to fade. It was Gynt who had presented Diana with her Korda diploma, kissing her on each cheek and announcing that she had all the makings of a great star herself – and now here she was, unbilled and playing her maid! *The Calendar* may not have drawn the crowds to the cinemas in droves, but it was important for Diana in that it introduced her to the first great love of her life. Egil Woxholt (1925–91) was one of the trainee cameramen, and also Greta Gynt's younger brother: a tall, handsome blond, he would subsequently achieve some recognition as an underwater photographer, most notably with *The Heroes of Telemark* and several of the Bond films. With Egil there were no preliminaries, no wooing, wining and dining as had happened with Guy Rolfe. Two days after they met he booked them into a hotel room. The next morning, when they arrived at the studio together, Diana was no longer a virgin. Many years later, she attempted to glamorise the event, writing in the first volume of her memoirs, 'If you are determined to lose your virginity – then what better place to do it than in the beautiful dales of Yorkshire.' Egil Woxholt, however, always maintained differently.

One week later, Diana left the YWCA, and with Egil's help found a small bedsit off the King's Road. She may have had a steady boyfriend, but this did not stop her from flirting and several times almost coming unstuck. She claimed that Fredric March, filming *Christopher Columbus* on an adjacent lot, had one day grabbed her as she had been walking past his dressing room, dragged her inside, and tried to have his way with her – though why she should have been walking past there in the first place she never elaborated on. 'I struggled free and ran out of the door,' she recalled, 'and ever after that he became extremely sullen, glowering at me whenever we passed each other.'

The exact identity of the 'chief executive' who is supposed to have invited Diana to his home at around this time – with a view to offering her the part which would make her a household name, while all he was really interested in was getting her into bed – is unclear. Names that have been suggested include David Henley, director Robert Siodmak and producer David Lean, with whom she would work next. The likeliest candidate, however, was J. Arthur Rank himself – in her memoirs Diana described her would-be seducer as 'the respectable man who controlled our destinies and careers'. The man, she said, informed her that it had been brought to his attention that she was putting on a little 'puppy fat'. Therefore, would she mind going into the next room and stripping naked so that he could see for himself? She added that at the time she had no idea *why* he wanted her to take her clothes off, but that she had started to do so, terrified of having her contract terminated unless she obeyed – suggesting that if this was not Rank, then it was someone with sufficient power within the organisation to end her career. Her honour and the situation were saved, she concluded, when the doorbell had rung announcing the arrival of his secretary – with whom he was cheating on his wife!

David Lean, a serial womaniser who would go through six wives, *did* make 'drawing room overtures' to Diana while casting *Oliver Twist*, his second stab at Dickens in the wake of the hugely successful *Great Expectations*, released the previous year. Diana rebuffed him, but got the part anyhow: Charlotte, the obnoxious undertaker's maid who mistreats the boy hero while he is lodging with her employers. It was a dowdy part to say the least – with the make-up department blackening her face with coal dust and dressing her in rags – but one she relished, she said, because her whole reason for attending LAMDA was with a view not to end up typecast in glamorous roles. 'Diana Dors endows Charlotte with all the baseness which Dickens wrote into the character,' the press release observed. Journalists who had never seen her before were surprised – shocked, even – when she turned up at the press conference looking every inch the movie star, in the same outfit she had worn for the Swindon premiere of *The Shop at Sly Corner*. Rank's publicist, Theo Cowan, seized the opportunity to announce that even at just 18 (supposedly), she had already turned down seven marriage proposals, including one from a European nobleman.

It was all hogwash. Diana was still with Egil Woxholt, but two-timing him with Kip Gowans, a 17-year-old assistant runner. Kip hailed from Ruislip, and on weekends if Egil was working he would take Diana home to visit his parents. On an evening, she said, after a trip to the cinema or their favourite restaurant, he would steer her towards Ruislip Woods and try to seduce her in the long grass – always ending up frustrated and covered in gnat bites in the wake of a heavy-petting session which always ended with Diana slapping his wrist, rearranging her clothes and announcing that it was time to go back to the house. Needless to say, the young man soon gave up on her. A few years later, Kip

Gowans embarked on a distinguished career as an assistant director – one of his triumphs, in 1956, would be *Reach for the Sky*.

Oliver Twist was a box-office smash. John Howard-Davies played the title role, and David Lean's then wife, Kay Walsh, was Nancy. Alec Guinness terrified younger audiences as what many believe to have been the definitive Fagin, while Anthony Newley excelled as the Artful Dodger. Then, immediately after this mini-masterpiece, it was back to the dross, and more typecasting when Diana played 'The Blonde' in *It's Not Cricket*, a forgettable tale of upper-class twits Basil Radford and Naunton Wayne posing as amateur detectives. The names of their characters, Major Bright and Captain Early, give some indication as to how daft this was.

In the summer of 1948, Diana appeared back to back (in each her character was called Diana, but with a different surname) in two sequels to *Holiday Camp* – *Here Come the Huggetts* and *Vote for Huggett*, scripted by Sydney Box and directed by Ken Annakin, which picked up more or less where the first film had left off. Now, the loveable odd-bod family are back on the home front with their three daughters: Petula Clark, Susan Shaw and Jane Hylton played these, again with first names the same as their own – with some cynics suggesting that their acting was so wooden, they would have been confused otherwise. Diana was the flighty family black sheep. Anthony Newley was also in the film, playing Petula's boyfriend. Despite both appearing in *Oliver Twist*, he and Diana had appeared in no scenes together and were now meeting for the first time. Dreadfully dated today, both storylines were positively vacuous – ranging from the mayhem brought about by the Huggetts installing their first telephone at a time when most working-class families did not have such things, Diana wrecking their car, and Mr Huggett (Jack Warner) standing for MP. Another *Huggetts* film would follow, though not with Diana.

Much better was *A Boy, a Girl and a Bike*, shot on location in Halifax and the Yorkshire Dales, though again Diana's contribution was not substantial. Directed by Ralph Smart, the film is interesting for its depiction of life in a Northern mill town before commercialisation set in. A precursor of British kitchen-sink dramas such as *Room at the Top*, the scenario centres around the lives and loves of a cycling club, the Wakeford Wheelers, which are turned upside down with the arrival of a Southern toff and a deserting soldier on the run from the police. The stars were John McCallum and future *Avengers* girl Honor Blackman. Thora Hird and Anthony Newley supported, while Diana played 'bad girl' Ada Foster.

A rough-and-ready kid from the wrong side of the tracks – almost a modern-day equivalent of the Artful Dodger he had portrayed so well – Anthony Newley was one month older than Diana, and apparently as keen to lose his virginity to her as she had been to lose hers to Egil Woxholt. Born in Hackney to unmarried parents, he had been raised by his Jewish mother and evacuated during the Blitz, whence he had struck up a friendship with a now forgotten music-hall entertainer, George Pescud, and been bitten by the acting bug. At 14, working as an office boy for the *Telegraph*, Newley had answered an advertisement for boy actors, and been taken on by the prestigious Italia Conti Stage School as a student-cum-errand-boy. His first part had been as Dusty in *The Adventures of Dusty Bates*, a popular Saturday morning cinema serial. This had been followed by a bit part in *The Guinea Pig*, which had brought him to the attention of David Lean. Newley would set a precedent for Diana's fascination – a trait she shared with all the blonde-bombshell movie sirens – with gay and bisexual men, though she would not always be subtle when discussing them, frequently coming to the conclusion that a man could not possibly be both gay and manly.

Diana's second volume of memoirs, *Behind Closed Dors* (like its predecessor, *For Adults Only*, an A–Z of her observations on life), included a section entitled 'Homosexuals' – which cynics noted was *non*-alphabetically wedged between 'Hitler' and 'Hell'. This was written in a tone unlikely to adhere her to today's gay community and supporters of overt political correctness, and while one might excuse the list of 'pre-John Inman' put-downs for gay men, one feels slightly uncomfortable reading such quips as, 'A more amusing type of person one cannot wish for. They also make marvellous friends and fans for women.' Equally inappropriate is the observation, 'Some manage to conduct their private lives quietly and with dignity, and some pretend that they are actually normal, which to my mind is hypocrisy.' This *was*, after all, 12 years after homosexuality had been legalised in Britain, and some of Diana's gay fans actually turned against her for suggesting that being gay was not normal. Diana promised to make amends to anyone she might have offended when writing its successor, *The A–Z of Men*. In fact, she only succeeded in making matters worse by declaring, 'Some of my best friends are homosexuals. But when I imagine them in the act of having sex together, I'm afraid it does cast a somewhat dark shadow on my feelings towards the matter.' And if her gay fans did not mind being referred to as 'confirmed bachelors', they balked at the term 'embroiderers'.

Though he would eventually have three wives, including Joan Collins, Newley was also known to have been supported by a succession of sugar daddies during his early career. He and Diana travelled to Yorkshire on the same train, escorted – a legal requirement as both were under 21 – by the film's producer, Ralph Keene. This was Diana's first location, an exercise she later described as 'a group of people combining good looks, talent, and skill at their craft...forced to live and work for weeks at a time, whilst trying to resist the temptations of the flesh'. The youngsters stayed in adjacent rooms at the Fells Hotel in Grassington, but if Newley was hoping to have his way with the pretty blonde, he had another thing coming when he turned up on set the following afternoon. There was Egil Woxholt, newly arrived from London with the crew – wearing skimpy shorts and helping the cameramen. 'As I watched him moving around, stripped to the waist,' Diana recalled, 'I became aware of his gorgeous muscular body and long brown legs...and I fantasised about Gil from that moment on.' She did not let on, however, that she already knew Egil or that they were lovers. Later she romanticised the scenario, claiming that she had been lying alone on her bed, in mental turmoil, when Egil had walked in – cynics have observed to relieve her of her virginity for the second time. 'If ever any moment was the right time, this was it,' she wrote in her memoirs. 'The time had come for me to venture into that unknown world of womanhood... I was ready to throw caution to the winds and give myself completely to the boy I desired!'

Diana's romantic bubble burst, however, once the film company returned to London. Making love in the shabby King's Road bedsit with the cooking smells and din from the unruly children next door, she decided, was not the same as it had been in Yorkshire, when in post-coital mood she and Egil had stared at the darkened moors outside her room window. In fact, it was Egil who effected a parting of the ways. He had had enough of her flirting with other men on the set, and now found himself another less flighty (he hoped) girlfriend.

Diana, meanwhile, turned her attention to James de la Mare, a former actor and descendant of the poet, Walter. This ended quickly when she learned that he was in the middle of a messy divorce. Therefore it was back to Anthony Newley, who despite her reckless behaviour still only had eyes for her. The fact that she began sleeping with him, however, did not make her treat him less shabbily. Newley may have been great in bed, but he was an uneducated and (she thought) vulgar young man she did not wish to be seen with in public – certainly one she did not wish to introduce to her new society friends on 'home' territory. Courtesy of Maxwell Reed, she had been inducted into the 'Chelsea Set', a precursor to the Sloane Rangers and similar in its concept to the Existentialists of post-war Paris, but lacking the philosophical and intellectual clout: 'We met alcoholics, criminals, drug addicts, pimps and prostitutes, impoverished members of the aristocracy, writers, painters, cashiered ex-Army officers and con-men who could sell anything from a dozen pairs of nylons to somebody's house, if they could get their hands on the deeds,' she recalled. Booze and drugs were also the order of the day with most of the Chelsea set, though Diana was rarely tempted by either, confessing that she got drunk a couple of times before deciding that throwing up and hangovers were not her scene – and that she had been decidedly unimpressed with her drugs experiments: including marijuana, dropping aspirins into Coca-Cola, and sniffing amyl-nitrate to enhance arousal during sex.

This group of thespians and music-loving odd-bods mostly gathered in the piano lounges of the Cross Keys, the Star in Belgravia, the Connoisseur Basement Club or the S&F Grill in Piccadilly – initials which were believed to stand for 'stage and film', or 'shit and fuck' in honour of all the cursing which went on, but were actually the initials of the owner! Diana, already the *coqueluche* or darling of the Piccadilly gay set, though she was not always reverent towards them, became particularly pally with one of their leading lights: Brian Desmond Hurst was an Irish-born director whose most accomplished film – Alastair Sim's *Scrooge* –

was yet to come. Openly and flagrantly gay, Hurst feted his discoveries at his home and, if sex did take place – as happened with Dirk Bogarde – it would be in his boudoir where the bed was surrounded by carved images of saints. 'He always had a penchant for beautiful boys, loving to have them around all the time,' Diana recalled. 'Brian always insisted that in order to gain his favour, *everybody* must be pretty!' There were certainly a lot of 'cuties' around to tickle Hurst's fancy: actors Edmund Purdom and Laurence Harvey were two Chelsea Set regulars, as was one Dennis Hamilton, of whom much more later. The group's stooge was the character actor Denis Shaw (1921–71), famed for portraying slimy villains, and who took pride in his self-professed reputation as 'the ugliest bastard in British films'. Shaw's trick, when it was his turn to buy a round of drinks, was to walk around the pub or club with an empty pint pot after the musicians had finished playing, claiming that he was collecting for them – then pocket the proceeds.

It was at one of these society watering holes that Diana met one of the key figures in her early life: Michael Caborn-Waterfield, known to his friends as Kim. Their first encounter took place on New Year's Eve at the Cross Keys, on the eve of Kim's 19th birthday. 'His dark good looks were almost beautiful compared with the characters and eccentrics around him,' she later remembered, adding that he had deliberately ignored her – *not* the kind of trait she admired in the opposite sex! Quite likely the young man had heard of her reputation, and may have deliberately steered clear of her. Later that same night, she bumped into him again at a post-pub party, with pretty much the same result – which only made her more determined than ever to have him.

Bedfordshire-born Kim Waterfield was the archetypal society dropout who had absconded from public school and run off to London, where after living rough for a while he had found employment as office boy to film producer legend Alexander Korda. Since then he had turned his hand to many things, mostly without success, including a stint as a junior jockey and another as a bit-part actor. If photographs taken at the time are anything to go by, he was by far the best looking of Diana's men: additionally, he slotted perfectly into the mean and moody, irascible category which she seemed to draw towards her like a magnet. Like Guy

Rolfe he was a Capricorn, which she later regarded as her 'downfall zodiac sign in the love department'. Unlike her, Kim tended to believe rather too much in his self-professed genius, boasting to Diana that while she had had to be satisfied with a mere third-billing in her last film, *he* had just signed a Hollywood contract to work with former child prodigy Margaret O'Brien.

This was nonsense: Kim's film career had peaked with a walk-on in Peter Ustinov's burlesque *Vice Versa* in 1948. Coincidentally, this had featured Anthony Newley in his first major role – Dick Bultitude – a name which, on account of the actor's alleged prodigious appendage, Diana considered could not have been more apt. For weeks, Diana had been deliberating over whether to end her relationship with Newley, who extant of the bedroom had always been restricted to meeting her at the local pub or greasy spoon, and never at her society haunts. She kept him hanging on, however, until the right man came along – her theory being that it was better to be 'getting it' from an embarrassment like Newley than not at all. Kim knew about Newley – indeed, Diana is believed to have delighted in discussing their nocturnal activities down to the most intimate detail – but he also wanted to get her away from the likes of Denis Shaw, who had a tendency to get friends to confide in him about their love lives, then broadcast it to all and sundry. As their affair blossomed, Kim began entertaining Diana at the St John's Wood flat he shared with his best friend, 25-year-old Patrick Beresford, or at his mother's house where they were waited on hand and foot by a coterie of servants. When they socialised, instead of mixing with the Chelsea Set, it would be at the finest clubs and restaurants in the West End, to which Kim would drive her in one of his six second-hand cars. What Diana did not find out until some time later was that her 'wealthy' boyfriend was living way beyond his means, much of the time borrowing money from his mother or from Patrick Beresford or other friends to offer her a good time, terrified that he might otherwise lose her to his 'Artful Dodger' rival.

Ultimately, Diana's mind was made up for her over which of her beaus was best for her – by Kim, who broke into Newley's flat, intending to give him a good hiding and warn him to keep away from her. Newley was tired of her flirting with every handsome chap who crossed her path, yet was unwilling to give up on her without a fight. Kim managed to get in the first punch, after which Newley went berserk – beating Kim black and blue, and smashing what little furniture there was in the room. Needless to say, after this incident Diana regarded Kim as her knight in shining armour, and opted to have nothing more to do with Newley. A few days before Christmas 1948 she began shooting her next film.

Diamond City was promoted as a 'British Gold Rush Western' – save that the gold and the Klondike were swapped for the late-19th-century diamond fields of the Transvaal, and filmed on location at Denham! David Farrar, fresh from his success in *Black Narcissus*, was hoping for further glory as the British entrepreneur who exploits the South African workers, while attempting to maintain law and order in the anarchic situation he has brought about. Honor Blackman was his Salvation Army love interest, and Diana, in her first starring role, played brazen barmaid Dora Bracken who – in a poor emulation of Marlene Dietrich in *Destry Rides Again* – sings (dubbed by Maudie Edwards), dances the cancan, plays the piano, shouts a lot, and banters with the rough-and-ready, primarily male clientele. The film was directed by David MacDonald, who that same year worked with Fredric March on *Christopher Columbus* and with Dennis Price in *The Bad Lord Byron*, both better than this one. Diana hated her role, eager as she was to get away from the typecasting which appeared to have returned since *The Calendar*. Indeed, she was only cast as Dora because Jean Kent, then one of the studio's biggest stars, had turned it down. She also got carried away during the saloon catfight scene with Blackman – modelled on the one between Dietrich and Una Merkel in *Destry*, though instead of this ending with the protagonists doused with a bucket of water, this pair only stop scratching and spitting when sprinkled with pepper – hitting her rival for real and ripping out her hair until the director yelled for her to stop! Her most embarrassing moment, she said, came after she had filmed a love scene with David Farrar – when a delighted David MacDonald bellowed down his megaphone in front of the whole set, 'There's no way Diana could have played that scene like that if she was still a virgin!'

Shooting had barely wrapped, when Diana collapsed on the set. David MacDonald was sufficiently concerned to want to send for the studio doctor, but Diana insisted upon being driven straight to her parents' house in Swindon. It seems that she was terrified that she might be pregnant, and that if this was the case it would be better to keep the matter private until she had decided upon her next move. It turned out, however, that she was suffering from nothing worse than the flu and a stomach upset, and a few days later she returned to London. Here, there was more drama when she could not get into the King's Road bedsit – the landlord had changed the locks and evicted her, following complaints from the neighbours over the noisy parties which for weeks had raved on until the early hours. For a while she moved in with Kim Waterfield and Patrick Beresford, though Kim assured her that this would be a temporary measure because they would soon find a place of their own – what he did not let on was that Patrick Beresford was about to move out because funds were running low, and that his mother Yvonne Waterfield, who disapproved of him 'living over the brush with a showgirl', was now paying the rent on the flat in St John's Wood. The option was there, of course, for him to ditch Diana and return to the family home, but Kim did not want this. Within a week he had found them a small flat in Jermyn Street, with a single window at the rear which looked out on to a brick wall.

Once they had settled in, Diana and Kim threw a housewarming party to which they invited her parents and his mother. The Flucks refused to attend. Mary had spoken to Kim on the phone and had taken an instant dislike to him, while Bert declared that he wanted nothing to do with a 'snooty opportunist' who gave the impression of having no intention of ever getting a regular job. The fact that Kim had recently given Diana a ring also riled her parents: they were convinced that he had only done this to soften her up, as a prelude to scrounging off her the way he had everyone else. Likewise, Yvonne failed to show up, having denounced her son's girlfriend as a 'common little tart' whose reputation preceded her wherever she went. Kim was further accused of bringing the Caborn-Waterfield name into disrepute by living in such a 'lowly' part of town: to this end she compromised by finding them a better apartment in the more upmarket Earl's Court, then crossed her fingers that nature would take its course – Kim would perceive Diana as she did, and return home.

In those early days of their relationship, Diana and Kim led a frugal but reasonably contented life. Rank offered her several days' work in *Dance Hall*, a tedious tale of factory girls seeking romance at their local dance palais: heading the credits were Donald Houston and Bonar Colleano. She also half-achieved an ambition she had nurtured since that afternoon she had stepped on to the platform at Paddington Station at the start of her LAMDA adventure – advertising Drene shampoo, not on a hoarding like Margaret Lockwood, but in a city newspaper. The fee was paltry, but the company gave her a year's supply of the product, which she sold 'wholesale' to a local shop to raise money for furnishings for the new flat.

No sooner had she finished shooting her scenes in *Dance Hall* than Olive Dodds packed Diana and fellow Rank starlet Barbara Murray off to the Connaught Theatre in Worthing for 10 performances of *The Cat and the Canary* – a common practice within the British studio system, as part of the young actors' development and training. She was clearly unwell but struggled through the run, returning to London to rehearse at once for *Lisette*, a musical comedy by Douglas Sargeant. Heading the credits was the now forgotten French revue star, Marcel Le Bon, then the boyfriend of Audrey Hepburn. However, much to Le Bon's chagrin, by the time the show opened in Brighton on 3 October, producer Norman Wright had effected a change to the proceedings: Diana's photograph had replaced Le Bon's on the playbills, and *she* was now promoted as the star of the show.

Wright may have been willing to sing Diana's praises to the local press, but his attitude towards her changed drastically when, halfway through the week in Brighton, she began experiencing nausea and dizzy spells and let slip that she might be pregnant. A doctor's examination organised by Wright confirmed this, and Diana assumed that once she had finished the run in Brighton, he would release her from the play. Wright argued that he had spent a good deal of his own money having the playbills and programmes reprinted, and that Diana would have to grin and bear it – and in any case, the paying public were interested only in her, which meant that if she left the production, the rest of the tour would have to be cancelled. When the production progressed to Margate, she became so ill that the doctor she saw there advised her that there was a very real chance of her miscarrying unless she gave herself up to complete bed rest. At this stage, she called Kim and he tried to reason with Wright – only to have the producer contact the police and have them issue a restraining order prohibiting him from coming within 50 yards of any theatre Diana was appearing in. Diana was further threatened with exposure of her 'dirty life' to the press, should she refuse to do as she was told. She struggled on, and the company moved on to Eastbourne, where *Lisette* closed on 22 October, the eve of her 18th birthday.

Riding the crest of a wave and having received rave reviews for *Lisette*, Diana decided that the last thing she wanted right now was a child. Almost certainly the baby was Kim's – at least, he believed this, and supported her decision not to have it. A friend – named by Diana as Oona, her understudy at Rank, made the arrangements and Yvonne Waterfield provided the cash. During the first week of November, Diana visited a back-street abortionist, where for £10 her pregnancy was illegally and agonisingly terminated by 'a fat, grubby little woman' on a tabletop in a Battersea kitchen.

No sooner had Diana recovered from this ordeal than Rank whipped the rug from under her. Faced with stiff competition from the big American studios, whose recent releases were trouncing theirs at the box office, the company announced that it had suffered tremendous losses over the previous 12 months. As such, they were shutting down studios, cutting staffing levels, and letting some of their less-important contract players go. Diana might have remained on their books had she conducted her personal life with a little more decorum, but news of her abortion reached Olive Dodds, who had no option but to report the matter to J. Arthur Rank. Like his Hollywood counterpart, Louis B. Mayer, Rank was a stickler for family values. He gave the instruction for Diana to be sacked.

Fortunately, until she hopefully signed with another studio, Diana had her albeit limited stagecraft to fall back on. Kenneth Tynan (1927–80) – who soon would be hailed the most influential if not controversial critic of his generation and, like Diana, was always a law unto himself – had taken a shine to her and in the spring of 1950 cast her in the play he was producing: H.M. Tennent's *Man of the World*. The previews took place at the Shakespeare Memorial Theatre, Stratford-upon-Avon, after which it transferred to the Cambridge Arts Theatre, and finally the Lyric Theatre, Hammersmith, where it did great business. Appearing with Diana were Ursula Jeans and Lionel Jeffries, who became a lifelong friend and confidant. The reviews were excellent: *Theatre World* gave her her first accolade, their Actress of the Year Award.

Gongs and good reviews, unfortunately, did not pay the bills. Diana was earning good money, but she and Kim were living way beyond their means. On New Year's Day 1951, Kim turned 21 and, along with the hangers-on which perpetually surrounded him, anticipated earning a fortune from his late father's estate. The upkeep on Yvonne Waterfield's homes and her own expensive tastes had put paid to this, and all he received was £50. Those friends from the Chelsea Set who had attended Diana and Kim's lavish parties paid for 'on the never-never' were now conspicuous by their absence. Evicted from the Earl's Court flat now that Yvonne could no longer afford the rent, they spent a week sleeping on the floor at a pal's house before renting a bedsit in Collingham Road, South Kensington – a move which coincided with British Lion Pictures offering Diana a part in their next production, *Beauty Queen*, scheduled to begin shooting in the spring. With it came a hefty, unprecedented fee of £800, certainly for eighth billing. Had she signed the contract just one week earlier, there would have been no need for them to move at all! In the meantime, she was paid considerably less for third billing in the film adaptation of R.F. Delderfield's West End play, *Worm's Eye View*, the somewhat lame story of a group of World War II airmen who are billeted at a family home against the owner's wishes. The stars of the film were former George Formby regulars Ronald Shiner and Garry Marsh.

'It's Spicy! It's Daring! It's Titillating!' proclaimed the tagline for the British Lion film, which by the time Diana began working on it had had its title changed to *Lady Godiva Rides Again* to commercialise on her presence. It was supposed to be a comedy, but despite the presence of Stanley Holloway, Sid James and other such character actors, it dwelled more on the sinister element of beauty contests. A working-class girl (Pauline Stroud) wins a Festival of Britain Lady Godiva contest, which has been rigged. Money and the promise of a film contract come her way, but her obvious lack of talent soon see her scratching around for any work she can get, including nude reviews. Interestingly, the cast included Joan Collins in her very first film role – unbilled, as a beauty contestant – and the tragic Ruth Ellis, of whom more later. Diana played Dolores August, a.k.a. 'Bikini Baby'. This was the title under which the film was released in the USA, where it immediately hit a snag with the censor because, among all the lovelies on display, Diana was the *only* one wearing a bikini. Moralists and religious groups were still fuming over Jane Russell's 'antics' in *The Outlaw*, and the Catholic League of Decency still ruled the roost. Though they could not actually ban a film, they could stir up enough fuss to deter cinema chains from renting and showing it. British Lion had anticipated such a problem and shot some of the scenes twice with Diana sporting an old-fashioned pyjama jacket in one scene, which completely covered her top half, and in another a 'fuller figure' two-piece that concealed her cleavage and navel. Prior to the film's release, Diana had auditioned for the part of Miss Smith in the Broadway production of Ben Wolfe Levy's farce, *Springtime for Henry*, whose title would some years later be co-opted as the sequence 'Springtime for Hitler' in *The Producers*. The controversy over *Bikini Baby* put paid to this: for the time being she would not be 'cracking' America.

Chapter Three

The Curse of Dennis Hamilton

While shooting the film, Diana was befriended by one of the bit-part actors and introduced to her boyfriend – a meeting which would have gone unrecorded were it not for future events. Osteopath Stephen Ward (1912–63) would achieve infamy as the doctor who committed suicide in the wake of his involvement in the Profumo scandal. Rumour had it that Ward was involved with procuring women, including Ruth Ellis, for sex for his friends. He certainly mixed with a strange crowd, not unlike the Chelsea Set. Diana spent some time with him at this time, leaving Kim pretty much to his own devices. But if Ward found her attractive and hoped she might provide him with the next notch in his bedpost, she claimed not to have liked him at all. 'He looked devious and was something of a show-off,' she wrote in her memoirs, though she could of course have been saying this in the wake of the scandal, fearful that some readers may have suspected her of being one of his call girls.

Stephen Ward was certainly no worse – and a good deal less psychotic – than the other opportunist she encountered at around this time, March 1951, at the S&F Grill. Dennis Hamilton lived in the same street as she and Kim, and was a friend of Kim's brother, John. Diana had often seen him driving by in his powder-blue sports car, but not met him until now. And over the course of the next few years, she would frequently wish that she had never met him at all. 'I was the only woman in his life to whom he gave his heart,' she said, 'for basically he hated women and often spoke of his contempt for them.'

Welsh-born Hamilton was an out-and-out louse: a thug, gigolo and serial philanderer who treated even his friends and most especially his girlfriends despicably, while always seeming to get away with it. In her memoirs Diana relates terrifying episodes from his past: his pathological loathing of the Welsh, how he had beaten up his headmaster at school, how when working as a bricklayer he had dropped a full hod of bricks on his foreman for ticking him off over some minor misdemeanour. Hamilton could also be a sadistic practical joker, which Diana found amusing, doubtless because while he was playing pranks, someone else was at the butt of his warped imagination and not her. He had a particular fondness for making anonymous telephone calls: one, she said, was to accuse a local scoutmaster of sexually abusing boys in his charge, which by sheer coincidence turned out to be true. On another occasion, he called a meat-processing factory and pretended to be a public health inspector investigating claims about its nonexistent filthy condition, subsequently causing the manager to sack his workforce and close the place down. She also recalled how, 'just for the hell of it', he had painted a large penis on an elderly lady's front door and almost caused her to have a heart attack. And yet, there is no doubting that without this man, Diana's career would not have seen so meteoric an ascendancy. Like the mothers of Judy Garland and Maria Callas, like Beryl, the wife of George Formby, Dennis Hamilton firmly believed that cruelty, manipulation and a twisted mind were the essential components of the perfect Svengali figure – and, in Hamilton's case, having a protegée who was not just willing to be knocked around, but actually encouraged and appeared to enjoy the process.

He had been born Dennis Hamlington Gittins on 23 October 1925, but had changed this by deed poll. Diana was the first to confess that he frightened the life out of her much of the time – in common with Joan Crawford and Edith Piaf, she would always nurture a fondness for violent, unpredictable men – but that there had been something about his callous, sinister and hostile mien which she had found irresistible:

It was Dennis's personality which really bowled me over. Added to that a dazzling smile which charmed everyone, regardless of what they thought about him, his motives or his principles. Not that he had any of the latter, as I was to discover. I never fell in love with Dennis nor loved him in the true sense of the word. Rather I was the fly caught in the spider's web. Yet now that I'm older, and I know more of the ways of the world, I cannot help wishing he was still here to look after me.

Diana, who of late had become addicted to reading her horoscope in as many publications as she could lay her hands on, regarded Hamilton as a lucky omen: not only did he have the same birthday as herself, but Hamilton's father and Mary Fluck shared the same birthday, and the elder Flucks and Hamiltons had the same phone number. Hamilton boasted to everyone that he was an actor, but his only known excursion into this field had been as an extra in Olivier's *Hamlet* back in 1948. Diana stressed in her memoirs that he was 'most definitely not' gay, but this does not explain why he had spent several years taken under the wing of the distinguished thespian Eric Portman (1901–69), a promiscuous homosexual renowned for championing the young men he slept with. Diana, for all her later worldliness, was certainly naive when explaining how one day Portman – with whom Hamilton had been living at the time – had dragged his protegé into a church and made him *swear* loyalty towards him – a strange thing to do, one would assume, had their relationship been merely platonic, even if Portman *had* permitted Hamilton to bring girls back to the house from time to time. To be regarded with equal suspicion was Hamilton's connection with Diana's film director friend, Brian Desmond Hurst, at whose home he had frequently stayed the weekend. This particular liaison ended when Hamilton had waited until Hurst was away: he and a friend then broke into the place and stole hundreds of pounds' worth of antiques – and then had the gall to confess the crime to Hurst and dare him to call the police! 'Brian, being the lovable and kind old rogue that he was, eventually forgave Dennis, so irresistible was that Hamilton charm,' Diana observed. In fact, he did nothing of the kind. Hamilton had almost certainly threatened to blackmail him, and Hurst was simply trying to avoid a scandal, fearful of having to explain *why* he so frequently allowed young men to stay the night at his house.

Since leaving Portman, Dennis Hamilton had as a front for his fraudulent scams and double-dealing officially earned his crust selling dodgy water-softeners, needless to say never covering the same patch twice. The evening he met Diana at the S & F she had been about to head home to Kim Waterfield, himself up to his neck in a perfume-selling scam. Hamilton had two tickets to see Danny Kaye at the London Palladium, and as his date had obviously stood him up, he insisted upon Diana accompanying him. That same night, their affair began. As for Kim, a few days later he was arrested and ordered to appear before a local magistrate. Hamilton gloated over the whole sorry episode, and rubbed salt into Diana's wounds by driving her to court to hear Kim being sentenced to two weeks' imprisonment. This, coming in the wake of their self-inflicted financial struggle, more or less put paid to Kim and Diana's relationship, something she would always regret:

> Borrowing a few pounds here and writing more post-dated cheques there, it would have seemed incongruous if anyone had prophesied the vast fortunes we would make separately in the years ahead. If only we could have accumulated all those millions at the time when we were still in love and knew what we wanted to do with our lives, there would no doubt be a different story now.

Diana and Kim had been together for almost three years, yet within days – taking advantage of Kim's absence – Hamilton was proposing marriage: traditionally, on bended knee, and with a stolen ring he had bought cheap from a friend. Diana had told him about the £800 fee she was being paid for *Lady Godiva Rides Again*, and that she might be getting the same amount for its successor, *The Last Page*, and clearly as the archetypal sponger he knew that he was on to a good thing. 'In a confusion of lost dreams, bruised ego and romantic flurry, I said yes,' she recalled, adding that she was also aware that her fiancé was seeing other women behind her back. He had, she said, even flirted with Yvonne Waterfield! However, as she was only 19 and a minor, she would not be permitted to marry Hamilton without her parents' permission. The Flucks, who had never liked Kim, approved of Hamilton because they believed he was in regular employment, and therefore able to provide for their daughter should her career flounder, as had happened with so many of the Rank starlets. They did not, however, agree with the proposed date for the wedding – 3 July 1951, five weeks to the day since the couple had first met – because this clashed with their annual trip to Weston-super-Mare, which had already been booked and paid for. Hamilton refused to compromise. He needed to have the banns read and the ring on Diana's finger before she had the chance to get back with Kim – therefore he forged the Flucks' signatures on the application paper.

The ceremony at London's Caxton Hall was a dramatic affair, to say the least. Hamilton had been cited as co-respondent by an irate husband in a messy divorce case, and needed to get the ring on Diana's finger before this became public knowledge and blew up in his face. In fact, she found out about it on the morning of the wedding when informed by one of his friends that the thwarted wife, unable to face life without Hamilton, was planning to end it all on the steps of the building unless he called the whole thing off! Fortunately, the spurned woman failed to turn up, though when Diana reached Caxton Hall, the registrar informed her that he had received an anonymous telephone call informing him of the forged application form. According to Diana, this could only have been Kim, who since his release from prison she was still seeing, though only in the capacity of confidant. As such, she claimed, the registrar refused to officiate – until Hamilton grabbed him by the scruff of the neck and growled, 'You'll marry us, otherwise I'll knock all your fucking teeth down your throat!'

No sooner had the rice settled than the rot set in. There was no honeymoon – just a small gathering at an Italian restaurant in Chelsea, where the guests were asked to pay for their own meals. With Diana paying, the couple rented a new place in Knightsbridge – Diana's first house, in Beauchamp Place. She had begun working on *The Last Page* with George Brent, the actor she had so admired as the psychopath in *The Spiral Staircase*. Leaving Hamilton to his shady devices, she left the house very early for Bray Studios, and often did not return home until midnight – meeting up with Kim after the day's shooting, and pouring out her troubles. Kim begged her to ditch Hamilton and move back in with him, but as much as Diana realised that she had just made the biggest mistake of her life in marrying this odious man, she felt there had been enough controversy in her life already without adding a public scandal to the list. 'I was married to a virtual stranger,' she recalled. 'It was so sickening that I began to hate Dennis almost as much as I hated myself for being so stupid.' Hamilton very quickly turned into a control freak, who ordered her around every minute they were together and kept tabs on her when they were apart. He had found out about Kim, and friends would later be asked to spy on her not just when she was with him, but when she was working, and to report back if she was seen in the company of another man, even if this was only the producer or director. Rather than complain, he delighted when the press referred to him as 'Mr Dors' each time they reported some scrape he had gotten into – which was often – because this kept Diana in the public eye during the odd hiatus in her career when less money was coming in than he would have liked.

The Last Page was an authentic *film noir*, directed by Terence Fisher for Hammer Films: the company was then in its infancy, and with Fisher at the helm of the studio's biggest productions it would go on to corner the British horror market. The words, 'Introducing Diana Dors' appeared at the end of the credits, despite this being her 17th film – this one was made with a view to launching her on the US market as a latter-day Jean Harlow. Like Harlow, she was by now a 'fully fledged' bottle-dyed platinum blonde, and to go with this and the brassy image the American distributor changed the title to *Man Bait* and added the tagline, 'The Cards Are Stacked...Against Any Man Who Falls For Her Kind Of MAN BAIT!' Scripted by James Hadley Chase, the story centred around John Harman (George Brent) the married owner of a second-hand bookstore who falls for his sexy assistant, Ruby (Diana), only to have her blackmail him. When she is accidentally killed by her partner-in-crime, rather than tell the police the truth, Harman goes on the run. In its day it was not a bad film, but today looks and sounds terribly dated. It also contains the plum line, pronounced by George Brent, which perfectly summed up Diana's feelings towards Dennis Hamilton: 'Whoever invented marriage must have been some sadist in the barbaric ages!'

'As he had made it to the altar four times by then,' Diana observed, 'I realised it was a sore point, and I figured in his experienced way he was trying to give me some advice. Sadly, it turned out in the end that George Brent was right.'

Diana was paid £450 for the film. Her fee, and a couple of photography sessions for a top London studio, enabled her to settle the debts she had accrued over the last few months. Once again, and to no avail, Kim Waterfield urged her to leave her brutal husband – he was not the only friend to do so, having witnessed the make-up department work wonders to conceal the constant stream of black eyes and bruises. Ultimately, he decided that rather than watch her suffer it might be better to put some distance between them and head for France – to do what, he had yet to decide – his theory being that if he was no longer there for her to come running to each time Hamilton had 'had a go' at her, Diana might hopefully see sense and follow him across the Channel. Diana insisted on paying his fare and Hamilton, keeping a watchful eye on her finances, saw the discrepancy in her bank account. Diana recalled: 'Never had I seen anyone turn from being a warm, amusing person into a screaming monster...His first blow sent me crashing across the room, and as one punch followed another he screamed that I was a "faithless whore", which I learnt later was how he regarded his own mother!'

Like many wife-bashers, Hamilton was frequently filled with remorse after an episode – alternatively blaming Diana for winding him up in the first place, or bursting into tears and begging her to forgive him, swearing that it would never happen again, which of course it would. This psychotic behaviour also spilled over into the couple's sex life. Hamilton liked things rough and daring, as did Diana. Sex was often a rumbustious affair, which invariably brought complaints from the neighbours, or other guests if they were staying in a hotel. There were reports of them having sex in the back of the Rolls, even in broad daylight. Hamilton liked to watch others having sex, and did not mind who might have been watching him.

A few weeks later, Diana received word from Paris: Kim was staying with friends, and apparently doing well for himself. Not long after this, she learned that he had sailed for New York, where he was earning a fortune promoting his newly discovered 'English dandy' image, selling Oscar Wilde-style clothes to gullible Americans. Diana also claimed that he alone was later responsible for launching the Teddy Boy cult in Britain.

The Last Page, meanwhile, was previewed in New York in February 1952 and received sufficient applause from the invited audience – mostly critics – for its American producer, Robert Lippert, to offer Diana a one-film Hollywood deal. Lippert (1909–76), the son of a hardware store owner, had founded Screen Guild Productions in 1945. This had subsequently become Lippert Pictures Inc, releasing 130 B-picture Westerns and low-budget adventure films between 1948 and 1955. Lippert, who had launched Shelley Winters, recognised the same rough-edged potential in Diana, and had earmarked her for the part of Princess Mari in *The Jungle,* a story of white hunters in India featuring Cesar Romero. If this worked out, she was told, there was every chance of her being offered the standard seven-year contract with one of the major studios. There was, however, one condition: she would have to divorce Dennis Hamilton! Like everyone else who worked with her, Lippert had seen the bruises, reason enough to want to protect her. His real reason for wanting Hamilton out of the picture, however, was purely linked to promoting Diana Dors, the commodity, as an 'eligible bachelorette', which made her suspicious that she might be jumping out of the frying pan into the fire – by making herself available to every elderly lecher in the film capital. Lippert next attempted a compromise: she could divorce Hamilton, get him to undergo psychiatric counselling, then remarry him once her first American film was in the can and her popularity on the other side of the Atlantic established. Still she would not budge: the idea was dropped, and Lippert gave Diana's part to the former Miss Utah, Marie Windsor.

Living in opulent surroundings at Beauchamp Place soon ran away with what little Diana had spare at the end of each week, and with Hamilton contributing not one penny towards running the place, she soon fell behind with the rent. Her husband's solution was to do a 'moonlight flit' – throwing their belongings into the back of his Opal car and driving out to Dunsfold, Surrey, where he had found them a cheap cottage off the beaten track where he hoped no one would find them. Then he contacted the press and announced that Diana had left London for a few weeks to mull over her next move – *she* had rejected the American contract, he said, because they had only offered her $15,000 a week, which was an insult for an artiste of her stature! He further declared that henceforth *he* and not Gordon Harbord would be acting as his wife's agent and manager. To prove a point he traded in the Opal as part-payment on a 1931 Rolls-Royce, which he bought for £350 in Diana's name – the idea being that when an impresario or producer saw her arriving in such style, he would be sufficiently impressed to offer a higher salary. When the cheque for this and the first month's rent on the cottage bounced, the couple relocated once more, this time to a rented house in Esher. Not long afterwards, the owner of the house in Dunsfold caught up with the couple and served them a summons for unpaid rent – a problem Hamilton solved by faking a robbery, smashing the windscreen of the Rolls and claiming £300 on the insurance for 'stolen' jewellery.

The move coincided with Diana being offered the part of Jenny in Peter Brook's film adaptation of John Gay's *The Beggar's Opera*, Laurence Olivier's only musical. It had been done before, of course, and much better. Lotte Lenya had created the role in Brecht and Weill's *The Threepenny Opera*, and much as Diana might have revelled in the role of the dockside doxy – Mack the Knife's girlfriend who dreams of killing everyone who sails into the harbour – compared to the original, the Arthur Bliss–Christopher Fry reworking was poor, and she was wise to turn it down, her excuse being that she had been offered the part of Cuddles, the sexy man-eater in Terry-Thomas's television series, *How Do You View?*

Scripted by the comic (the title was a play on his catch phrase) and Talbot Rothwell, who later achieved fame with the *Carry On* films, this was broadcast live at fortnightly intervals between 1950 and 1953. Diana pocketed a tidy £250 for an hour-long rehearsal and a few minutes of screen time, more than she had made so far in most of her films. It was, however, a one-off. The next day the BBC were inundated with calls and letters from irate viewers complaining that they had not gone to the trouble of investing in this new medium to watch smut: though her pouting and purring would seem harmless today, the moralists drew the upper hand, and Diana was informed that she had probably blown her chances of ever appearing on the television again. There was also an unpleasant, totally unnecessary coda to the episode. The previous year, Swindon Hockey Club had made her their honorary president. Now she was relieved of the post, the club's reason for this being that she was not a resident of the town – which had not prevented them from appointing her in the first place. She later learned that the Mayor of Swindon had privately accused her of bringing the town into disrepute, which was of course utter nonsense.

At the end of 1951, Diana was signed by David Dent Productions for third lead in *My Wife's Lodger*, but when shooting was rescheduled for the late spring of 1952, she elected first to return to the boards in the Finn Boe comedy revue *Rendezvous*, a box-office smash in Norway which had recently been translated into English. The producer offered her £25 a week, which she accepted. Then halfway through rehearsals, Dennis decided that this was insufficient and demanded that the fee be doubled to £50. When the ruse failed, he pulled her out of the show, which could not have delighted Diana more – she was pregnant again, and this time wanted to keep the baby. Hamilton would not hear of this, and booked her an appointment with a 'top notch' abortionist such as starlets and the occasional major star consulted when their publicists announced them to be suffering from appendicitis. Diana paid for the procedure herself with a modelling assignment arranged by him, and immediately afterwards sank into a brief but profound period of depression which Hamilton declared would only be cured by hard work. Unable to replace her at the last minute, the producer of *Rendezvous* had agreed to a compromise – she would be paid £40 a week.

Rendezvous opened in Brighton at the end of March, playing there for one week before transferring to the London Comedy Theatre, where it played to packed houses for a month. The stars of the revue were Walter Grisham, Roberta Huby and Chili Bouchier – big names at the time – but the critics were interested only in Diana, who appeared in two very distinctive tableaux. In the first, she wore her hair in pigtails and played an 'innocent schoolgirl' who, after warbling 'I Want to Be a Gangster's Moll', drew a gun from under her gymslip and shot the pianist! In the second she was Little Miss Muffet, who sat on her tuffet reciting poetry in 12 different regional accents. Her friend Kenneth Tynan, now working as a reviewer for the *Evening Standard*, enthused,

Beneath her robust and open-hearted physical allure, Miss Dors conceals the soul of an ugly duckling, a boisterous and jolly child eager to be liked. She is an unabashed parodist of desire...I cannot guess whether Miss Dors has any real talent, and I do not violently care. What is clear is that her personality is a blessing to our theatre and could easily develop into a legend... Miss Dors is a landmark rather than a performer, and I expect the National Trust already have their eyes on her.

Laurence Olivier visited Diana backstage at the Comedy Theatre, in a final attempt to get her to change her mind about appearing in *The Beggar's Opera*, but her answer was still the same, while Dennis Hamilton growled that no wife of his 'would be seen dead playing a fucking whore'. Early in May she began shooting *My Wife's Lodger*, a dull tale, and the first of a trio of films directed by Maurice Elvey (on record as Britain's most prolific director – over 200 films in a 40-year career). It was a paltry production with a silly story played out by a group of unknowns – today, the only identifiable name among the cast is Diana's. A soldier (Dominic Roche, who wrote the script) returns from the war to find his home turned into a boarding house: he engages in a series of scuffles with a character called Roger the Lodger, resulting in a slew of tired old jokes, but all ends well when Roger turns out to be a criminal, and the soldier inherits a farm in Texas!

For some reason, news of this film reached across the Atlantic, and Hollywood beckoned once more when she was suggested for the part of the native girl, Dalabo, in *His Majesty O'Keefe*, featuring Burt Lancaster as the adventurer who heads off to Fiji to seek his fortune. Lancaster was currently in London, and invited Diana to dinner within the intimacy of his suite at Claridge's. Dennis Hamilton wanted to handle the negotiations, but was overruled: Lancaster had insisted upon seeing Diana alone, or not at all. His reason for this was only too obvious. 'He was one of the most handsome, gorgeous specimens of manhood I had ever seen,' she recalled, 'and as the evening went by, it was inevitable that he should try to take advantage of it. But desirable and attractive as I found the American star, the spectre of Dennis waiting below spoilt the entire scene so far as I was concerned.' Diana actually got as far as making a screen test, darkening her skin and donning a sarong and black wig, only to have Hamilton turn down the part on her behalf. It subsequently went to another British glamour girl, Joan Rice, and remains her best-known role.

Diana's next offer was far less exciting. Though she absolutely loathed the place, she accepted summer season in Blackpool. Bernard Delfont, Britain's biggest impresario at the time, proposed £135 a week for a twice-nightly 20-minute variety spot in one of the end-of-the-pier shows, which would then tour theatres up and down the country. Dennis Hamilton made so many extraneous demands that the deal fell through, with Delfont swearing never to have anything to do with either of them again. Even so, Blackpool was still interested and Diana was offered a part in *Life with the Lyons,* on the same salary. The Lyons – Ben Lyon, his actress wife Bebe Daniels and their children Richard and Barbara – had started off in American vaudeville, but relocated to London during World War II and launched their phenomenally successful radio (and later television) series of the same name. The revue played to packed houses in Blackpool for three months and featured the entire family, along with their no-nonsense Scottish housekeeper, played by Molly Weir, and an assortment of odd-bod friends and neighbours. The British public adored the Lyons, though away from the spotlight they were a pretty unpleasant bunch – Bebe in particular. Back in the 1920s she had worked with Rudolph Valentino, and had thrown so many on-set tantrums that during one love scene he had exacted his revenge by spitting raw garlic into her mouth!

The money she earned from *Rendezvous* had enabled Diana to rent a house in Chelsea. Hamilton told the press that she had bought it, cash in hand. According to him she also owned the two-seater plane they had hired to fly them up to Blackpool – not only this, but that she had piloted the craft herself! 'Much faster and more economical than the Rolls,' he told reporters, 'and Dors has a pilot's licence, now!' This boasting backfired on the couple when Diana was served with a writ on behalf of Westminster County Court, for unpaid rent on the house at Beauchamp Place. Hiring a local solicitor, she tried to put off the hearing until after the Blackpool season, declaring that attending would be impossible without spending the night in London, and breaking her contract. The counsel for the prosecution suggested that, as Diana had flown to Blackpool, she could easily fly herself to London, attend the hearing, and be back in Blackpool before curtain-up. Forced to confess that her husband had made up the story about the plane, she was told that the case would be dismissed providing she called into Blackpool Magistrates' Court and settled the debt within the next 24 hours, which she duly did.

On 23 October 1952, Diana celebrated her 21st birthday, and Hamilton his 27th. Hamilton had opted to turn her into the 'English Errol Flynn', in that she would henceforth be portrayed as a controversial figure, eternally getting into scrapes to keep her name in lights – a precursor to celebrities such as Katie Price and Naomi Campbell, in that her every move would be monitored and chronicled by the media. No matter how attractive the offer, now or in the future, Hamilton declared, Diana would never give up her beloved country for the artificial glamour of Hollywood. Flynn, who Diana would meet several times, had spiced up the parties at his Mulholland Drive home with lovers of both sexes, liquor, drugs and two-way mirrors. Diana's shindigs, which took place at every home she shared with Hamilton, would be minus the narcotics and the sex would be strictly of the heterosexual kind because, though she claimed to be tolerant of her gay pals' lifestyles, she was anything but – while Hamilton, who had enjoyed sexual relationships with men in the past, was now content to denounce such lifestyles as 'perverted'.

For their birthday party, Hamilton decorated every room of their house with hundreds of Christmas lights, and invited 80 'unshockable' guests, along with 20 top-notch prostitutes – if there were not enough of these to go around, he declared, some of the guests would have to share. Yet Diana claimed not to have spent much time at the party, once the caterers had left and the expensive food demolished: impresario Jack Hylton had offered her a part in a West End play, *Remains to Be Seen*, and she had an early rehearsal. Not that she was able to sleep. Later she recalled being awakened by an argument coming from downstairs – when she got up to investigate, she found Hamilton brawling in the kitchen with one of the guests, and heard the man threaten, 'I'll tell Dors the truth about you! I'll spoil your meal ticket!' Diana said how she initially assumed the man had been referring to her husband's nefarious business activities, which she already knew about – therefore she had quietly tiptoed back upstairs. He had actually meant Hamilton's womanising, with which he hit her for six – literally – not long afterwards when the couple were in Poole, Dorset, where they had just bought a small yacht, and where Diana was judging a beauty contest. Leaving her alone in their hotel room that evening after the event, Hamilton went out 'on business' and, her suspicions aroused, Diana waited up for him, sitting at the window with the light off. Sure enough, she watched the car pull up and witnessed Hamilton kissing his mistress goodnight. Afterwards, he confessed to having had sex with her in the back of the car – and promptly punched Diana in the mouth. 'It was one more nail in the coffin of this marriage that I often hated so much,' she later said.

In his memoirs, *Crying With Laughter*, Bob Monkhouse remembers being invited to the Hamiltons' joint birthday bash and entering the living room while the guests were settling down to a porn film. Not that they stayed there for very long before pairing up and having sex themselves – some discreetly retiring to another part of the house, others putting on a public show of their own in front of the screen. Hamilton fixed Monkhouse up with a young dancer, who led him upstairs to one of the bedrooms. The comic's suspicions were aroused, however, while they were cavorting on the circular bed – she kept looking up at the mirror on the ceiling. Monkhouse then realised that he had been set up and, without finishing what he had set out to do with his female partner, made a hasty exit. It subsequently emerged that the woman had been hired by Hamilton, who did this sort of thing on a regular basis, gathering friends in the loft space above the mirror to gaze down and participate in a 'circle jerk'. Diana always denied being involved in her husband's 'mutual little wanking sessions', and claimed that Monkhouse, along with two of her 'regulars', had been in on the stunt but chickened out at the last minute:

> I never found it particularly interesting. Funny, yes, but certainly not exciting in a sexual way. More often than not I would let them get on with their little 'wardrobe games' as I called them, and find myself something better to do. It was of course essential that the man in the lovemaking duo knew what was going on, as otherwise one or the other would have turned out the light

and plunged themselves, along with the spectators, into total darkness, thus spoiling the fun!

Years later, Diana would hypocritically denounce the very men she had formerly invited to her home – well aware of what they had been getting up to and not disapproving back then – with another group of 'hated' individuals:

> Voyeurs! These sick men are almost as bad as gay vicars, but at least they have the decency to keep their behaviour private. I can find it in my heart to forgive the odd vicar who, through inescapable circumstance, falls in love with someone else's wife and runs off with her, therefore creating an appalling scandal and a bad reputation for religion. But GAY vicars? NEVER, NEVER, NEVER!

Diana never named these 'regulars', as most of them were still alive when she published her four volumes of memoirs, though she did give away enough clues to identify one: show-business columnist and trombonist Jack Bentley, who a few years later married the actress Wendy Craig. She also wrote of her amazement – feigning disgust – over how far some women would go, sexually, to please visiting movie stars who ended up with them on that infamous circular bed, adding that *should* she name all the well-known people who had had sex in her house, she would be able to write her own *Who's Who*.

On the face of it, *Remains to Be Seen* bore all the markings of a great success: its writers, Russel Crouse and Howard Lindsay, were responsible for innumerable Broadway hits, including *Anything Goes* and *Call Me Madam*. The screen version was currently being shot in Hollywood, with June Allyson and Van Johnson. The stage version, however, which opened in Oxford on 10 November 1952, turned out to be a dud. Its feeble storyline, set in New York, centred around the police investigation into the murder of a wealthy collector of erotica – and around the 'cutie' band singer (Diana), who is having an affair with the manager of the apartment block where he lived. Diana's co-stars were comedians Dickie Henderson and Newton Wayne, and tossed into the mix – the publicity boasted – was a 'hilariously funny

Chinese houseboy' who subsequently drew no laughs. The local press lampooned it, and the London critics had already sharpened their quills when it opened in the West End on 16 December. 'A more resolute kimonophobe I have rarely seen,' quipped the reviewer from the *Evening Standard*, of Diana's insistence in 'flaunting' herself in a different bathrobe each time she walked on to the stage. The Broadway production had packed out the theatre for seven months: this one folded after seven performances.

Chapter Four

It's a Grand Life

Diana's first film of 1953, which premiered at the end of January, was *The Great Game*, a comedy-drama set in the world of First Division football. James Hayter, best known for his portrayal of Mr Pickwick in *The Pickwick Papers* (1952) played the wealthy manager who sparks off a scandal when he dishonestly tries to purloin a top player from another team. Maurice Elvey directed, and the locations were shot in Griffin Park, home of Brentford FC. Several real-life footballers appeared in cameos, including Tommy Lawton. There was a fleeting appearance by Jack Howarth, who later played resident grouch Albert Tatlock in television's *Coronation Street* – and another by Dennis Hamilton. During a break in filming, Diana herself appeared in a cameo in Hammer Films' *The Saint's Return*, starring Louis Hayward. She should have gone straight into a radio series for the BBC's Light Programme (subsequently Radio Two) with Tony Hancock, but Hamilton poured cold water on this by demanding that her name appear above Hancock's in the billing, and the producer dropped her. Not to be outdone, Hamilton negotiated a last-minute engagement as part of a variety bill with singer Monte Rey.

It was a *big* mistake for Diana to make her debut as an 'all-round entertainer' at the Glasgow Empire – nicknamed 'the artistes' graveyard' on account of its tetchy, hostile audiences – and an even bigger mistake for Hamilton to book her there for a whole week. Though American stars such as Judy Garland and Vic Damone could do no wrong there, the crowd was decidedly anti-English. 'I was in a foreign field, and trying to cash in on a screen name at what was to prove to be the toughest theatre in the world,' she recalled. When she arrived at the venue for an afternoon rehearsal, she was pleased to see the long queue winding its way from the box office out into the street – only to be barked at by the manager that these people were not buying tickets to see her, but for an all-Scottish gala the following week. Much of the emphasis, naturally, was on Diana's costumes: like Eve Boswell and Yana, she loved sequins and skintight fishtail dresses that emphasised her hourglass figure. Just before going on, she stood in the wings and witnessed Monte Rey being put through the mill. Mistaking him for an Italian (despite the name, he was British) one heckler stood up and yelled, 'I shot at Eyetie bastards like you during the war!'

The first thing Diana saw when the curtains swung open were rows of people eating fish and chips, completely oblivious to what was happening on the stage! She opened with 'I Feel So Mmm', a sexy, suggestive piece written especially for her – then sang 'Put the Blame on Me, Boys', which Rita Hayworth had performed (or rather mimed) so memorably in *Gilda* (1946), before executing a little song-and-dance sketch which included an impersonation of Ava Gardner. She closed with the Rose Murphy novelty number, 'Brrp, Brrp, Busy Line'. And after each item, an almost glacial silence broken only by someone shouting, 'Git yer tits oot, lassie!' Diana rushed off the stage in tears, and begged her husband to cancel the rest of the tour so they could go home. Hamilton was all for doing just this, until the manager interjected that the evening had been a success – because no one had thrown anything at her! A backhanded compliment indeed, though this and the piece which appeared in the next morning's *Daily Record* convinced them not to give up:

> The reason for her failure last night lay in the faintly nasty and singularly witless number which Miss Dors had specially written for her opening. She would have done so much better merely to have come on and given us a bibful of old sentimental tunes... For the gal can sing! She has presence and aplomb, and she could have charm too if they put different lyrics in her mouth!

The next evening, instead of being on stage for 30 minutes, Diana told a couple of anecdotes and performed just the *Gilda* and Rose

Murphy songs, and was slightly better received. The rest of the tour, which took in Birmingham, Hull, Portsmouth and Brighton, was a success – she netted almost £2,000 for five weeks' work. Throughout the rest of the year, working around film commitments and with an act which became progressively longer – more sketches and hit songs of the day – her confidence grew and she made over a hundred variety appearances, including a memorable one in May at the Swindon Empire, where on home ground she broke all previous box-office records. The *Swindon Advertiser* enthused: 'Miss Dor's act is a skilful blend of showmanship, cleverly written and tailored to her personality. It is not original, but it shows that Miss Dors has versatility of talent, and knows how to make the most of good material. She should go far in the entertainment business.'

Then it was back to the studio for her next film, *Is Your Honeymoon Really Necessary?* With a cast headed by David Tomlinson and Bonar Colleano, this was a dull sex comedy directed by Maurice Elvey which Diana loathed making – though she did not balk at the £1,000 fee for just a few days' work. The money, barring personal expenses, was handed over to Dennis Hamilton to invest in their recently formed company, Diana Dors Ltd, where it stayed until he reinvested it, along with some of his ill-gotten gains, into 'property renovation'. This involved buying up old terraced houses for a song – paying the current market price as defined by one of his dubious 'surveyor' contacts – then modernising them and selling them on at inflated prices.

Arguably the shiftiest of Hamilton's friends who entered his life at around this time, and whom Diana positively loathed, was Perec Rachman, more familiarly known as 'Polish Pete', and a thoroughly reprehensible individual. Rachman (1919–62) had evaded capture when the Nazis had invaded Warsaw during World War II, escaping to Russia where he had been captured and interned in a labour camp. He had arrived in London in 1949, and over the next few years acquired vast wealth by means of any number of nefarious activities, primarily as a crooked landlord – enabling a new word, Rachmanism, to be added to the Oxford English dictionary as a derisory term for greedy, unscrupulous landlords. Rachman operated mainly in the Notting Hill and Westminster districts of the city, buying up mansion blocks – forcing out the white tenants by hiking the rent at a time when there were no strict laws against this, then letting and subletting flats and rooms to migrant workers and prostitutes, the latter sometimes by the hour. Non-payers would be turfed out on to the street, or worse. Short, balding and plump, Rachman had an insatiable appetite for women – it was only after his death that Mandy Rice Davies and Christine Keeler were revealed to be among his mistresses – and for voyeurism in particular. Whenever there was a two-way mirrors party at the Hamiltons' home, the first to be invited would always be Polish Pete.

Not long after its formation, Diana Dors Ltd was investigated by the Inland Revenue (as part of their bigger investigation into Rachman), who suspected Hamilton of paying insufficient tax on his wife's earnings, and of stashing away his ill-gotten gains in some secret location. Nothing was found regarding the latter, and an examination of the company accounts, along with Diana's contracts, revealed that Hamilton had merely lied about her earnings to the press, as a means of inflating her value to prospective producers.

Diana's next film was her best for some time. Indeed, *It's a Grand Life*, produced by Mancunian Films and shot in and around Manchester, is feted as one of the great British post-war comedies. For Diana it was also a triumph of mind over matter, for it saw her working with a man she truly detested: Frank Randle, in what would be his final screen appearance – he died four years later of a combination of alcoholism and tuberculosis. 'A dirty, disgusting old drunk' was how she described this hugely talented and immensely popular comedian. Randle (born Arthur Hughes, 1901–57) was born in Wigan – the only thing he had in common with his greatest rival, George Formby, for while Formby was the archetypal cheeky comic with a fondness for double entendre delivered with gormless and cheerful innocence, Randle was a deeply unpleasant individual whose coarse, unadulterated humour went straight for the jugular. Towards the end of his life, ploughing through two bottles of Scotch and a crate of Guinness every day, Randle was worshipped by fans but loathed by most of those who worked with him – though they never knocked back doing so because of the prestige this brought them – because they never knew what he was going to do next.

Randle had started out as a circus tumbler. Then in 1939, having been declared unfit for military service, he had turned his hand to stand-up comedy and making films – earning upwards of £1,000 a week, whence his popularity had successfully transcended the feared North–South divide. His stock-in-trade characters included the Hitchhiker (a vulgar octogenarian in baggy shorts who spat cherry pips into a tin bucket) and a knobbly-kneed Scotsman in a kilt whose catchphrase was 'I dunna knoo where that draught's coming from, but I knoo where it's a-gooing!' Today this seems like pretty harmless banter, but at the time such jokes were considered extremely offensive, and frequently saw Randle arrested at the stage door and charged with obscenity. Blackpool's Chief of Police held a particular grievance against him, which resulted in Randle hiring a private plane and 'bombing' the police station with toilet rolls. On another occasion, when the manager of a hotel he had accused of poor service refused to knock a few pounds off the bill, Randle set fire to the building! He also had the habit of carrying a starting pistol in his pocket, which he would pull out and fire at people when they were least expecting it – and wholly unaware that it was not a real gun. In the days before unruly rock stars he was the first to go regularly berserk in his dressing room, usually over the slightest criticism of his act, wrecking the place with the axe he kept in his suitcase, but always paying over the odds afterwards for the damage he had caused. A few days before commencing shooting *It's a Grand Life*, Diana went to see Randle in Blackpool and was appalled when, after someone heckled, he spat out his dentures and flung them into the audience – something he had been doing for years, and apparently always getting them back after the show!

Quaintly dated in parts, the film centres around accident-prone, fast-talking Private Randle and his attempts to save pretty truck driver Corporal Paula Clements (Diana) from the unwanted advances of lecherous Sergeant Major O'Reilly (Michael Brennan), so that she can be with the man she truly loves, Private Green (John Blythe). Randle himself commissioned the opening credits, where he describes himself as 'The Stage & Screen's Most Famous Comedian', and his co-star as 'Britain's Most Beautiful & Glamorous Diana Dors'. We see her in the opening scene as the new recruits disembark from the train and head towards the Army

Training Camp, filmed from behind but instantly recognised by way of her platinum-blonde hair. From then on, over the next 30 minutes, the emphasis is on Randle, obsessed with smoking his favourite Woodbines and getting away with as much 'smutty' innuendo as the censor would allow: soldiers entering the lavatory in pairs, the gay private as per the edicts of the day portrayed as a bumbling sissy – the men wolf-whistling at Diana and Randle's response, 'Very nice of you, boys, but I'm not that way inclined!' And the clip which was cut from some prints of the film when Randle nods towards the tiger-skin rug and barks the order, 'Look after the pussy!' The other gags are pure slapstick, taken from Randle's stage act: 'No smoking allowed!' – to which he retorts, 'I'm not smoking aloud, I'm smoking a-quiet!' It is that kind of film. When Paula arrives late for training and gets on the wrong side of O'Reilly, he threatens to make her life hell unless she accompanies him to the weekend dance, which is where Randle steps in to protect her. At the dance, she performs a first-class jitterbug and afterwards, in the film's only high-drama sequence, is followed back to the barracks by O'Reilly, who menaces her on the canal bridge. She (or rather stunt-double Patricia Phoenix, later immortalised as alter-ego Elsie Tanner in television's *Coronation Street*) falls into the water, and is rescued by Randle. The film ends with him replacing the disgraced O'Reilly as sergeant major, and speaking with a Scots accent – to get in the 'draught' joke. Randle is guest of honour at Paula and Green's engagement party, where the entertainment is provided by piano legend Winifred Atwell, who plays her big hit of the day, 'Britannia Rag'.

A surprise visitor to the set was Albert Pierrepoint (1905–92), Britain's chief hangman, who during his career would carry out some 450 executions including those of Ruth Ellis, Derek Bentley, John Christie, Lord Haw-Haw, and 200 Nazi war criminals. Diana was advised not to speak to him about his 'work', and later described him as looking more like a bookmaker than a hangman. 'A tubby little man wearing an ordinary suit, pork-pie hat, loud hand-painted tie and sporting a large cigar stump in his mouth... But then with hindsight I realised he would hardly be likely to walk around wearing a black hood over his head.' After the day's shooting Diana, Hamilton and Frank Randle accompanied Pierrepoint to the pub he owned on Manchester's Oldham Road, where they experienced his sardonic sense of humour – pinned to the wall was a notice, 'No Hanging Around The Bar' – and sat looking through the scrapbook which included clippings and photographs relating to his gory profession.

On Friday 17 July 1953, Frank Randle collapsed with suspected alcoholic poisoning, and director John Blakeley closed the set for the weekend. Taking advantage of the break in filming, Diana and Hamilton drove to Blackpool and checked in at the Mayfair Hotel, where after a beach barbecue an all-night bottle party took place. To ensure there would be no complaints from the other residents, Diana invited them all to the bash, along with 20 or so friends and acquaintances she and Hamilton had met during the run of *Life with the Lyons*. When one of these – Frank Rogers, who ran a baby boutique – failed to show up, Diana, Hamilton and a jeweller named Freddie Markell decided to leave the party and fetch him. Rogers was not in, therefore Hamilton – an expert in such matters – prised open a window and let the others into the ground-floor flat, where they proceeded with a party of their own, downing almost the entire contents of Rogers' cocktail cabinet save for several bottles which they filched. Then, to assure Rogers that he had not been burgled, Diana left him a note – while Hamilton scrawled a pornographic image on his desktop pad. The joke backfired when Rogers came home later that evening and called the police – no one had seen the trio entering the building, but a neighbour had witnessed them leaving via the same window, each clutching bottles.

The next day, the Hamiltons' hotel room and car were searched, and the missing bottles found: Diana, Hamilton and Markell were subsequently arrested, charged with breaking and entering and theft, photographed, fingerprinted and bailed. Before the incident reached the press, an anonymous caller – almost certainly a friend of Hamilton's, and put up to it by him – called Diana's parents in Swindon and informed them that their daughter had been arrested for burglary. Needless to say, she caused a furore of interest among the police station's usual Saturday night collection of brawlers and drunks – even the two officers who interrogated her could not resist being photographed with her and asking for her autograph. The situation became more embarrassing when Rogers learned that Freddie Markell – a former lover he had shared a home with

– had been involved in the break-in. Markell begged the chief of police to intervene, claiming that Markell had always had his own key to the flat. However, as they had not used the door, the burglary charge stood and all three were summoned to appear in court the following week.

Dennis Hamilton was currently negotiating a contract for Diana with a theatre in Hulme (which subsequently fell through), and to acquire publicity for this, the manager put on a chauffeured Rolls-Royce to drive her to the hearing. Local shops had supplied her with various items of apparel: fur coat, dress, high heels and a pair of massive hoop earrings. Diana defended herself against the charge of theft by arguing that there was no proof how much liquor had been in Frank Rogers' cocktail cabinet, and explained they had taken the bottles as a practical joke. Rogers was so mean, she said, that he would never have brought a bottle to the party like everyone else – therefore, when he eventually turned up at the hotel, he would be surprised to find that someone had brought one for him! She certainly worked her magic on the magistrate, who gave her an absolute discharge because she had had the courtesy to leave Rogers a note – while Hamilton and Markell were each fined £10 and ordered to pay costs. Hamilton was further reprimanded on account of the dirty drawing.

Only weeks after this episode, Diana received word from France that her former beau, Kim Waterfield, had also got into a spot of bother with the law. The globetrotting conman had recently taken up with film mogul Jack Warner's 18-year-old niece Barbara. The family owned a villa at Cap d'Antibes, to which the youngsters had been invited, and while Warner had been spending an evening at the Casino de Monte Carlo, Kim and a friend had rifled the safe, relieved their host of £25,000 in cash and jewellery, and fled. The next morning they caught the boat-train to England. Warner had immediately applied to the French police for an extradition order, though it would take him years to see justice done.

Diana, meanwhile, began working on her next film. When asked about this, on the eve of the Blackpool hearing, she had joked, 'I'll be shooting it in prison – whether as an actress, or a guest of Her Majesty's pleasure remains to be seen!' *The Weak and the Wicked*, directed by J. Lee Thompson, was based on his wife Joan Henry's *Who Lie in Gaol*. Heavily censored for cinema audiences, this film centres around a group of women from different backgrounds who, one by one, recall in a series of flashbacks how they came to be in prison. 'The Sensational Naked Shame Exposé Of Women's Prisons!' screamed the tagline, which was of course grossly misinterpreted.

The film opens with Jean (Glynis Johns) being made an example of by the judge, who jails her for 12 months for bouncing a cheque to pay off her gambling debts, then trying to fiddle an insurance claim – a crime for which she has been set up. In prison she befriends Betty Brown (Diana), who is there for fencing stolen goods – her boyfriend, who she swears will come for her some day but who never does, has let her take the rap. 'Give us a fag, there's a pal!' she barks, before telling Jean the story of her life. Pat (Rachel Roberts) is having a baby, at a time when being pregnant and in prison was regarded by moralists as truly shameful, and when it was customary to remove them from their mothers when nine months old and put them up for adoption. Babs (Jane Hylton) is there because she went out on the razzle with her lover, and left her children home alone – the youngest choked to death in his cot.

The emphasis of the film was promoting the benefits of open prison and rehabilitation, as opposed to the hardline tactics of institutions such as Holloway. The fictitious Grange, to which Jean and Betty are transferred for good behaviour and to prepare them for life back on the outside, was based on Askham Grange in Yorkshire, the governess of which was hired by Thompson as technical adviser. Thus for several minutes the film becomes a documentary, singing the praises of this more humane treatment of wrongdoers who all look like they are on holiday, rather than serving time at Her Majesty's pleasure. The governess in the film (Jean Taylor-Smith) also more closely resembles a friendly mother superior – persistently addressing Betty as 'my child' – than the boss of a corrective facility. All ends well, however. The two women are allowed an unsupervised day of freedom – shopping, dining in a fancy restaurant and even visiting a funfair – before being released, and though Betty considers making a break for it when she sees other sweethearts kissing while knowing that her own boyfriend has dumped her, she opts to be a good girl from now on and there is a happy ending of sorts.

The Weak and the Wicked may seem dated nowadays, but it was a good film for its time, though the critics were divided in their opinion. *Monthly Film Bulletin* found it 'of dubious taste' on account of Henry's injection of comedy into some scenes to prevent it from becoming a *film noir*. *Picturegoer*, however, liked this, declaring, 'Some of the characters are figures of tragedy, but others equally are figures of fun. That's life, and that's the film's strength... Call her blatant, call her tough, call her anything you like. But can you *ignore* a character like Diana?'

After completing the film, Diana began a stint in what was then Britain's highest-rating radio series, *Calling All Forces*, written by Bob Monkhouse and Dennis Goodwin, and broadcast each Sunday from London's Garrick Theatre. In her first broadcast she risked a reference to the Blackpool fiasco, telling listeners, 'I finally got the handcuffs off and made it to the theatre!' By now, life with Dennis Hamilton was virtually intolerable – he was still knocking her around, cheating on her persistently and suffering from uncontrollable mood swings which today would almost certainly see him diagnosed with bipolar disorder. Inevitably, Monkhouse provided a welcome shoulder to cry on, and the pair embarked on a brief affair – one that she claimed did not involve sex. When Hamilton found out about this, he trashed their living room and gave Diana yet another good hiding, and not for the first time she considered divorcing him:

> People saw in me a young woman mesmerised by this dominant man. A blonde glamour machine who went through the motions of film acting or performing on stage as if propelled by his dynamism... Our success was the envy of many. But beneath the whole facade I felt stifled and cornered like the captive mouse. Dennis still frightened me with his violent tantrums... I had a continuous desire to run away, to be free and to find someone with whom I could fall in love before I grew old.

By now, Dennis Hamilton was too wrapped up in his 'business' enterprises to devote himself to Diana entirely – save for advising her what to do with her money – so she hired an agent, Al Parker. The BBC had reversed their decision (in the wake of her controversial appearance alongside Terry-Thomas) never to have her on the television again, and booked her for a guest slot on *The Frankie Howerd Show*, scheduled to go out live on 10 September. Parker had been offered 25 guineas, but only hours before the broadcast, Hamilton overruled him, declared that this was not enough, and announced that she would not be appearing. Any attempt to blacklist Diana failed, however, and she was back on the screen on 8 December in an episode of *Douglas Fairbanks Presents*. 'The Lovely Place' was directed by Leslie Arliss, whose proudest moment had been Margaret Lockwood's *The Wicked Lady* (1945). Diana's co-star was Australian actor Ron Randell, now best remembered as the centurion in *King of Kings* (1961). That same month she made her pantomime debut, playing the lead in *Aladdin* opposite Wee Georgie Wood's Widow Twankey at the Boscombe Hippodrome, Bournemouth. She had just released her first single – 'A Kiss and a Cuddle' with 'I Feel So Mmm' on the B-side – songs she had been performing since her variety debut in Glasgow, and which were included in the production. Hamilton had a bit part, and trashed her dressing room one evening upon seeing the huge basket of flowers sent by Bob Monkhouse. Neither was Wood excused from his deplorable behaviour: when he saw the diminutive comic winking at Diana he decided to 'teach him a lesson' by hiding heavy lead pulley-weights in Widow Twankey's laundry basket, causing Wood to pull a muscle in his back and almost have to drop out of the show.

A few days before Christmas, Al Parker was contacted by Carol Reed, who had famously directed *The Third Man*. Knighted the previous year, he was one of only two directors at the time to receive the honour, the other being Alexander Korda. Reed (1906–76) had seen a preview of the soon-to-be-released *The Weak and the Wicked* and wanted to test Diana for his new film, *A Kid for Two Farthings*, scheduled to begin shooting in July 1954. According to Diana, some time before she and Hamilton had been driving through London when Reed's car had pulled up alongside them at the traffic lights. Hamilton had pointed to the director and told her, 'One day, Dors, you'll do a film for him, I promise, and that will make them all sit up!' Maybe this was just another of her tall tales, as was the one where she claimed that Reed made her sweat it out for 10 days before offering her the part, on a non-negotiable salary of £1,700.

In the meantime, as a favour to her friend J. Lee Thompson, Diana accepted a cameo as a showgirl in his musical drama, *As Long As They're Happy*, starring Jack Buchanan and Thora Hird's daughter, Janette Scott. In her scene she sings Frankie Yankovic's ultra-camp accordion hit, 'The Hokey-Pokey Polka'. Against her better judgement, she allowed Al Parker to push her into *Miss Tulip Stays the Night*, a quota-quickie directed by Leslie Arliss, of which perhaps the least said the better. Starring husband-and-wife team Jack Hulbert and Cicely Courtneidge, who loathed Diana because her name appeared above theirs in the credits, this was a tepid murder 'mystery' – the clear giveaway to the killer's identity being that Courtneidge played identical twins, one syrupy and the other psychotic.

In 15 months, Diana had hardly taken a day off work, and Dennis Hamilton – not she – now decided that as they had no time for a holiday, the next best thing would be relocating to the country. He settled on Brook Cottage, a large house in Bray, Berkshire, built next to the Thames but within easy commuting difference of London and all the major studios. A few years later, many big stars would move here, including Dorothy Squires, Marian Montgomery, Max Bygraves and celebrity crimper Raymond 'Mr Teasy-Weasy' Bessone, of whom more later. Diana paid £7,000 for the five-bedroom property with its own boathouse, set in three acres of landscaped gardens. Later, she would allow Hamilton free range with the renovations, which included a 'swimming-pool sized' sunken tub in the master bedroom, a tennis court and a huge tropical aviary. Because the 1931 Rolls-Royce looked 'lonely' in the massive garage, Hamilton bought (with her money) Diana a powder-blue Cadillac convertible, with her initials embossed on each door in solid silver. There would also be a 22-foot Delehaye, which Hamilton boasted had set him back £4,000, a tremendous sum for the time. The car was customised with a gold-plated steering wheel and accessories, and though capable of reaching speeds of 150 mph it was a real gas-guzzler that only did six miles to the gallon. It mattered little to Hamilton that Diana still had her L-plates: the car was a status symbol, which would only increase her value as the commodity she was in his eyes. When she finally passed her driving test after the third attempt, Hamilton presented her with a Mark-7 Jaguar – which only he was permitted to drive.

Shortly after moving into Brook Cottage, Diana was introduced to one of the most talked about photographers of his day. London-born Horace Roye (1906–2002) had spent time in South Africa as a diamond smuggler before relocating to Paris. Here, in 1931, he began snapping the great female stars of the day – including Francoise Rosay and Arletty – more as a paid hobby before moving on to the nude studies he became renowned for. These were never vulgar, rendered innocuous by cautious airbrushing or strategically placed objects, pretty much like the *Calendar Girl* shots of today. Then in 1938, while war clouds were gathering over Europe, Roye had caused a furore in Britain with his study of a naked woman wearing a gas mask and 'nailed' to a crucifix. The French, however, regarded him as a hero. During World War II they had employed him as a propaganda photographer: his mock-ups of Nazi officers depicted in compromising positions with prostitutes had sold by the thousand under counters in the Occupied Zone. Therefore, as Roye was right up Diana's street where causing controversies were concerned, she did not think twice when he asked her to pose for him. He had recently pioneered the Roye–Vada 3-D technique, and the result of their two afternoon sessions was *Diana In 3-D*, a glossy magazine complete with cardboard and plastic 'glasses', which hit newsstands during the autumn of 1954 – only days before Diana began shooting *A Kid for Two Farthings*.

At once the press made comparisons between Diana and Marilyn Monroe, while a few labelled her the English Bardot. In truth, she was like neither: she always had been and always would be herself, emulating no one. In London the new venture was more or less tolerated, but in some provincial towns she was branded a pariah: newsagents' shops were raided by the police and copies of the magazine confiscated. One or two were taken to court for peddling obscene publications, but no charges were ever made to stick. As is usual with such issues, many were willing to haul Diana over the coals without ever seeing beyond the imperious, pouting image on the cover. Inside, there were no naked photographs at all – just studies of Diana, in an assortment of costumes, which could just as easily have been stills from her films: at home in her bedroom or at her cocktail bar, or posing on her patio. And when one newspaper suggested that Horace Roye should be prosecuted for this 'filth', he was defended by no less an organisation than Scotland Yard. Only recently he had been employed by them – helping to track down porn merchants and other photographers genuinely flaunting the country's obscenity laws. Roye gained more from the *Diana Dors In 3-D* fiasco than she did, for whereas she had been paid a flat fee of just £175 for her contribution, he collected royalties from the many thousands of magazine copies sold as a result of what had effectively been a fuss over nothing. It added to his prestige, and the commissions that came his way because of it enabled him to retire a wealthy man in 1959. Hoye lived to the ripe old age of 96, when he was stabbed to death by an intruder who broke into his Morocco home.

Carol Reed was displeased with all this adverse publicity, and tore a strip off Diana within the privacy of his office. The last thing he wanted, he told her, was a scandal on his hands simply because she had been incapable of keeping her clothes on. Diana showed him a copy of the offending publication, then reminded him that he should have been used to scandals, particularly as he had been born on the wrong side of the blanket – the son of the distinguished actor Sir Herbert Beerbohm Tree and his mistress, May Pinney Reed. The director backed down, and the film was completed in an uneasy atmosphere.

So as not to add fuel to the fire, Diana resisted having an affair with her hunky blond, six-feet-two co-star, 'Tiger' Joe Robinson. Born in Newcastle in 1927, Robinson was a real all-action hero: a stuntman, judo champion, karate black belt, and a professional wrestler who in 1952 had defeated Olympic champion Axel Cadier to win the European Heavyweight title. Then, after a back injury had put paid to his wrestling career (though he performed all his own stunts in the film), he had studied with RADA and began an acting career that would see him appearing in numerous 'sword and sandal' epics, a Bond film, and on television in *The Saint* and *The Avengers*. Diana said that he reminded her of Burt Lancaster (who he subsequently portrayed in a television documentary), and some years later Robinson confessed that kissing her on the screen represented one of the most exciting moments of his life. Diana's friends have also said that, had Robinson been aware that her husband had been knocking her around, he would have made short work of him.

A Kid for Two Farthings, scripted by Wolf Mankowitz from his novel, is a real feel-good movie in the same league as *It Happened One Night* and *A Wonderful Life*. It is also a deliberate feast of homoeroticism. When Joe Robinson dons his skimpy trunks, the fans see him *au naturel* – no 'taping under' as per the requirements of the day. Astonishingly, the close-ups of his 'package' managed to get past the censor, but if some critics and picture-goers believed that he may have been taking his 'Health and Strength' image a little too far, the closeted gay fans could not get enough of him!

Interweaving fantasy with reality, the allegorical story delivers a blow to prejudices of the day – not just against homosexuality, at a time when directors were risking career suicide by tackling such issues, but anti-Semitism, where the story champions the plight of European Jews who have survived the holocaust. Mankowitz's theory was that gay or bisexual men should never be typecast as lily-livered degenerates – the exception here being the gay *and* Jewish 'Madame' Rita, the 'Yiddish Dior' proprietor of the milliner's shop. Regarding the attempted destruction of an entire culture by the Nazis, he reminds us that good will always triumph over evil providing one applies the precognitive dream – the fact that all will turn out well so long as this is what one wishes. Thus the resurrection of the Jewish faith evident by almost all the characters in the Petticoat Market scenario being Jewish, and by the appearance at key moments in the story of the rabbi, pushing a phonograph on a trolley while reading from the Torah. By contrast, Mankowitz's lovers stand out from the crowd *because* they are the perfect, blond, blue-eyed specimens dreamed of by Hitler as representative of his Master Race.

Within the shadow of the Unicorn public house, the shopkeepers and stallholders go about their daily business and dream of how they would like life to be. The elderly tailor, Kandinsky (David Kossoff), slaves away with the flat iron and dreams of the day when he might own a modern steam-press. His friend Joanna (Celia Johnson), who lives above the shop, dreams of getting a letter from her errant husband who she thinks is in South Africa, making plans for their future. Her small son, Joe, never had much luck with pets – they have all quickly died on him, and now he dreams of owning a unicorn, having been regaled with stories from Kandinsky that the mythical beast's magical powers can make dreams come true. The tailor's assistant, Sam (Joe Robinson), sits at his sewing machine – not regarded as suitable employment at the time for a gung-ho, supposedly straight man. And while the other males in the district wear pullovers and coats, Sam wears a skimpy white vest, which highlights his superb physique, and leaves his machine only to flex his muscles, or to add a photograph of some other near-naked hunk to the collection on the wall behind his bench.

Sam dreams of marrying his milliner fiancée, Sonia (Diana). The trouble is, though they have been engaged for four years, he is yet to buy her a ring, which he says he will be able to afford only if he wins the Mr World contest he has been training to enter for as long as anyone can remember. Friends hint that this is not the real reason why Sam has been biding his time, and why Sonia has to make a sterling effort to sustain his interest. Basically, she hungers for male flesh, of which Sam has more than his share (and on display most of the time) – but, being a decent girl, she would never dream of having sex with him until after the church wedding with all the trimmings. Firstly she has dyed her dark hair platinum blonde, bringing the quip from the jealous rival who fancies Sam for herself, 'Everybody seems to be going blonde around here. Marilyn Monroe is come out like a sort of rash!' Secondly, Sam may not be as 'manly' as she thinks he is – judging by the looks he gets from the gay couple who run the shop which Sonia drags him into, to bounce-test the mattress she has her eye on. Others cast doubts on his masculinity. Blackie (Lou Jacobi), the agent he encounters at the gym, assures him that he stands a better chance of earning the money he needs to marry Sonia by becoming a wrestler than he will by winning a contest: 'Mr World, high in the sky – and afterwards a muscle-bound hunk of stale male cheesecake!' And champion wrestler Python (Primo Carnera) – the Hitlerian bully to Sam's Aryan hero – derides him by calling him 'pretty bum' and 'cream puff', while vowing to steal Sonia from him because what she needs is a real man. Indeed, she too appears to have her doubts about him, rebuking him after her attempts to seduce him fail, 'Don't torture yourself, Sam. Go back to the shop and do some sewing!'

The fate of all the protagonists is changed by the boy, Joe – actress Rosalie Crutchley's son, Jonathan Ashmore, in what would be his only film role, and who sticks out like a sore thumb with his clipped Colonial accent. When his pet chicken dies and Kandinsky gives him money to buy a dog, he instead buys the 'unicorn' which has been his sole topic of discussion since the film began – a sick little goat kid which has just one twisted horn in the middle of its forehead. It is this cute little animal which inadvertently makes everyone's dreams but his own come true, for as the goat's life ebbs away, Sam takes on the bigoted Python in the ring, flattens him, and uses his winnings to buy a ring for his girl (from conman Sid James in an early role) and the trouser press for Kandinsky, who repays his kindness by making him a partner in his business as the credits prepare to roll on this inspired chapter of British film history.

A Kid for Two Farthings was chosen as a UK entry for that year's Cannes Film Festival, while moralists bemoaned the fact that its London premiere would take the form of a charity evening to be attended by the Queen and the Duke of Edinburgh. Kenneth Tynan offered a backhanded compliment by way of his review in the *Evening Standard* which concluded, 'In the new Carol Reed picture she has the chance of playing an ingénue who is neither a doll nor a slut. But even if [the film] has failed to turn her into a great actress, I for one shall not mind. To expect her to act as well is like expecting the Boulder Dam to play chess.'

The 'British Monroe' tag amused Diana at first, because when Marilyn had first hit screens in Britain *she* had been labelled 'The American Diana Dors'. Now, another 'sex kitten' had emerged: 20-year-old French star Brigitte Bardot, currently shooting *Doctor at Sea* at Pinewood with Dirk Bogarde. Like Diana, Bardot had been saddled with a tyrannical husband – the director Roger Vadim, who had discovered and launched her in *Le Trou Normand*. As this translated as 'The Norman Hole' – which one critic ungallantly suggested referred to a certain part of Bardot's anatomy! – the film had been released in Britain as *Crazy for Love*. The French star was on the receiving end of one of Dennis Hamilton's pranks when, having been asked to sing in the Bogarde film, she rehearsed the number in the dressing room which just happened to be next door to Diana's, by singing along to a demo-disc she had made and which she played full-blast for hours on end. When Diana politely asked her to turn the sound down and

Bardot refused, Hamilton sneaked into her dressing room while she was out, destroyed the valuable recording, and left a note telling her exactly what he thought of her. Bardot swore to have her revenge (not that this would amount to much).

The purists loathed the fact that the world's most famous blonde bombshells, and one brunette – Dors, Monroe, Bardot and Claudia Cardinale – were instantly recognisable by their double initials – DD, MM, BB and CC – monikers which flipped easily off the tongue and represented all that was bad with the cinema. A particularly nasty attack on Diana was launched by John Balfour, a gay journalist whose ersatz moralist rantings claiming to 'expose the shocking truth about our celebrities' in the populist rag *Daily Sketch* deflected attention from his own questionable private life. Balfour was utterly charming while interviewing Diana; his feature should have been headed, 'Meeting Diana Dors', but he subsequently changed it to 'Are British Films Going Too Far?' and all but singled her out as the supreme example of human degradation. Group Films had just released pre-publicity photographs purporting to be from her next film, *Value for Money*, for which she was to be paid £8,000 – her highest fee so far. In fact, these had nothing to do with the film – they were just a series of shots of Diana wearing as little as possible without actually being branded as indecent. In one, she stands provocatively behind a bathroom door: though little flesh is on display – her face, part of her shoulder, one leg – it was pretty obvious that she was naked, which meant of course that she had stripped for the photographer. When Balfour had asked her about this, Diana's response had been that censorship was 'not her baby'. 'This kind of pose has turned France's film industry into a nightmare of banned reels and X certificates,' he now pontificated, 'and we don't want that *here!*'

Balfour's attack could not have come at a worse time. Diana's mother had been ill for some time. Mary and Bert Fluck had spent the 1954 festive season at Bray – an uneasy time, for they had witnessed Dennis Hamilton's tantrums first-hand, and come to fear for their daughter's safety, albeit that Diana was so stubborn and defensive whenever he was criticised, like everyone else they had left her to her own devices and hoped that one day she might see sense and leave him. In April, 65-year-old Mary had been admitted to a London hospital for a routine hernia operation. Less than a month later, just as doctors had pronounced her on the road to recovery, she suffered an unexpected heart attack and died. Diana was devastated, not just upset over losing her mother but feeling guilty that she had neglected her over the last few years – yet the career she held responsible for this, which unbeknown to her was about to reach unprecedented heights, had been Mary's only reason for living when Diana had been a child. *Miss Tulip Stays the Night* had just gone out on general release, *A Kid for Two Farthings* was two months off its premiere, and she was about to begin shooting *An Alligator Named Daisy* – publicised as a 'Carole Lombard-style slapstick comedy'. Working with a director of Carol Reed's eminence had, albeit temporarily, regained Diana a great deal of respect from the film industry, and Al Parker was approached by J. Arthur Rank with an offer she would have been foolish to refuse.

The deal was for a five-year, non-exclusive contract: one film a year at £7,000 per film, and each one with a shooting period which would not exceed 10 weeks, enabling Diana to do whatever she liked for the rest of the year, whether this be variety appearances or making films for other studios. Dennis Hamilton shunted Al Parker aside once more, and attempted to turn the offer down on his wife's behalf, boasting to the press that as *he* had arranged the Rank contract, then he could just as easily reverse the process – but as she had already signed the contract there was not much he could do. Rank had offered Diana £100,000, he lied, which she had rejected because she could earn much more than this working independently. Furthermore, from now on *he* would be producing her films, to which aim he had set up a new company, Diador Ltd. For her first project, he had hired Ida Lupino to direct Diana opposite Edward G. Robinson in *The Rough and the Smooth*, scripted from the bestselling novel by Robin Maugham. Tagged as 'A Shockingly Adult Film!' this would recount the 'harrowing' story of a British archaeologist, about to be married, who has a passionate affair with a German nymphomaniac – to be played by Diana, naturally.

Hamilton *had* contacted Lupino, along with Robinson's agent, but neither of them were remotely interested in making a film with him at the helm. Six years later, *The Rough and the Smooth* would hit the screen, directed by Robert Siodmak and starring the less illustrious Tony Britton and Nadja Tiller. As for Hamilton, his boasts resulted in Diana being subjected to another visit from tax officials, who concluded that if she could afford to turn down a £100,000 contract, then maybe Hamilton had not exaggerated her earnings prior to their initial investigation. Again, he was revealed to have lied to inflate her value, yet, hard-faced as ever, he denied this when asked by reporters – on the very morning of Mary Fluck's funeral – how his wife was bearing up in the wake of the tragedy. 'She feels great,' he replied, 'and we're going to be rich. Only Vivien Leigh is getting bigger offers than Dors is getting, right now!'

Chapter Five

Yield to the Night

It was courtesy of Weston Drury, the casting director instrumental in getting her into LAMDA, that Diana tested for the part of 'easy lay' nightclub dancer Ruthine West in *Value for Money*, directed by her old friend Ken Annakin with whom she had worked on the *Huggetts* series. Annakin told reporters how he was looking forward to working again with one of his favourite actresses, but met up with fierce opposition from the producer, Sergei Nolbandov, a feisty but prudish Russian who had recently scored a big success with *The Kidnappers*. Nolbandov had been told of Diana's fondness for changing in front of the cast and crew, once even stripping down to her undies to give the technicians an eyeful. Initially, he declared that he would not have a woman of such reputation on any set of his, and was all for having her fired until Annakin stepped into the breach to defend her. Diana was, he declared, the most consummate professional he had ever worked with. She was punctual, she never complained or argued with the director no matter what he asked her to do, and there was not one person who had worked with her in the past who did not adore her. Indeed, all these things were true. Furthermore, he stressed, if Nolbandov fired Diana, he would have to find himself another director.

Following John Balfour's attack in the *Daily Sketch*, the film's content had been reassessed by Arthur Watkins of the British Board of Censors, the man who in 1951 had introduced the X-certificate. Watkins' attention had been drawn to the paragraph in Balfour's feature that referred to the still of Diana peeking around the bathroom door:

Even as an advance publicity still the pose is cheap, and it is not the kind of cheapness Mr Rank's studios can afford to indulge in. Nor for that matter can Miss Dors herself, just at a time when her genuine talent as an actress is being recognised. I look to Mr Watkins, a fair and far from prudish censor, to save Diana and her employers from themselves!

The 'offending' still had by now been removed from circulation, and many fans were disappointed not to see the much talked about scene. In fact, this scene had never been there in the first place. What they did see was a homely tale, much of it shot on location in Batley, West Yorkshire. A local man (John Gregson) inherits a fortune, takes his first trip to London, and comes close to eschewing the comfortable life – and girlfriend – back home after experiencing the city's nightlife and falling for hoofer Ruthine West, who is only interested in parting this fool from his money. Interviewed on location, Diana professed to disliking her part: she was, she said, getting weary of being typecast as the 'brassy blonde broad', adding that she had never wanted to play such roles in the first place, but rather she had been pushed into them by money-grabbing producers. This of course was not true: since the age of 13 when she had flaunted herself in front of the GIs, Diana had played the siren on and off the screen. And when asked what part she really would like to play she replied, never more seriously, 'A nun!' Also, she declared, she wanted to write – not her memoirs, much to the relief of many, but a book of children's stories. Some years earlier, while a child star, Elizabeth Taylor had published *Nibbles and Me*, a ghostwritten account of life with her pet chipmunk. What Diana had in mind was a tome entitled *Tales Tweetie-Pie Told Me* – about her budgie. The book never materialised.

Diana's love of animals was carried over into her fifth film release that year, *An Alligator Named Daisy*, though even she would have balked at owning such a pet! Directed by her old friend J. Lee Thompson, it saw her working opposite Donald Sinden, and alongside a veritable *Who's Who* of British character actors, mostly in cameo roles. Peter Weston (Sinden) is on his way home from Ireland when a fellow passenger asks him to look after his pet alligator, Daisy, for a moment – then promptly disappears.

When the police and a local pet shop refuse to take Daisy off his hands, he abandons her in Regent's Park but, feeling guilty, returns to rescue her. The pair bond, but with disastrous results – after causing him to lose his job, Daisy comes between Weston and his fiancée, Veronica (Diana) having crawled into his suitcase when he goes to visit her well-heeled father (James Robertson Justice) at his mansion. Veronica breaks off their engagement, and Weston ends up with Irish colleen Mona (Jeannie Carson), who has always been sympathetic towards the little creature. A silly story, but younger audiences loved it.

Some of the £7,000 Diana earned for the film was put to good use – by Dennis Hamilton, who decided that he wanted to go into the espresso coffee-bar business, a big craze in America but a relatively new concept in Britain. He had come across a cheap property in Maidenhead which, he boasted, would revolutionise the café scene there. His original idea was to transform the place into what would have been a precursor of the Rain Forest Cafés across the Atlantic – an indoor aviary-eatery where rare imported tropical birds would fly around freely, while cages containing small monkeys would dangle from the rafters. Initially, the local council refused to grant planning permission for the enterprise – not on account of the animals and birds, but because Hamilton wanted to dress his waitresses in sarongs. It was only when Diana vowed this would never happen that the operation was eventually given the go-ahead.

During the first week of September 1955, while Maidenhead Council were deciding the fate of Hamilton's latest folly, Diana and the cast of *An Alligator Named Daisy* were invited to the Venice Film Festival. Though their film had not been included in that year's line-up, Rank believed their appearance would help sell their other productions to foreign buyers. Also included in the package were John Gregson, Jack Hawkins and Diana's nearest rival, Belinda Lee. When the organisers informed Hamilton that there would be no seat on the plane for him or any of the other spouses, he announced that Diana would not be flying either – taking the scenic route, they set off two days before everyone else and drove across Europe in the Cadillac. Each town on the route was pre-advised of their arrival, ensuring a welcoming committee for Diana, who never wore the same outfit twice.

While the other Rank stars had to make do with being photographed in the airport lounge, Diana's arrival in the centre of Venice caused an almighty fuss – men of all ages, along with a few protesting Catholic priests, reacted as if they had never seen a woman before, chasing after the Cadillac as it drove through the streets to the Excelsior Hotel. Here, in the forecourt, Hamilton was shunted aside as dozens of photographers swarmed around Diana. She was asked if she would be taking a punt along the Grand Canal in a gondola and, indicating her Christian Dior twin-set, the top of which barely contained her bosom, replied, 'Of course, but first of all I'll have to change into something a little more appropriate!' Twenty minutes later she emerged from the hotel entrance – sporting a mink bikini, which all but caused a riot between the hot-blooded Latins and the clergy, several of whom held up placards inscribed with the equivalent of 'Diana Go Home!'

'My husband has always refused to buy me a mink coat,' she purred, cautious not to divulge Hamilton's theory that only whores wore the fur, 'so I'm afraid I had to make do with this little number!' With this she climbed back into the Cadillac and made her way to the Grand Canal, where she grabbed the pole from the gondolier and attempted to navigate the vessel herself, steadied by the muscular young man regarded by many to have been the luckiest in all Italy – particularly when she slipped and he had to wrap his arms around her to prevent her from falling into the water.

Several Italian newspapers branded Diana's performance 'obscene' – not that this prevented them from publishing pictures of the event. 'Anybody would think they'd never seen a pair of tits before,' Dennis Hamilton told one journalist. In Venice, there was also a massive row between the couple when Diana learned that Burt Lancaster was in town, promoting *The Kentuckian*. Lancaster called Diana and asked her to dine with him in his hotel suite – as before, Hamilton was excluded – but this time she politely declined, much as she was 'hungering to get laid' by the charismatic American, as she later confessed to Dorothy Squires. Even so, Hamilton decided to teach her a lesson by spending the night with the actress Mary Ure, currently dating playwright John Osborne – they would marry two years later – then boasting about it to reporters in the hotel bar the next day. Another drama involved a photographer who sneaked into Diana's suite while she was out and hid in the walk-in bathroom closet, hoping to snap her in the shower. Fortunately she heard him moving about, called security, and he was ejected from the building.

The rows continued throughout the journey back to England. Only days later, the Hamiltons' marital problems were exacerbated by an incident at London's Embassy Club, where Diana had secretly arranged to meet old flame Kim Waterfield, back in town and, she suspected, involved in some new scam or other. In fact, subsequent press reports suggest that Diana was thinking of leaving her husband and moving in with Kim, currently unattached. To her dismay, Hamilton insisted upon driving her to the club, and when Kim saw the latest bruise on her face, he turned on Hamilton and a fracas erupted. Kim, who started the fight, was ejected from the premises by security men and the matter should have ended there. Hamilton rushed out into the street after him, and Kim's misfortune was again getting the first punch in – laying his rival out on the pavement just as a policeman happened to be passing. Arrested, he spent the night in custody, and one week later was brought before a judge and fined for causing a public disturbance.

Diana, meanwhile, moved on to her next project. Since shooting *The Weak and the Wicked*, Diana had stayed in touch with Joan Henry, who back then had promised to write a sequel of sorts especially for her: the story of a woman sentenced to death for murder. This would prove inadvertently more controversial than anticipated. On 13 July 1955, Albert Pierrepoint had executed 28-year-old Ruth Ellis in Holloway for killing her lover, David Blakely. She was to be the last woman to hang in Britain, and public condemnation of her death – along with the backlash from *Yield to the Night*, based on Henry's novel of the same name – would contribute towards the abolishment of capital punishment, which finally happened at the end of 1965.

Ellis (born Ruth Nelson) had much in common with Diana, and in retrospect was always a tragedy waiting to happen. Aspiring towards a career in show business, she had worked as a photographer's model and nightclub hostess, appeared in a film (*Lady Godiva Rides Again* – ironically with Diana), had one child out of wedlock and at least one known abortion, and she had experienced no little trauma at the hands of the men in her life. Her husband, George Ellis, was a thug from whom she had received regular beatings: both he and Ruth's son committed suicide after her death. Blakely, an ex-public schoolboy racing driver three years Ruth's junior, had also knocked her around. A heavy drinker, no less violent and obnoxious than Dennis Hamilton, Blakely had punched her in the stomach, causing her to miscarry their baby. On Easter Sunday 1955, having had enough of his cruelty and cheating, Ruth had waited outside the Magdala public house in Hampstead, drawn a gun and pumped four bullets into him. She had at once handed herself in to the police, and at her trial told the prosecution, 'It's obvious when I shot him I intended to kill him.' Sympathisers argued that Blakely had got no less than he had deserved, and that had this been the Continent, it would have been regarded as a crime of passion. There was no such ruling in Britain: the crime was deemed to have been premeditated, Ruth was shown no clemency, and it had taken the jury just 14 minutes to convict her.

Though Joan Henry's book had been published the year before the Ellis–Blakely drama, Henry and the director *must* have had Ruth at the forefront of their minds while making last-minute changes to the script to capitalise on the still-delicate situation. Henry had initially been approached by Rank, with a view to casting Margaret Leighton as Mary Hilton, but the author was having none of this – she had written the screenplay *only* with Diana in mind, and refused to accept anyone but her in the part. J. Arthur Rank, however, wanted nothing to do with Diana Dors, his excuse being that such a dramatic part might affect Diana's future with the studio: she was famed for her flirty comedy roles, and he feared that playing a young woman about to go to the gallows would kill off her blonde-bombshell image in one fell swoop. She, of course, knew she *had* no future with the studio, and Rank's nastiness only made her more determined than ever to play Mary, which many consider the greatest moment of her career. Henry had therefore taken the project to Associated British Pictures (Kenwood) who nevertheless had been unable to resist the pre-publicity tagline, 'HERE SHE IS! That Eye-Filling, Gasp-Provoking BLONDE

BOMBSHELL!' It was hardly appropriate for this kind of production.

Kenwood moved swiftly, announcing that shooting would begin at Elstree on 23 October, Diana's 24th birthday. Two weeks prior to this, she discovered she was pregnant. This time Dennis Hamilton – who eventually wanted to have children with her – had no say in the matter. Diana booked herself into a clinic and underwent her third abortion. Then, on 16 October, she was en route to the studio for rehearsals when her chauffeur-driven car slammed into the back of a truck. Fortunately she was sleeping in the back, but a shard of glass from the shattered windscreen shot over the passenger seat and embedded itself in her scalp. Because stitches would show up on camera, the cut was concealed by emergency plastic surgery.

Yield to the Night is a true *film noir*, one of those melodramas where one expects to see Joan Crawford engaging in battle with Zachary Scott via obtuse camera angles courtesy of Orson Welles, before valiantly yielding to a fate that has never been less than inevitable. It opens with Mary Hilton evening the score with wealthy love rival Lucy Carpenter (Mercia Shaw). Mary climbs out of her cab, strolls up to Lucy as she is unlocking her front door, and calmly plugs her seven times (strangely, cynical critics observed, from a six-chamber gun). The next key we see is opening the door to her cell where she awaits execution, unless there is a last-minute reprieve. The prison staff are mostly sympathetic, especially the warder MacFarlane – serenely portrayed by Yvonne Mitchell. Only the chaplain is the archetypal Job's comforter, advising Mary that if she accepts her fate rather than fighting it, death will be easier to bear. No one informs us that she is on suicide watch, but the warders stay in her room all hours of the day and night, she cuts up her food with spoons, and is not even allowed to take a bath alone. Without make-up, her dirty blonde hair fastened with a rubber band, she looks a mess – a far cry from the glamorous woman in the flashback scenes, as her story unfolds.

Like Ruth Ellis, Mary has fallen for a louse. Part-time pianist and serial cheat Jim Lancaster (Michael Craig) meets her at the department store where she works – he is there to buy perfume for his girlfriend, Lucy, but is immediately smitten by the pretty blonde, who is having marital problems and is in search of a friendly shoulder to cry on. They soon become lovers, embarking on a relationship which we know is only doomed for failure. Mary is paranoid that he will dump her some day, like all the other men she has known. He pretends to hate Lucy, but continues seeing her behind Mary's back because he needs the money she is paying him for sex. Of marriage he scathingly observes, 'You don't have to go down a coalmine to know it's dirty!' Like Ruth's lover, David Blakely, he is also unstable: following a failed attempt to gas himself, he plans to blow his brains out, changing his mind only when Mary relieves him of the gun and takes him in.

Meanwhile, back in her cell and well aware that the noose is dangling behind the door facing the foot of her bed, Mary is visited by prison reformer Miss Bligh (Athene Seyler), while the warders debate the death penalty. 'Of course I'm very sorry for the girl. But we mustn't forget the other one, the girl who was murdered,' one says, while the other responds, 'Oh, I don't forget her. But another death won't bring her back.' Mary dreams only of hearing the familiar footsteps of the governor, bringing news of her reprieve, but marks off her last days on her calendar just the same. We get to know why she was so eager to be loved and never left alone when she is visited by her estranged husband, her manipulative brother and her insensitive mother (Dandy Nichols) of whom she sobs, 'She doesn't care about me. She never did. She always said I'd come to a bad end. Now she just wants to gloat at me because she was right. I didn't *ask* to be born!' Then the story returns to that fateful New Year's Eve, where Mary waits for Jim to pick her up to take her to a party. He does not turn up so she calls his landlady, who delivers the horrific news that he has finally killed himself. With nothing left to live for, and blaming Lucy for the tragedy – Jim's suicide note was addressed to her – Mary makes up her mind to kill this awful woman using Jim's gun.

The final scenes in the film are profoundly disturbing, and truly delve into the tormented mind of the convicted killer when Mary's reprieve fails and she is told that she has just two days to live. The warders too are shocked and upset that this timid victim of circumstance is about to die. 'They all have that funny look in their eyes, like I had once,' Mary murmurs. 'They're going to kill someone too, only this time it's legal.' And finally, the door opens at the foot of her bed...

On 7 November 1955, the day after shooting the scene where Mary says goodbye to her mother – also the day she was voted Britain's Top Female Film Star – Diana attended the Royal Film Performance premiere of Hitchcock's *To Catch a Thief*. Dennis Hamilton was 'otherwise engaged', and her escort for the evening was Mexican actress Katy Jurado. In the reception area, they shared a table with mean and moody heart-throb actor Steve Cochran, and Ava Gardner, who told Diana after they had been introduced, 'I don't care who she is – I will not curtsey to your fucking queen!' Good to her word, she stood stock-still next to Diana in the alphabetical line-up after the screening, and while Diana chatted to the Queen about her new film, Cochran, standing on Diana's other side, covered his bulging groin with his hands – the excitement of peering down her cleavage having proved too much for him!

Yield to the Night wrapped a few days before Christmas. For Diana it had been a pleasant, stress-free experience despite the harrowing storyline – Dennis Hamilton had been absent most of the time, 'interviewing' waitresses for his coffee bar project. He also took it upon himself to go house-hunting, having decided that *he* no longer wanted to live in Bray. It mattered little what Diana thought, and when he saw photographs of Woodhurst, a 23-room mansion set in several acres next to the Thames near Maidenhead, and on the market for £12,000, he put down a deposit without even consulting her. Diana checked the place out on Christmas Eve, took an instant dislike to the place – with the exception of the huge, covered Romanesque swimming pool, the stables and squash courts – but was overruled by Hamilton. He had already made plans to turn the ground and first floors of the building into executive flats, and the stable into a cottage to bring in enough capital to cover the mortgage payments, while the top floor and roof area would become a penthouse for himself and Diana. The work would take just three months to complete, by which time Hamilton would have spent vast amounts of Diana's money on only the costliest furnishings. He even bought twin 'thrones', which he had set on a dais in the centre of the living room.

Studio executives who had seen the rushes for *Yield to the Night* – not just the ones from Kenwood, but from rival studios who had never liked her – were already raving that Mary Hilton was the best role she had ever played. However, as the film would not be released until July 1956, no one could predict what the fans and those all-important newspaper critics would have to say. Having had a taste of high drama, Diana was in favour of continuing with the theme. 'Just because a person is glamorous doesn't mean that they can't feel real emotions,' she told *Picture Post*, adding that she was getting fed up of being compared with Marilyn Monroe. Yet as 1956 progressed and no such roles came her way, she came to the conclusion that Mary had been a one-off, and that she would end up playing 'dumb blondes' until she was too old to sensibly do so without being considered a joke. Rank, irked at missing out on *Yield to the Night*, deliberately omitted Diana's name from their list of productions for 1956, though this did not worry her unduly – by the terms of her contract, they would have to offer her something. Or so she thought.

On 7 February Diana and another sexy blonde, Yana – famed for her sultry songs and fishtail dresses – joined the line-up for Bob Hope's television show, filmed in London and subsequently broadcast in New York. Topping the bill was the equine-faced French comic, Fernandel. Hope, who like Steve Cochran hardly took his eyes off her cleavage, offered her the part of Betty Compton in his next film, *Beau James*, a for once serious (though much Hollywoodised) drama centred around Jimmy Walker, the controversial New York mayor who during the Roaring Twenties had risked public disgrace by having an affair with the British showgirl he eventually married. There was, however, just one snag. Compton had been dark-haired, and Hope was expecting Diana to dye her trademark locks black, which she would never have done. Hope's director, Melville Shavelson, subsequently gave the part to Vera Miles. Diana was also briefly considered to play opposite Norman Wisdom in John Paddy Carstairs' *Up in the World*, but decided she did not want to do screwball comedy immediately after *Yield to the Night*.

On 13 March, the Variety Club of Great Britain held a charity luncheon in Diana's honour, and awarded her their Showbusiness Personality of the Year Award. The event was clearly the dividing point so far as her relationship with Dennis Hamilton was concerned. He had used her, and she him, and he had served his purpose. The mood-swings, she said, had become more frequent and severe since moving to Woodhurst because the opulence of the new surroundings had turned him into a despot. He would insult her and take a swing at her no matter where they were, call her a 'dirty fucking whore' if she so much as smiled at another man, yet he was sleeping around indiscriminately. His alcohol consumption was spiralling out of control – whenever Diana sensed one of his drink-fuelled 'turns' she would escape to the bedroom and lock herself in. (Later that year, in the summer of 1956, she sought out her old pal Bob Monkhouse for no other reason than a shoulder to cry on. Her husband got wind of this and collared Monkhouse at a party the Hamiltons had also been invited to. In his memoirs, the comic explains how Hamilton had slammed him up against a wall, and produced of all things a cut-throat razor, threatening to slit his eyeballs unless he kept away from Diana. Monkhouse also had it on good authority that Hamilton had taken out a hit on him. 'For three years, I walked around looking over my shoulder,' he wrote, 'and the best thing of all was, I had done nothing!')

On 16 April, during the last big party thrown at Bray before the move to Woodhurst, Hamilton truly overstepped the mark when one of the guests drew his attention to an earlier newspaper article which referred to him as 'Diana Dors' suede-shod Svengali' – a double-edged term relating not just to the fact that many regarded him as her bullying mentor, but a slur on his sexuality. Both descriptions were of course apt: though there is no evidence of him being involved with other men during his marriage to Diana, it had always been an 'open secret' among the Chelsea set that her husband swung both ways. Intent on having her defend him on both counts, Hamilton had invited two reporters to the party, but these did not show up until after midnight, when most of the guests had left and Diana had gone to bed. By now blind drunk, Hamilton rushed upstairs to get her, dragging her out of the bedroom and barely allowing her time to cover her naked body with a dressing gown. At the top of the stairs, she protested weakly that she did not give interviews at this time of night, and Hamilton hit her so hard that she tumbled down the stairs and landed in a heap on the hall floor, her dressing gown wide open. 'Now fucking interview her,' she recalled him ordering the journalists. Diana staggered to her feet, answered a few questions, and 10 minutes later, while Hamilton was in another room, sneaked out of the house, got into her car, and drove off to spend the rest of the night with friends. Hamilton spent much of the next day ringing around until he found her, then went after her. His was the post-tantrum behaviour of the archetypal wife-beater: blaming her for making him lose his temper and, when the guilt trip failed to work, falling to his knees, clinging to her ankles and sobbing how sorry he was, begging her to forgive him and swearing that it would not happen again so long as she promised to return home. Like a fool, she believed him.

On 24 April, the Hamiltons were all fake smiles when the powder-blue Cadillac drew up in the forecourt of Cannes' plush Carlton Hotel – the car had been driven over from England, while this time they had travelled by plane. *Yield to the Night*, ahead of its UK premiere, was the only British film entered in that year's film festival. Diana formed part of the delegation sent over by Rank – though *Yield to the Night* was not a Rank production, she provided ideal 'decoration' for the studio. She was not afforded the privileges of the studio's other stars, however: instead of sitting with them for the official reception dinner, she was relegated to the table reserved for the press corps, and even had to cover half of her expenses, and all of her husband's. Even so, the publicity afforded to her was priceless.

The film was not tipped to win: the favourites were Hitchcock's remake of his own *The Man Who Knew Too Much*, with Doris Day and James Stewart, and Jean Delannoy's *Marie-Antoinette, Reine de France*. In fact, neither won. The Palme d'Or went to Jacques Cousteau's *Le Monde du Silence*, while the Jury's Special Prize was awarded to Henri-George Cluzot's *Le Mystere Picasso*. Susan Hayward won Best Acting Award for *I'll Cry Tomorrow*. The Festival's surprise success, however, was Albert Lamorisse's *Le Ballon Rouge*, a 34-minute fantasy about a boy (the director's own son) who finds a helium-filled balloon that follows him everywhere. In some British cinemas, this would be shown on the same bill as *Yield to the Night*.

Diana did not participate in the *Montée des Marches* ceremony, where traditionally all the major stars climb the stone steps up to the Palace: spouses were barred from doing this, and Hamilton decided that if he would have to enter the building via a side door with the minor actors and the audience, then so would she. Once through this door, however, Hamilton was taken to one side by officials while Diana, wearing a three-quarter-length white dress and looking more naturally beautiful than her over-made-up, over-coutured American and European counterparts, took her place in the line-up to be introduced to that year's special guests, writer-poet Jean Cocteau and legendary French actress Arletty. Standing near Diana was Brigitte Bardot who, still fuming over Dennis Hamilton's prank at Pinewood the previous year, pulled a sour face and turned her back on her – the sum total of the revenge she had sworn the previous year.

While in Cannes, Diana – along with Bardot, Ginger Rogers, Susan Hayward and Richard Todd – were invited to a sumptuous luncheon party thrown by the 78-year-old, fabulously wealthy Aga Khan, at his villa overlooking the town. The food, she recalled, was served on solid-gold platters. Afterwards, she was taught a valuable lesson in humility when she drove Ginger Rogers back to the Carlton Hotel. While dozens of fans clamoured around her, demanding her autograph as she entered the building, her famous passenger remained unrecognised, and was unfazed by this lack of attention. She recalled, 'I realised that as popular as I was then, there would come a day when I too would be ignored in the rush for some newer star. I hoped that when this happened, I would conduct myself with as much dignity as Ginger did.'

There had been no press presence at the Aga Khan's villa, a far cry from the event on 2 May when Diana turned up for the world premiere (six weeks ahead of the British one) of *Yield to the Night* wearing a strapless, fur-trimmed turquoise fishtail dress, on to which had been sewn 250,000 sequins. With some difficulty she managed to get out of the Cadillac – her breasts almost popping out when she stopped to gather up her train – and for several minutes she posed for photographs while a festival aide attempted to explain to her husband, as before, that the palace steps were for the stars only. Having been 'thwarted' once, Hamilton was having none of this until Diana shrugged free of him, and he was held back until she had entered the building. As the film finished, an ecstatic audience treated her to a 10-minute standing ovation, though the French media were not so enthusiastic. When a producer approached her with a view to appearing on a live television programme with Bardot the following evening, so that viewers could make up their own minds who was emulating who, Diana politely informed him, 'Thank you, darling, but I think I'll give that one a miss!'

In Cannes, the Hamiltons had argued virtually nonstop: on more than one occasion he had made as if to hit her, then laughed the whole thing off as an example of their clowning around. In England, his violent streak was well known among the show-business cognoscenti. Yet Diana steadfastly defended him against every critic, even to her closest friends, maintaining that their marriage was solid as a rock and that with Dennis Hamilton she really had found that elusive crock of gold at the rainbow's end. On 12 May she wrote in *Picturegoer*:

I am married to a rather wonderful guy. I've always known it – but at Cannes last week it was brought home to me. It isn't the easiest thing being married to someone like me... For there I was last week – being photographed and leered at, peered at, cosseted, feted, wined and dined. And always in the background, there when I wanted him, was Dennis. If you think any husband likes his wife being asked about her bust measurements by inquiring reporters, you're crazy. But Dennis takes it all in his stride and rarely loses his temper. We have a formula. Share everything: laughter, tears and problems...

On and on she went, singing his praises. In Cannes, while Hamilton had been off adventuring with another woman, Diana had lunched with Anna Magnani, Italy's greatest ever actress, who had recently made *The Rose Tattoo* with Diana's idol, Burt Lancaster. Magnani had been party to a bust-up the previous day when Hamilton had told his wife, 'One of these days, I'm going to break your fucking spine!' Afterwards, Magnani had told her about some of the men in her life, who had *always* been secondary to her career, which was why at the slightest sign of threatening behaviour, she had sent them packing. 'I can do without a man, but I just cannot do without my work,' Magnani had concluded, to which Diana now responded, 'Phew, I would hate to be *that* dedicated!'

And yet, deep in her heart, she knew that her marriage had floundered almost beyond redemption.

Chapter Six

The Great American Misadventure

Mere days after arriving home from Cannes, Diana received a transatlantic call from Louis 'Doc' Shurr, Bob Hope's agent, with an offer she could scarcely ignore. Shurr had been in talks with RKO Pictures, who had apparently had their eye on her for some time. Subsequently they had commissioned a comedy script especially for her, which they claimed would be 'right up her street'. Her fee was set at a staggering $125,000, and Shurr agreed to represent her while she was working in America.

The studio had recently signed the television comedian George Gobel to an exclusive actor-producer contract, in the wake of his top-rating series with CBS. Having already cast him in *I Married a Woman*, which he was producing for his own company, Gomalco, they were in search of a leading lady as extroverted as he was shy and retiring. Louis Shurr had suggested Diana, and on the strength of her appearance on *The Bob Hope Show* this was accepted. Gobel (1919–91) had started out as a country singer. His stage act saw him starting off with a song, which he never finished, always getting sidetracked into a monologue or comic situation. His catchphrase, 'Well, *I'll* be a dirty bird!' had entered television folklore. Gobel's delivery was as relaxed as those of contemporaries Jack Benny and Milton Berle were loud, earning him the nickname Lonesome George. Paramount had only recently put him into his first film, *The Birds and the Bees*, co-starring Mitzi Gaynor and David Niven, which had bombed at the box office. RKO were unfazed by this: with Diana playing his foil in the film, they were certain they were on to a winner.

In fact, there was an ulterior motive for her being chosen above dozens of American actresses who could have played the part just as well. Diana was picked for no other reason than Marilyn Monroe had just been assigned to her first British film, *The Prince and the Showgirl*, directed by and co-starring Laurence Olivier, due to begin shooting at Pinewood. Naturally, the publicity machine that surrounded and frequently stifled Marilyn did not want her British 'rival' hanging around while she was there, sharing the attention. Effectively, Diana was being shunted out of the way. She was still under contract to Rank, who on account of her controversial lifestyle had already opted never to work with her again, but who were not averse to striking a loan-out deal to RKO and earning a great deal of money for themselves in the process. At no stage in the proceedings was anyone hoping to turn George Gobel into an international movie superstar. He just happened to be in the right place at the right time, and RKO were far more interested in her, once the deal had been clinched, than they had ever been in a man who was as dull as Diana was vibrant and exciting.

The tabloids on both sides of the Atlantic vied for exclusives, mostly exaggerated, about 'The British Marilyn Monroe' and 'The American Diana Dors'. RKO and Rank tried to set up an arrangement where the two stars would swap houses for the duration of their respective shooting schedules. Diana and of course Hamilton were fine with this: no sooner had the ink dried on Diana's contract than he was boasting, contrary to his assertion of four years earlier, that they were thinking of staying in Hollywood once they got there, as she had been inundated with offers of work. This was utter fabrication. Marilyn did not relish staying for 10 weeks in a house next to the Thames, opposite which tourist boats paused every hour for their guides to point out who lived there, and where she was terrified of becoming a target for kidnappers and other unwelcome visitors.

Shooting on *I Married a Woman* was scheduled to begin on 18 July 1956, four days after Marilyn was expected to arrive in London. To avoid the pair meeting, it was necessary to get Diana – but most especially Hamilton, who had also boasted that he would 'soon be fucking the bejesus' out of his wife's rival – out of the country as quickly as possible. Because flying the Hamiltons directly to Hollywood would have left RKO's publicity department with too much time on their hands, the couple set sail from Southampton on the *Queen Elizabeth* on 20 June. Hamilton, comparing the importance of their journey with those of Dietrich and Garbo several decades earlier, had arranged a press conference at the dockside and instructed Diana what to say. This was her greatest adventure, she enthused, the one which would make her a household name around the world. She was 25 years old now, she added, and planned on retiring in five years time to start a family – by which time, Hamilton chipped in, she would be a millionairess and financially secure for the rest of her life.

Five days later, the couple reached New York. Hamilton had cabled ahead, and even at six in the morning the harbour thronged with reporters and onlookers, anxious to see the woman hailed by her husband as England's answer to Helen of Troy. There were loud gasps as Diana descended the gangplank, smiling and swaying her hips, wearing a short white dress under which clearly there was no bra. After posing for pictures, she and Hamilton were whisked by Cadillac – what else? – to the Sherry-Netherland Hotel on 5th Avenue, with Diana persistently asking the chauffeur to slow down so that she could marvel at the sights of the city. She was exhausted after the long sea journey, she told pressmen waiting in the foyer, but would be down to answer their questions once she had had a nap.

There was no chance of this. RKO had organised a tight schedule, and she was given just 30 minutes to change into something more 'appropriate' – the last thing the studio wanted was a scandal on their hands before Diana had shot a single frame. The press conference however did not take place at the hotel, but in the form of a cocktail party at the 21 Club, which the studio believed would be more in keeping with what Diana was used to back home. Here, to her horror, she was introduced to the bevy of reporters not by name, but as 'The British Marilyn Monroe', as she recalled:

Nothing I had done, apart from the Bob Hope TV special, meant anything to these hard-boiled American reporters. *Yield to the Night*, the Cannes Festival, films, plays, variety – it all meant nothing as they compared me to her. This made me feel extremely insecure. For the first time in my life I experienced the sensation of people thinking and implying that I had copied someone else to attain success. In the minds of the American press, and soon the public, I was merely some British blonde without any talent who had jumped on Monroe's bandwagon. Even worse, to them I was a beginner in show business!

The New York reporters, several of whom had attempted to interview Marilyn and witnessed first-hand the extent of her paranoia when asked personal questions – frequently shrinking into corners, or rushing from the room in sheer terror – did not know what to make of her British counterpart, who clearly did not know the meaning of the term 'shy and retiring'. Diana repeated her earlier statement that it was her intention to make as much money as she could, then withdraw from the limelight. When asked about the comparisons being made between herself and Marilyn, she stuck out her bosom, declared her vital statistics, and suggested that the young man make up his own mind. 'And in any case,' she added, 'I've had more movie experience than Monroe. I started making films three years before she did.'

When told that Marilyn would soon be marrying the much older playwright Arthur Miller, and asked if the rumour was true that she had been invited to be a bridesmaid at the ceremony, Diana snapped, 'I wouldn't like to be a bridesmaid at anybody's wedding, let alone hers!' One reporter held aloft a copy of *Diana Dors In 3-D*, and she pointed to Hamilton and pronounced, 'That was his idea, darling – part of our five-year plan to clean up and retire!' And finally, having made it perfectly clear – no matter what her husband had to say on the subject – that she had absolutely no plans to live in America, Diana was asked what she thought about American men. 'Well, my love,' she responded, 'In the hour or so that I've been here, I haven't seen many. Better ask me the same question next week!' The headlines in the next day's papers were generally enthusiastic, an exception being the *New York Mirror*, who had seen through the charade and by way of a backhanded compliment tagged her 'A Fascinating Fabrication of Femininity'.

Two days later, the Hamiltons flew to Hollywood. Diana had dressed down for the occasion, and swanned into the airport lounge wearing pink slacks and a powder-blue sweater. Once the chorus of wolf-whistles had died down, she indicated this and purred, 'Nice colour, don't you think? I bought it to match my Cadillac back home!' Hamilton, standing behind her, was initially mistaken for her bodyguard, but soon made it known that he was in charge. He also took an instant dislike to RKO's head of production, William Dozier, who had instructed for Diana's suite at the Beverly Hills Hotel to be filled with flowers – but gone too far by presenting her with the fur coat Hamilton had always denied her. His first words to Dozier are reputed to have been, 'What are you trying to do, mate – make my wife look like a fucking whore?'

The fur coat incident subsequently resulted in Diana being forced to turn down the lead opposite Tom Ewell (Marilyn's leading man in *The Seven Year Itch*) in Twentieth Century Fox's gangster movie, *The Girl Can't Help It*. This one had the campest tagline of all: 'No Lights On The Christmas Tree, Mother – They're Using The Electric Chair Tonight!' The storyline of this was less interesting than the showcasing of many of the big rock-and-roll stars of the day, including Gene Vincent, Little Richard and Fats Domino. When Dennis Hamilton learned that Fox wanted Diana to play a gangster's moll, however, he put his foot down. One Hollywood mogul had wanted to make Diana look like a whore – now another wanted her to play one! The part went to another blonde bombshell – Jayne Mansfield, who Diana met soon afterwards. The two would stay in touch over the years and feign friendship in the best Bette Davis/Joan Crawford fashion, while actually disliking each other. 'I could not believe that this sweet cooing dumb blonde from Texas was really as dumb as she pretended to be,' she recalled, 'and in all the time I knew her she never let the mask fall once, until in the end I finally believed that she really did speak and think like a Kewpie doll.'

Because they had arrived in the film capital a day earlier than scheduled, and because RKO did not want Diana to give unsupervised interviews or even speak to the hotel staff for fear of the wrong stories ending up in the press, there was nothing to do on this first night but stay in their suite and watch television. Diana found this fascinating because there were more channels here than at home, while Hamilton threw a tantrum and argued that he had not come to America to sit in front of the 'goggle-box'. Therefore he descended to the bar, where he spent the evening boasting about his 'investment' and getting plastered.

The next evening, Hamilton was ordered to be on his best behaviour because RKO had organised a reception which would officially introduce Diana to Hollywood's elite – not just movie stars and moguls, but the all-important newspaper gossip columnists. Foremost among these were rival hacks Louella Parsons and Hedda Hopper, the undisputed makers and breakers of more careers than most who had crossed them cared to remember, and always on the lookout for some juicy titbit. Diana described Louella as 'a wrinkled crone with a voice to match', and Hedda as 'a fascist with a sharp tongue and an evil eye fixed on everybody'. Both were exceedingly wealthy: both owned collections of furs, jewellery, works of art and even Cadillacs to rival those of any movie star – gifts from potential victims hoping to keep them on side. Both hired lackeys to do much of their groundwork: both thought they knew more about the Hamiltons than the Hamiltons knew about themselves.

It took less than five minutes for this gruesome pair of harpies to sum up Tinseltown's newest arrivals. All Diana had to do was sashay into the room in her strapless dress and stick out her bosom to have Louella denounce her as 'too forward for her own good', and for Hedda to write Hamilton off as 'a greasy-looking heel'. At this reception Diana also met up with Bob Hope's manager, Doc Shurr, of whom she observed, 'He was an incredibly old character who looked like a garden gnome, who wore a rubber girdle to keep his paunch under control, and who had a roving eye for the ladies, including me!' Hope was working away from Hollywood, but Shurr informed Diana that he still wanted to make a film with her – this time one where she would not be expected to change the colour of her hair. What he had in mind, Shurr elaborated, was a remake of the Jean Harlow classic, *Platinum Blonde*. With her natural flair for comedy and for never taking herself too seriously, Diana would have been perfect for such a role. Sadly, nothing came of the idea.

After just two days, the American adventure had gone to the Hamiltons' heads, and over the coming weeks the pair would cause more than their share of problems for their peers on both sides of the Atlantic. Diana had signed a deal to pen a weekly column for British movie magazine *Picturegoer*: readers would be able to share her Hollywood experience as this unfurled, along with the latest American fashion and make-up tips, and also get to know who was dating who. Initially, Diana began writing this herself, but as her workload and party-going increased, the task would be passed to a ghostwriter, apparently without the magazine's knowledge. The contract was for just two months, for she had made it perfectly clear to the editor that she would never wish to live permanently in America:

> In that town I learned so many things new to me... The lack of privacy. The dislike of the British (in those days). The waiters, chambermaids, barmen, many of whom were on the payrolls of the ever-powerful columnists ready to report what the celebrities had for breakfast, and who with! The competition was so fierce too. A jungle compared with the steady pace of England, and the clichéd route through bedroom door to stardom or disaster, which I thought had all been over long since, was just as prevalent as it had ever been.

On the couple's third day in Hollywood, Dennis Hamilton called William Dozier and informed him that any potential parts for Diana would first have to be vetted and approved by him, as her manager and the 'protector of her interests'. Dozier's response was that while he might have been responsible for doing this in England, this was not how things were done in Hollywood: as an employee of RKO she would be put into whatever movies they saw fit. Hamilton saw red. Barging into Dozier's office, he yelled at the mogul that his wife had now changed her mind about working for RKO. She would make the one prescribed film for this 'tin-pot' studio which paid peanuts, after which as an independent star she would earn so much money that she would be able to afford to buy out her contract with RKO several times over. Not so, Dozier snarled back at the arrogant husband. Diana Dors would toe the line like every other star in town, or she would very quickly find herself blacklisted not just by RKO, but every other major studio in Hollywood.

Diana subsequently apologised for her husband's aggressive behaviour, and promised to stick to the rules. She had of course yet to prove herself, and the fact that she kept changing her mind over her future plans at each new press conference only confused

William Dozier, who was by now beginning to wish he had never heard of her. Dozier had wanted to assign her to the company's usual (in common with all the major studios) seven-year, seven-picture deal, but when Diana announced her plans to retire in five years' time, he realised this would be inappropriate and that for once an exception might have to be made. Hamilton then made a point which was, for once, valid. If RKO were hailing Diana as Britain's *equivalent* of Marilyn Monroe (though the press were not) and boasting that they were going to make a lot of money out of their investment, then she should be treated accordingly.

Even Hedda and Louella could not argue this point, and William Dozier made the first step by moving the couple out of the Beverly Hills Hotel and into a rented Spanish-style villa off Sunset Boulevard – until recently this had been occupied by Marlene Dietrich. Then, following an emergency meeting with his executives, Dozier re-negotiated Diana's contract. She was now offered a one-picture deal to follow on from *I Married a Woman*, with the possibility of a second one-picture deal if things worked out between everyone. Hamilton rejected this. Diana (or rather he) now wanted a five-year, five-picture, non-exclusive deal, otherwise they would be on the next plane home. Dozier held fast for three films over three years. It was agreed that Diana would be paid $125,000 for her first film, as promised, with a 10 per cent increase in salary for each one after that. Diana also offered a condition of her own: while working for RKO, they must desist from calling her 'The American Monroe'. This would never happen.

Dennis Hamilton's boasts that he had formed a company, Treasure Productions, to handle Diana's US earnings – and that her very lucrative contract would also boost her fees for television and personal appearances, therefore guaranteeing her millionaire status in less than two years – was welcome news for her detractors in Britain, always on the lookout for ammunition with which to attack her. In a piece headed 'Close That Dors!' the *Daily Sketch* columnist Candidus accused her of tax evasion and concluded, 'No doubt she will have a London premiere for her first American picture. Well, I am just as tired of Hollywood tax-dodgers nowadays as I was on Hollywood bomb-dodgers in 1939, and when that premiere comes along I hope not to be there. I also hope no one else will be there.'

Effectively, if Hamilton was to be believed, Diana was quickly heading towards the super-tax bracket, a situation she could only salvage by applying for US residency. Yet fame-wise she was in an odd position. In England, courtesy of *Yield to the Night*, she had recently entered the box-office Top Ten, whereas in America, despite the massive publicity afforded to her arrival, she had yet to prove her worth. Her second meeting with Louella Parsons at the columnist's home – attendance obligatory – made her aware of how fickle the Hollywood machine really was. One of the guests was Lana Turner, who had started out as a notch on a movie mogul's bedpost. Lana had been one of the lucky ones, Louella reminded Diana, having been discovered sipping soda at a drugstore counter, adding with sardonic glee, 'This time next year, Miss Dors, you and many other movie stars like you who *think* they have what it takes might just as easily be *serving* soda behind that same counter! You are not *that* special, dear, and you must not forget that!'

Soon after the brush with Louella, Diana was tricked into giving an interview with the man regarded almost as her British counterpart – Don Iddon, the *Daily Mail*'s highly paid resident US correspondent – unaware that Dennis Hamilton had spoken to him first. She had, she said, absolutely no intention of ever becoming an American resident. She owned properties in England which could be sold, and her pets could be brought to Hollywood if need be, but she had been born English, and would die so. Hamilton, on the other hand, told Iddon that though they *would* be returning to England once Diana had finished working on *I Married a Woman*, they would only be staying there long enough to sell their home and tie up all the loose ends. He had discussed the matter with his wife, he concluded, and she was perfectly happy with his decision.

No sooner had the ink dried on Iddon's piece than RKO began experiencing severe financial difficulties, partly due to the advent of television, partly due to the dross the studio had been churning out over the last 18 months. *I Married a Woman* very definitely slotted into this category. The tagline – 'What Happens To The Mouse When The Cheesecake Bites Back?' – said it all. In the film, George Gobel plays an advertising executive whose Miss Luxembourg Beer Beauty Contest sees him marrying the winner

(Diana), only to neglect her for his work, then spend the second half of the picture trying to woo her back into his affections. Woven into the silly plot was a Technicolor sequence featuring John Wayne, as himself.

At the beginning of August, Diana was informed that her second RKO project was to be *The Lady and the Prowler*, opposite Ernest Borgnine. Then, while the final touches were being added to the script, the studio announced they would be closing down operations and handing over their current productions to Universal, who would distribute them 'in order of merit'. *I Married a Woman*, halfway through shooting, had been scheduled for a January 1957 release, but when Universal demoted it to B-movie status, RKO were told that there was every chance of it not hitting the cinemas for another six months. In fact, it would not be released until the spring of 1958.

RKO were now faced with the dilemma of having a costly star on their hands, and with the likelihood of having nothing to show for their investment in the foreseeable future. Neither was it Diana's fault that one of the year's most applauded British releases, *Yield to the Night*, had not yet been granted a US certificate. Firstly, the American distributor had complained that the title sounded pornographic, and insisted that it be changed to *Blonde Sinner*, which of course sounded worse. Secondly, the Catholic League of Decency had protested that American audiences would find certain elements of the production too disturbing. As a result of this, 18 minutes had been trimmed from it, and Diana was now threatening to back out of promoting it unless it was restored to its original length. William Dozier therefore gave the go-ahead for shooting to commence on *The Lady and the Prowler* before *I Married a Woman* was completed – only to have Ernest Borgnine's manager pull him from the film, fearing that this one might also end up assigned to the RKO vaults. Not for the first time, Diana thought of throwing in the towel. 'All my life I had dreamed of going to Hollywood and being a star,' she recalled, 'and now I was there, none of it seemed important.'

In the meantime, the Hamilton's went house-hunting, and very quickly settled on Hillside House, a two-storey property set in four acres in Coldwater Canyon. The asking price was $50,000 and included most of the furnishings: RKO, who only weeks before had complained of feeling the pinch, loaned Diana the money. The couple then set about organising a house-warming party. This being Hollywood, William Dozier suggested that they think up a gimmick that would amuse the gossip columnists, who would of course have to be invited before everyone else.

It was Diana's idea to fly over the most famous crimper in Britain – Raymond 'Mr Teasy-Weasy' Bessone – to supervise the proceedings. The press reported how she was personally forking out $10,000 to treat herself to the most expensive hairdo in Hollywood history. In fact, Teasy-Weasy was footing the bill, with the intention of hopefully launching his own Hollywood career, using Diana's party as a platform to drum up business in a community that frequently had more money than sense.

Born in London in 1911, Teasy-Weasy is generally regarded as Britian's first celebrity hairdresser – his nickname came courtesy of the way he back-combed guests' hair on his Saturday evening television show: 'We'll do a teasy-weasy here, and a teasy-weasy there!' The undisputed Liberace of the salon, as a child he had been mollycoddled by a mother who had dressed him in velvet and lace, which he had still been wearing when he began his career making fake beards in his father's Soho barber's shop. And when, having decided not to follow in his macho father's footsteps but instead become a ladies' coiffeur, a friend had suggested that only 'queens' became hairdressers, the young Raymond had opted to 'go the whole hog' – sporting a pencil-line moustache which made him look like the baddie in a silent movie, satin suits with a blue carnation buttonhole, vivid red nail varnish and lipstick, and smoking monogrammed, pink filter-tip cigarettes. The transformation was finished off with a fake French accent, while the 'Parisian' flavour extended to his salon, a veritable pink palace of gilt mirrors, chandeliers and champagne fountains. Once, when questioned about his effeminate mannerism, he had publicly exclaimed, 'I *am* homosexuality!' Effectively, despite his marriages and alleged female conquests, Teasy-Weasy was a gay man, if not by natural inclination than by force of will, different only in that he was a gay man impersonating a straight man pretending to be gay.

The Hamiltons had just moved into Hillside House when Teasy-Weasy breezed into town, accompanied by his wife Jennifer, and several assistants. He had cabled ahead to RKO to instruct them that *only* he would have any say in the 250-strong guest list, therefore it was 'tough titties' if he invited anyone the studio disliked, or if any particular favourite was left out. RKO agreed to this, their only condition being that Hedda and Louella be invited. He readily agreed; as the town's official spokeswomen, if Teasy-Weasy got them on side and earned himself a favourable mention in their columns, he would have the customers flinging themselves at his feet.

The party was fixed to take place on 19 August, and among those invited were Zsa Zsa Gabor, Ginger Rogers, Lana Turner, Doris Day, Debbie Reynolds, Dinah Shore, Edith Piaf (who 'deeply shocked' Teasy-Weasy by informing him that she had better things to do) and Dorothy Squires, who said, 'Just so that he wasn't the only princess at the party, he invited Liberace.' The other males on the guest list included George Gobel, Adolph Menjou, John Wayne and Eddie Fisher.

Dennis Hamilton and Teasy-Weasy boasted that their party would be the most talked about 'ding-dong' of the year, and they were not wrong. The hairdresser 'marked his patch' by buying 500 of his favourite blue carnations, which were used to spell his name in the pool. Chinese lanterns were hung from the trees and trellising, and as the guests arrived they were welcomed by a mariachi band. Diana's entrance, at 8pm sharp, was not as spectacular as everyone expected: she wore a simple outfit comprising turquoise three-quarter-length slacks, a matching open-necked blouse and beaded slingbacks. Around 30 minutes into proceedings she, Hamilton, Louis Shurr and a couturier named Howard Shoup posed in front of the pool for photographs. They were all laughing at one of Hamilton's crude jokes when, suddenly, the pressmen surged forwards, there was a scuffle, and all four toppled backwards into the shallow end. All but Hamilton appear to have seen the funny side of the incident: climbing out of the pool, Diana's furious husband yelled that he would give $5,000 to the first person who stepped forward to name the culprit who had pushed them into the water. When this did not happen he grabbed the nearest press photographer – 32-year-old Stewart Sawyer – punched him to the ground, and repeatedly kicked him in the head. According to Sawyer, a sopping-wet Diana kicked him too – though with her slingbacks she could not have inflicted nearly so much damage as Hamilton, who was dragged away screaming while an unconscious Sawyer was carried into one of the bedrooms. Who called the police is not known. Suffice to say, not wishing to be further implicated in the scandal, by the time they arrived, almost all of the guests had left.

The next day, Diana's picture was splashed across the front pages with the kind of headlines she had least wanted. Stewart Sawyer had been taken to hospital with severe concussion, cuts and bruises, a cracked rib and a suspected broken nose. Diana had sprained her back, and her arms were covered in bruises. Over the next few days, there were several versions of what had actually happened at the pool party. Hamilton had threatened to punch one of the cops. Initially, Diana denied attacking Sawyer, until witnesses came forward stating that the bruises on her arms had been caused by her being restrained while kicking him. She claimed that she had seen Sawyer 'deliberately and violently' push Shoup and Shurr into herself and Hamilton, sending all four sprawling backwards into the water. Sawyer denied this, adding that he *may* have accidentally bumped into the group because, like everyone else that evening, he had been a little tipsy. His wife defended him, claiming that he had been nowhere near them – but she had, she swore, witnessed Diana laying into him. 'I'll get back,' she told one reporter, 'and when I do, I'll kick the lady where it hurts the most!'

Hedda Hopper and Louella Parsons were kicking themselves for not making it to the party, but had their say all the same because each had had a spy in the camp. Their opinion was that the whole incident had been yet another of Dennis Hamilton's pranks, and they made it clear that if he was used to getting away with this sort of thing in England, he was in Hollywood now and the piper would have to be paid. Hamilton refused to apologise for the incident, but confessed that it had been meant as a joke – his intention, he said, was to have Zsa Zsa Gabor fall into the pool, but Diana had gallantly taken her place while the others had been lining up for the shot. Hedda concluded that no one had pushed anyone into the pool – Hamilton had *pulled* them in. Meanwhile, in his stage act, Louis Shurr's number-one client, Bob Hope, made light of the situation by adding a new gag to his routine: 'Louis Shurr's just ordered his party costume for the season – white tie, goggles and a snorkel!'

Hedda and Louella were beaten to the attack in the gossip columns by Lewis Onslow, writing for the supermarket trash-mag, *National Enquirer*. Onslow had planned an exposé on *Dracula* actor Bela Lugosi, who died three days before the Hamilton party, but could not pass up on this very different horror story. And, like his harpie rivals, he pulled no punches:

> They are a bizarre, boisterous couple who have thrived on publicity, good and bad, and whose zany, riotous exploits have reverberated on both sides of the Atlantic... Miss Dors is Britain's busty answer to Marilyn Monroe. Dennis Hamilton is her husband, and nobody's answer to anything... The [pool] exhibition was sheer bad manners. Inexcusable bad manners, even if the whole thing was a publicity stunt. We have enough bizarre characters in this country without importing others who have no regard for the common standard of decent behaviour!

The feature, splashed across the publication's cover, was headed, 'Ms Dors Go Home – And Take Mr Dors With You!'

Chapter Seven

Point of No Return

Only days after the party, Diana registered with a Beverly Hills medical centre for thrice-weekly sessions for stress-control. Teasy-Weasy had left Los Angeles in a huff, blaming the Hamiltons for sabotaging his US career. Diana cared less about this than she did the fact that her fate was now in the hands of the RKO executives, who during the police investigation had consulted with their lawyers, ridiculous as this might seem today, with a view to having the couple kicked out of the country.

Like every other studio employee, Diana's contract contained a clause prohibiting 'moral turpitude' – this harked back to the days of clean-up campaigner Will Hays' Motion Picture Code and basically meant that stars and personnel should conduct their private lives with decorum at all times. Hay's famous Black Book was still in existence and contained the names of over 200 stars – the worst offenders being Mae West, Tallulah Bankhead and Errol Flynn – who had at some time been blacklisted for 'inappropriate' behaviour. Diana however had not once stepped out of line since arriving in America: though Stewart Sawyer had accused her of kicking him, he had done so outside of the police investigation and any beef the journalist really had was with Dennis Hamilton, who was not on any studio payroll. RKO therefore could not hold Diana responsible for her husband's actions: the most they could do was to bar him from the set of any of her future films.

This happened when shooting began on *The Lady and the Prowler* in September 1956. At the helm was director-producer-screenwriter John Farrow (1904–63), husband of former *Tarzan* actress Maureen O'Sullivan and father of Mia (one of seven siblings), who later married Frank Sinatra. Australian-born Farrow had recently scripted *Around the World in Eighty Days* for Mike Todd, which would win him an Oscar the following year – a mammoth effort which nevertheless caused him considerably less stress than this film, though Farrow himself was never an easy man to work with. He was also very much a womaniser, which in view of his subsequent attitude towards Diana saw her denouncing him as the ultimate bigot. Tagged, 'HALF-ANGEL, HALF-DEVIL, She Made Him HALF-A-MAN!' the film tells the ubiquitous story of vintner Paul Hochen (Rod Steiger), who meets loquacious blonde siren Phyllis (Diana) in a bar. They marry, she soon tires of him and becomes the mistress of a rodeo star (Tom Tryon), and plots a murder which goes disastrously wrong.

The locations were filmed in California's Napa Valley vineyards. Though Dennis Hamilton travelled to San Francisco with Diana, he was not allowed within a hundred yards of her when she was working and, while he went off in search of pleasure elsewhere, she found herself growing increasingly close to her co-star. Steiger (1925–2002) had been brought up by his alcoholic mother, and during World War II had run away from home to join the US Navy. In peacetime he had taken up acting, studying Method and joining an elite but eccentric group that included Marlon Brando, Montgomery Clift and James Dean. In 1953 he had caused a sensation in the television adaptation of *Marty*, the story of the mild-mannered, lonely butcher looking for love. Ironically, he turned down the film and the studio had given the part to Ernest Borgnine, who won an Oscar for Best Actor. And now he was playing another coveted role, one rejected by Borgnine!

Steiger's most recent triumphs included *On the Waterfront* and *Oklahoma!* in which he had played the villainous Jud Fry. Based in New York, he was reputedly happily married to Broadway actress Sally Gracie (the first of five wives – a more famous one would be Claire Bloom), five years his senior, and the couple had a small daughter, Claudia. Steiger claimed that he found Diana fascinating because, like himself, she was a rebel: unafraid of denouncing the artificialities of Hollywood and some of its famous residents, even to their faces. For the first time, Diana found herself playing her serial adulterer husband at his own game. Unlike Hamilton, Steiger treated her like a lady instead of a meal-ticket and punchbag, taking her for picnics and long romantic walks and sometimes reciting poems by his favourite, e e cummings, or odes he claimed to have penned just for her. Later she would learn that he did this with all the women he had affairs with, and that the poems had been around for years. 'I saw in him someone I thought would fill the emptiness of my life,' she recalled. 'Here was no hustling manager who treated me like a commodity. Rod made me feel like a woman, not a child, and in him I imagined I saw a real man.' Diana also admired Steiger for having a mind of his own when it came to his work: like all the Method actors, he was unafraid of doing something more adventurous than merely following the director's instructions to the letter. One afternoon, she watched him 'psyching up' for a scene that called for him to lose his temper. Instead of merely interpreting what was printed in the script, he stamped his feet on the floor for 10 minutes, then ran around the set screaming at the top of his voice before instructing the cameraman that he was ready for the take!

Dennis Hamilton suspected that Diana was involved with one of the actors from *The Prowler and the Lady*, as did Hedda Hopper and Louella Parsons, but after seeing photographs in the press of the Steiger family – the actor was smiling radiantly, something he rarely did – their suspicions fell not on their obvious choice but on the second male lead, Tom Tryon.

While Hedda and Louella's spies hung around the set in the hope of acquiring some sort of scoop, so too did the ones employed by the current scourge of the movie world, *Confidential* magazine. For years the studios had been feeding the press with mostly fictitious stories about their stars, but as the power of the moguls declined along with the credibility of their press offices, a new form of exposé was launched for a public greedy for scandal and titillation: the trash-mags, cheaply produced periodicals where readers could find pictures of their favourite stars accompanying lurid, no-holds-barred accounts of their indiscretions – wedged between advertisements for impotency pills, personal horoscopes, slimming aids and other mostly useless paraphernalia. With titles such as *Whisper*, *Tip-Off* and *Inside Story*, and with self-explanatory headlines such as 'The Wild Party That Helped Sinatra Forget Ava Gardner', they could be found stacked on newsstands everywhere: in supermarkets, Laundromats, gas stations, and mostly outside cinemas where they were screening the films of whichever unfortunate happened to be splashed across the cover of that week's issue.

Confidential was the most horrendous and feared publication of them all. Its motto, 'Tells The Facts and Names The Names', appeared on the cover beneath the title. It was launched in 1952 by Robert Harrison, who got the idea because of his infatuation with the top-rated televised crime investigations hosted by Senator Kefauver. America, Kefauver declared, was gripped in a wave of vice, gambling scams, corruption and organised crime, and Harrison decided that the epicentre of this 'den of iniquity' was Hollywood itself. Thus far, Harrison had managed to stay one step ahead of organised scandal-mongers Hedda, Louella and 'holy terror' Elsa Maxwell. What everyone detested most about him were the devious methods he employed to obtain some of his exclusives: whores of both sexes were paid huge sums of money to coerce stars into compromising situations while a tiny machine whirred away in the boudoir, capturing not just the sex act but the all-important post-coital small talk. Jealous or thwarted stars were encouraged to rubbish rivals so they could step into their shoes when important parts were up for grabs. For 'special' cases such as Elvis Presley and Rock Hudson (homosexual affairs, real or invented), Errol Flynn (two-way mirrors) and Lana Turner (sharing lovers), Harrison supplied his 'detectives' with tiny, sophisticated infrared cameras. 'We all read it,' Marlene Dietrich told me. 'Not because it was any good – it was rubbish and worse even than some of the garbage you get on newsstands nowadays – but to find out if we were in it. Sometimes you never got an inkling until it was too late.'

Robert Harrison had learned of Diana's fondness for two-way mirrors, and since arriving in Hollywood Dennis Hamilton had never stopped boasting about his own sexual exploits. Harrison had always suspected that Diana must have been as promiscuous as her husband, and when one of his tip-offs informed him that she *was* having an affair – having ruled out Rod Steiger on account of the previously mentioned family photographs – he too jumped to the conclusion that her mysterious lover could only be Tom Tryon, particularly as the two had been seen socialising after work. What no one suspected was that Diana had been acting as the actor's 'beard'. Tryon (1926–91) was gay, but would remain intensely discreet about his preferences until the early 1970s – by which time he had quit movies to embark on a successful career as a very fine writer of mystery thrillers, and entered into an open relationship with gay porn star Casey Donovan. Diana's biggest mistake was to tell her husband the truth about her and Steiger after Hamilton threatened to give Tryon a good hiding – mindless of the fact that the American was much tougher and brawnier than he was, and with an even worse reputation for brawling.

The day after hearing this news – and according to Diana, though no one else reported this, brandishing a shotgun – Hamilton barged past RKO's security men, yelling for Steiger to come out and face him like a man. Steiger was not on the set, so Hamilton turned on Diana: if he was no longer good enough for her, he declared, then he would return to England and leave her to her own devices. Diana's response to this was, 'Fine, darling. Just let me know when you want me to drive you to the airport!' Two days later – 27 September – she did just this, and RKO breathed a huge sigh of relief. Twice during the last few weeks, after an argument with Diana, Hamilton had gone berserk and wrecked his hotel room and the studio had fought to keep this out of the press. Yet no sooner had he left than John Farrow received a call from Louella Parsons, demanding that Diana get in touch with her at once and explain what was going on. Swallowing her pride – and no doubt biting her tongue – she called the woman she only ever referred to as 'that interfering old crone', and explained that her husband had returned to England to supervise the sale of one home there, and the renovations of another. For the time being, she was believed.

Robert Harrison's interpretation of Dennis Hamilton's sudden departure led him to believe that *he*, and not Diana, had been misbehaving and that maybe she was not having an affair with Tom Tryon after all. Therefore, for the time being, *Confidential* turned its attentions elsewhere while, each from their own corner, Diana and Hamilton gave identical statements to the press as to why he had made himself scarce. No, they had not had a row. Indeed, they had never been so in love! And no, their 'separation' had nothing to do with the events at the pool party. What she had told Louella Parsons was true, save that there had been a major change to their plans – once the work had been completed, they would be staying on at Woodhurst and not returning to Hollywood. Hamilton was already negotiating Diana's next film with Rank, which was expected to be *The Long Haul*, co-starring Robert Mitchum. 'The fee's only around £20,000, nothing compared to what Dors earns in America,' he told reporters, 'but she's feeling so homesick, what else can we do?'

The British press swallowed the story, while the Americans were sceptical. Hamilton received an angry summons from John Farrow, forced to contend with the daily calls from Hedda and Louella, who were demanding to know the truth now that photographs of Diana and Rod Steiger had begun popping up in the newspapers. In fact, these were publicity stills from the film: both columnists knew this, but were still baying for blood. Today, of course, such interfering busybodies would find themselves barred from the set, or just ignored, but such was the power of these two – much as the all-powerful New York theatre critics could with one scathing review close a Broadway show after just one performance – that their every whim had to be pandered to unless one wished to kiss goodbye to one's career. Farrow was not just thinking about Diana when he ordered Hamilton to board the next plane back to Los Angeles, but his own position in Hollywood. For if it was proved that Diana and Steiger *were* involved, and Farrow was shown to have known about this all along and to have taken no action, then he too would find himself blacklisted by the Catholic League of Decency and have difficulty working in the film capital again.

By now, RKO, Farrow and Louella Parsons had decided that Diana Dors was no lady, so the title of the film was changed from *The Lady and the Prowler* to *The Unholy Wife*, which they believed suited her more – it was what they and most of Middle America believed she was (Bosley Crowther, who later slated it in the *New York Times*, preferred to call it *The Unholy Mess*). Hamilton arrived back in Los Angeles on 2 October and was met at the airport by Farrow's chauffeur. Everything was stage-managed: aware that they were being trailed by reporters, he stopped the car at the nearest florist's shop and ordered red roses to be sent out to his 'beloved' wife, filming a scene on the RKO lot with Tom Tryon – who had been driven there that morning by his girlfriend, a.k.a.

a bit-part 'beard' hired by Farrow, who must have known that Tryon was gay. Rod Steiger had been given the day off to spend with his family. Then, Hamilton changed his mind again: mindless of his exhaustion he could not wait to see Diana, so he asked the chauffeur to follow the florist's van to the lot, where he and Diana fell weeping into one another's arms as if they had been apart for years.

The next morning, Farrow accompanied the Hamiltons to Louella's house, leaving rival Hedda Hopper fuming. Louella had already spoken to Diana over the phone, and heard her deny any affair with Rod Steiger, when clearly this was not true. Now, she was told by Farrow that in Louella's eyes, her greatest sin was not adultery, but deceit, and as such it was now her duty to genuflect, apologise and beg the hack's forgiveness. If she did not, Farrow elaborated, Louella would make her feelings on the matter known to her group, the Women's Catholic Guild of America, who would join forces with the Catholic League of Decency and have the Hamiltons ejected from the country. Years later, after converting to the religion, Diana would still loathe this movement. 'There are good Catholics and there are also bad,' she observed. 'The Women's Catholic Guild of America, for instance, who see fit to crucify anyone who transgresses in their opinion.' Diana was further advised by RKO's William Dozier that unless she humbled herself and donned the proverbial hair shirt, Louella would make an example of her, as she had fellow Englishman Rex Harrison. In 1948, while still married to Lilli Palmer, Harrison had been secretly seeing Carole Landis. Louella had denounced them on national radio and, unable to cope with the public shame of what had been a very private affair, Landis had killed herself.

What made John Farrow the arch hypocrite was that as a supposed devout Catholic he had denounced Diana over her involvement with Steiger, while not exactly practising what he preached. For weeks he had been having an affair with Diana's stand-in, a Marilyn Monroe lookalike she names in her memoirs as Dee. The story she recounts is that every red-blooded male on the set of *The Unholy Wife* had lusted over Dee, but that 'Fearless Farrow' had ended up with her. After stalking Dee late at night and watching her through the motel window having sex with the second assistant director, Farrow had barged into the room, wrenched her from the other man's arms, and 'with a shout of triumph' walked off with the prize. And if this was not hypocritical enough, the next morning Farrow had dragged the young woman off to the nearest Catholic church to confess *her* sins!

Diana remembered this particular meeting with Louella as one of the most sickening events of her life:

> I have never liked to crawl, and as we waited for her to make her entrance, I felt inwardly nauseous... I had been drilled as to what to say, and delivered my lines with all the aplomb of Bette Davis. Eventually after a lecture from the old crone, with her religious shrine lit up in pastel-shaded lights glowing in on us from the garden, she wagged her finger at me like a schoolteacher, and pronounced her forgiveness of my terrible behaviour, making me swear it would never happen again – or if it did to let her be the *first* to know before Hedda Hopper.

Yes, Diana confessed to Louella, she *had* slept with Steiger, something she now very much regretted. She and her husband had been experiencing problems, but this was all behind them now. The meeting ended with Louella patting both on the head and giving them her blessing for the future. Farrow further agreed that when shooting resumed on *The Unholy Wife*, guards would be posted outside Diana's and Steiger's motel rooms and location trailers so that no more 'romantic funny business' would take place other than in front of the camera. The pair were indeed watched like hawks, but only while on location. Once the production company were back in Hollywood and working on the interiors and Diana had squared up to Farrow, and threatened to expose his own philandering unless he minded his own business, the director left his stars to their own devices. Diana returned to Hillside House, where she remained for just 24 hours before rejoining Steiger at his rented hideaway beach cottage in Malibu. 'I knew our affair was doomed,' she recalled, 'yet something kept pushing me towards him, always in optimism that we would win through.'

There were further problems when Diana inadvertently got on the wrong side of columnist Mike Connolly – like Hedda and Louella more or less a law unto himself, and almost as feared.

Chicago-born Connolly (1914–66) had famously scripted the film version of Lilian Roth's autobiography, *I'll Cry Tomorrow* – starring Susan Hayward, it had featured alongside *Yield to the Night* at Cannes. He was however better known for his column in *Hollywood Reporter*, and his vociferous campaigns against prostitution and Communism. According to his biographer, Val Holley, 'Such campaigns were attempts by Connolly, a gay man, to feel part of the homophobic Hollywood mainstream.'

Reading between the lines of Connolly's column, and the not-so-subtle innuendo which may still have gone above the heads of the then naive general American public where homosexuality was concerned, one gets a clear story of the gay goings-on in the film capital. There was, however, no innuendo when he curiously branded Diana a fascist (rather than a Communist) under the headline, 'Up The Hammer & Sickle Girl: Gather Those Yankee Dollars While You May!' Diana was still contributing to *Picturegoer*, but of late had been too busy to check the content with her ghostwriter before giving the go-ahead for the column to be submitted to the editor – or so she claimed. What made Mike Connolly see red, literally, were her sympathetic comments about Dawn Adams, prohibited from working in Hollywood for appearing in a film with known Communist Charlie Chaplin. According to Diana, Adams and Chaplin had been wrongly accused of being 'Reds', and should be welcomed back into the movie colony with open arms. Connolly's attack on Diana raged on for days, until she found herself summoned to an emergency meeting with the RKO executives, where she was forced to sign a declaration that *she* was not a Communist. The move saw her dropped by *Picturegoer*.

Dennis Hamilton waited until this heated debate had died down somewhat, and on 23 October – purposely timed to miss Diana's 25th birthday – he flew to London. Again, the press were led to believe this was a business trip, save that this time Diana had not driven him to the airport for that fake kiss goodbye. No sooner had he left than Hillside House was broken into – the intruders, almost certainly 'reporters' from *Confidential*, stole nothing and had the audacity to call Diana and inform her that the purpose for their visit had been to rifle through drawers and cupboards in search of evidence regarding her complicated love life, now that

Tom Tryon was no longer a 'suspect', and that Rod Steiger was 'under control'. A rival trash-mag, *Suppressed*, had unearthed stories from Diana's past – the sex parties involving two-way mirrors and circle jerks – way too obscene to even *consider* for publication.

Diana took advantage of Hamilton's absence to spend a little more time with Rod Steiger in Malibu – effectively, to close the door on their romance, because he had decided to return to his wife and daughter in New York to salvage what was left of his own wrecked marriage. She stayed on at his cottage for just over a week, until the lease ran out, and by 2 November had come to a decision about her future. Louella Parsons – who else? – was the first to be told that she and Hamilton had officially separated. The split had been amicable, Diana pointed out, and there were no plans to divorce – indeed, her husband would still be managing her affairs. Just how Hamilton planned to do this, with several thousand miles of ocean between them, was not elaborated on.

Chapter Eight

A Nice Kid At Heart

On 3 November 1956, the day after making her momentous announcement, Diana flew to London to shoot *The Long Haul*. Dennis Hamilton had negotiated a £20,000 fee, of which she would see only £1,000 – he needed the money, he said, for living expenses. Hamilton was still living in Maidenhead, so she stayed at the Dorchester until she had decided her next move. 'The house with the swimming pool belongs to Dennis,' she told reporters at the airport. 'He's welcome to it. I'll just find myself some other little place!'

A few days later, Diana (and not Hamilton) was invited to the first night of *Grab Me a Gondola* at London's Lyric Theatre. Written by James Gilbert and Julian Moore, this had been inspired by Diana's trip along Venice's Grand Canal, wearing her famous mink bikini. The story centred around blonde starlet Virginia Jones (Joan Heal), who arrives in the city with the intention of playing Portia in *The Merchant Of Venice*. She falls for a visiting journalist (Denis Quilley), here with his fiancée, who plays him at his own game by having a fling with a Venetian prince. The play ends with him seeing the error of his ways, but with Virginia ending up with the prince – exactly the kind of adventure, the writers claimed, that could have been befallen Diana Dors. Among the bit parts were Una Stubbs and Joyce Blair, sister of dancer Lionel. The songs, which included 'The Motor Car Is Treacherous', 'Rocking at the Canon Ball' and the one that upset Dennis Hamilton, 'I Want a Man, Not a Mouse', were instantly forgettable, but the production ran for an astonishing 687 performances, causing Diana to regret rejecting the part of Virginia.

Smiling radiantly, Diana was questioned about her financial status – the rumour that Dennis Hamilton had frozen her assets, and that she was so strapped for cash that she had been compelled to sell her Lincoln convertible to make ends meet. She dismissed the story as 'poppycock' – she had 'thousands in the bank', she said, and had sold the car solely to invest the money in a new Cadillac, which she would be collecting later in the week. On the subject of her marriage – she had removed her wedding ring – she confessed that this had been little more than a balance sheet, that despite all the money she had earned she had never been truly happy. 'Diana without Dennis is going to be difficult,' she declared, 'My mink bikini era is over.'

Even so, Hamilton did not appear to be out of the picture entirely. Over the years he had proved himself a more than worthy business manager, Diana confessed, a position she hoped he would continue to hold providing he could handle the careers of the *two* women in his life! The previous day the same reporters had tracked him down with his 'other' woman, 18-year-old starlet and former *Titbits* pin-up Shirley Broomfield, in a pub near Leicester Square, where he had been more than eager to pour out his woes so long as the drink had kept flowing. Diana, of course, was portrayed as the villain of the piece. For five years he had played the role of the dutiful husband, never so much as looking at another woman and always treating Diana like his very special princess. She alone was responsible for the break-up of their marriage, aided and abetted by Rod Steiger and a couple of evil gossip columnists: 'Women with hats that need a gardener, creating a cancer in the press!' Hamilton boasted of how he had spent over £1,000 on transatlantic phone calls while they had been apart, imploring Diana to change her mind and stay with him. He alone had put Diana Dors on the map. When they had married, she had secretly confided in him her dreams for the future, and he had enabled her to achieve them all – the big houses with swimming pools, the jewels and swanky cars (which he omitted to say she had paid for) and, most importantly, Hollywood fame. When questioned about the nature of his friendship with Shirley Broomfield (who later found fame as Shirley Anne Field), Hamilton was adamant that any relationship between them was strictly platonic. He wanted nothing more, he concluded, than to remain married to Diana Dors, and was confident that things between them would return to normal once she had been given time to cool down.

Before leaving Hollywood, Diana had fired her agent, Louis Shurr, claiming that as she was leaving America for good, she would not be needing him any more. Louella had had her say: now it was Hedda Hopper's turn to get even, sniping in her column, 'Miss Dors' popularity is slipping in the States, even before her first film is released, and the lady deserves nothing less than to be unknown here.' Hedda and just about every journalist who wrote about the couple were in agreement over one thing: the Hamiltons' marriage had not been kept alive by love and affection, but by greed. On 3 November, the day after Diana had announced their split, Marshall Pugh published an open plea to her in the *Daily Mirror*:

> We all know you're a nice kid at heart. We believe that in your own way you're also quite an actress. Maybe this harping on about cash-cash-cash is just another act, maybe it isn't. But here's some advice, free of charge. Why don't you just shake the dust of Hollywood off your feet, rub the gold dust out of your eyes, and leave this money-grabbing talk behind? It isn't cute or clever. It doesn't win friends or influence people. Why not give it a *permanent* rest?

Over the next few weeks, the tabloids and gossip columnists speculated over whether the Hamiltons would be reconciled. Dennis had not moved out of the family home. Diana was desperate to have a baby. Diana had faked the affair with Rod Steiger to get herself ousted from Hollywood so she could return to her beloved England. Diana was on the verge of bankruptcy. Diana was still holding wild parties at her home. None of these rumours were true – indeed, 'home' for her was still the Dorchester.

Hamilton had also recently been in the headlines, having been arrested after a road-rage incident. Driving along Maidstone High Street in Diana's Cadillac, he had attempted to overtake the car in front of him, sounding his horn and yelling for the other driver to pull over and let him pass. The man had ignored him, and a few minutes later Hamilton had cut in front of him, forcing him to stop, then jumped out of the car and punched the man in the face. The police had charged Hamilton with assault, and upon being told that he almost certainly would face jail if found guilty, the matter was settled out of court, with Diana paying and signing a bond to vouch for his future behaviour, even though this meant them getting together again. 'The bird was back in the cage – it's fight for freedom had failed,' she recalled.

The Hamiltons' reunion would prove not unexpectedly brief and stormy. After spending an uneasy festive season at Woodhurst, they spent two weeks in Malaga with friends Patrick Holt – he had appeared in three of Diana's early films – and his wife Sandra Dorne. Then it was back to work. Robert Mitchum's agent had persuaded him to drop out of *The Long Haul*, claiming that working with Diana would seriously damage his reputation. The storyline centres around American GI Harry Miller, who after being discharged from military service in Germany relocates to England with his wife and small son. Here, he finds work as a truck driver for racketeer Joe Easy (Patrick Allen), who gets his mistress, Lynn (Diana), to seduce him into joining his latest smuggling operation. Harry subsequently leaves his wife, but the fun stops when his son is badly injured in an accident. The director was Ken Hughes, who later achieved recognition with *Chitty Chitty Bang Bang* – and derision when he dragged 85-year-old Mae West out of retirement to appear in *Sextette* (1980). *The Long Haul* would be released as a double-feature with *The Hard Man*, starring Guy Madison, with the tagline, 'The Long Haul Will DELIGHT You – The Hard Man Will EXCITE You! – which saw both films being banned in parts of Europe and America.

Mitchum's replacement was 43-year-old Victor Mature, the hulking six-foot-three star whose speciality until then had been biblical epics such as *The Robe* and *Samson and Delilah*. Mature, the first to admit that he was one of the dullest actors around, had recently been investigated by *Confidential* magazine, and had earlier issued a warning via Hedda Hopper to colleagues who might be thinking of stepping out of line, 'If you're so concerned about your fucking privacy, don't become a fucking actor!' Now, he was reported to be 'on the prowl', having recently divorced his third wife – there would be two more – and Dennis Hamilton jumped to the immediate conclusion that Diana would soon be added to his roster of conquests.

In fact, as had happened with Tom Tryon, Hamilton – and the press, also well aware of Mature's track record – were watching the wrong man. Mature, when asked if he found his platinum-blonde co-star sexy, gruffed, 'Blonde? I'm colour-blind!' Diana, for her part, was not in the least amorously interested in him because she had already fallen for Tommy Yeardye, his stunt double in the film, who appears to have been equally dull, but not lacking in the 'trouser' department. Years later she would dismiss him almost as a nonentity, recalling, 'I once had an affair with a muscleman and nearly died of boredom! The only thing he was interested in was lifting his wretched barbells and improving his physique!'

Tommy Yeardye (1930–2004) had been born in Ireland into a family of peasant farmers – something Diana never failed to remind him of if ever they had a row – but raised in Mill Hill, London, by his mother who had moved here in search of work. To help out at home, as a child he had earned pennies taking photographs of tourists around Leicester Square and Piccadilly. As a teenager, he had hustled for sex in gambling joints such as Winstons, in Bond Street, where he had amassed a clientele of wealthy women – and allegedly more than a few men – while brushing shoulders with several kingpins of the criminal fraternity, including the Krays and members of the Charlie Richardson gang. Softly spoken but hard as nails, six-foot-four and tipping the scales at 200 pounds, Yeardye was a serial poseur, nicknamed 'Mr Muscles' by friends and enemies alike. He met Diana via one of Dennis Hamilton's shady underworld contacts, and for both it was love at first sight. 'Fists like bricks, eyes like emeralds, and the cock of a horse,' was how she once described him.

Over the last two years, Yeardye had supplemented his gigolo income by working as a bit-part actor and stuntman. In the summer of 1954, while visiting his family in Ireland, he had answered a newspaper advertisement from a film company who were looking for an actor to double for Rock Hudson, currently shooting the locations for the swashbuckling adventure *Captain Lightfoot*. Rock had taken to him at once, and the two men – who were exactly the same size, height and weight – had got along famously, stopping short of becoming lovers only because of Yeardye's jet-black hair– Rock's lovers *always* had to be blond. Indeed, it was while shooting this film that he fell for one of the extras, a hunky Italian named Massimo who is generally regarded as the greatest love of his life – the pair would stay together, off and on, for another 30 years. A few weeks after completing *Captain Lightfoot*, Yeardye had been hired as stuntman on the less enterprising *Dick Turpin: Highwayman*, but it was for being Diana Dors' lover, and later as one of the co-founders of the Vidal Sassoon hairdressing empire, that he will be remembered.

Dennis Hamilton found out about Diana's involvement with Yeardye by taking a leaf out of *Confidential* editor Robert Harrison's book. The Hamiltons' friends, Jon Pertwee and his actress wife Jean Marsh, were spending the weekend at Woodhurst while Pertwee was appearing in cabaret in Croydon. One evening, while the men were out – Pertwee working, Hamilton at the local pub – Diana and Jean engaged in a little 'girlie' talk, unaware that Hamilton had concealed a tiny tape recorder in the room. Subsequently, he captured a conversation wherein Diana had regaled her friend with intimate details of Yeardye's alleged humungous appendage and prowess in the bedroom. Later, while the two women were eating supper in another room, Hamilton listened to the tape and went berserk, smashing a plate-glass table with his bare fists before starting on the ornaments – then crumpling into a heap in the corner, wailing like a child. Diana and Jean fled from the house in terror, and Hamilton was still in the same position when Jon Pertwee returned, several hours later.

Diana spent several nights at the Pertwees' flat in London, until Hamilton called her and begged her to come home, with the usual sob story that he would never lose his temper again. Because he was officially her manager, she said, she had decided to stay with him only until *The Long Haul* wrapped: then, she and Tommy Yeardye would set up home somewhere, and she would file for divorce. Hamilton wormed his way back into her affections on 1 April by promising her an evening out she would never forget. Sophie Tucker, one of Diana's favourite singers, was appearing at the King's Theatre, Hammersmith, and he had managed to secure tickets to see her. As a safety precaution, Tommy Yeardye tagged along in case Hamilton turned nasty again – he followed the couple in his own car, though he too had been let in on the secret, and at the theatre introduced himself as Diana's bodyguard. And it was at this stage that she realised that she had been set up, for the curtains swung open to reveal not the great Jewish singer, but Eamonn Andrews, who pronounced the words, 'Diana Dors, this is your life!'

A few years later, footballer Danny Blanchflower would tell Eamonn Andrews exactly what to do with his big red book, and Diana came very close to doing the same. She and her husband were not speaking, she still bore the bruises from the latest thrashing he had given her, and she was not in the least interested in some of the 'friends' the programme had lined up to tell her how wonderful they thought she was, when the feeling was not always mutual. The first guest was her father, who she had not seen in a while, and an aunt and two uncles she had hoped never to see again. After the show, Bert Fluck snubbed Hamilton, who he had loathed since first setting eyes on him. Though Miss Leason, Diana's elocution teacher from Selwood House, turned up for the show, the Misses Cockey who still ran the establishment declined to appear, telling the producer, 'The fact that Diana Dors attended our school is something that we would prefer not to be broadcast to the world. We have not seen any of her films, nor would we want to!' Genuine, warm-hearted tributes came from co-stars and directors she had worked with, but someone Diana had definitely not wanted to see was the *Daily Mirror*'s show-business columnist Donald Zec, who in the past had written extended features about her under such titles as 'Blonde Gold Mine' and 'The Bosom of Bray' – not always complimentary, though he thought of himself as her friend. Diana was angry with him at the time, though towards the end of her life she would forgive him his trespasses. The banter between them on *This Is Your Life* was decidedly uneasy:

DIANA: (seeing Zec appear): I'd better leave, I think!
ZEC: Dear me! Let's face it, Diana. You *do* represent the most calculated, hard-boiled exploitation of sex I've ever seen in British pictures!
DIANA: Not really...

ZEC: Everything you say, everything you wear and everything
   you do is calculated to create a very big sensation. Sensations
   like falling into swimming pools by accident...
DIANA: Let's not go into that.
ZEC: And wearing mink bikinis, which I don't think *was* an
   accident!
DIANA: Hmm, and I remember *your* remarks on that!
ZEC: (apologetically): Diana, though I think at times you're
   brash, perhaps at times very outrageous, I'd also like to think
   you unique. No one can ignore Diana Dors. You have that
   rare quality which I admire and which I write about all the
   time. You're a *star*!

Some years later, Zec did not apparently consider Diana enough
of a star to warrant a mention in his memoirs – indeed, she was the
only major celebrity he had encountered in a lengthy career who
was conspicuous by her absence. Equally unwelcome, coming
straight after Zec's reference to the swimming pool incident, was
Stewart Sawyer, who sneeringly told her that he had flown 6,000
miles just to shake her hand. 'All the way from Hollywood to
reassert his innocence,' host Eamonn Andrews put in. Diana just
as coldly replied, 'If I'd have known *you* were coming, I'd have
put on a bathing suit!' Sitting next to her, Dennis Hamilton was
seen to clench his fists, and immediately after the live broadcast
Sawyer made a hasty exit from the studio, fearful of another
showdown with the still-irate husband.

No sooner had the applause died down on *This Is Your Life*
than Hamilton was back to bullying Diana, but wary of actually
hitting her because Tommy Yeardye had threatened him with a
fate worse than death should he so much as lay a finger on her
again. The last Friday in April, in the wake of one argument too
many, Diana told him to get out of the house and he did just this
– moving out of the penthouse, he set up a love nest in one of the
Woodhurst apartments, mere yards away, with the Anglo-Indian
woman he had hired to manage his latest foible financed by Diana:
El Dors, a Singapore-style restaurant in Windsor, scheduled to
open in May.

Diana was convinced that her marriage was well and truly over:
though Hamilton was living within spitting distance, so to speak,

he had never left *her* before, and the fact that he was now living with his mistress was a bonus. The next day, Saturday, she called her lawyer and made an appointment for the following Monday, with the intention of starting divorce proceedings. In the meantime, Tommy Yeardye moved into the penthouse. Diana had already arranged a party for that evening, and saw no reason to cancel this just because Hamilton would not be there. The next morning, she received a visit from a bubble-gum machine tycoon named John Hoey, who had been unable to make it to the party. To make up for this, he and his companion, a young actress called Shani Wallis who later played Nancy in *Oliver!*, invited Diana and Yeardye to go for a spin in his new Cadillac. The quartet returned at around 6pm to find that Hamilton had let himself into the penthouse. Exactly what happened next depends upon whose story one wishes to believe.

According to Diana, her housekeeper Frances Sholl – in whose eyes Hamilton could do no wrong – was waiting for them on the drive. Her husband was not here to cause trouble, Sholl told her: he needed her to sign important business papers and had insisted on seeing her alone. Diana entered the house and went upstairs to the bedroom. Hamilton had two files: one contained a document detailing their joint ventures, which included the coffee bar, the club in Windsor, two cars, a river-launch, movie equipment and the entire contents of the safe. There was also a coda assigning £19,000 of her £20,000 salary for *The Long Haul* over to him, to cover future tax bills. The other file contained a list of names and addresses of men Hamilton claimed Diana had had sex with, including the locations. The idea was that she should sign over her properties and ventures to him – aside from the penthouse and the powder-blue Cadillac, which he claimed *he* had bought her as gifts – and that in return he would not hand the list of her lovers over to the press!

Diana's version of events was that she signed the document, and that Hamilton had made as if to shake her hand – but instead punched her in the face, grabbed a double-barrelled shotgun which just happened to be in the room, smashed a window and aimed the weapon at Tommy Yeardye, who by this time was standing on the drive. The Irishman, mindless of the danger, barged into the house, took the stairs three at a time and bashed

Hamilton senseless, before slinging Diana over his shoulder and carrying her off like a damsel in distress – placing her in his car and driving her to his mother's house in Mill Hill.

Diana certainly did spend a week being cared for by Mrs Yeardye, until J. Lee Thompson found her a small mews house in Belgravia: the owners were on holiday and she stayed there for a month. Yeardye's own story differed from Diana's. Hamilton had been in the penthouse long enough to collect Diana's clothes and throw them out of an upstairs window on to the drive. The housekeeper had placed these in the boot of Yeardye's car, while Diana had gone into the house to speak to her husband, who had slammed the door shut after her and locked it. Yeardye had kicked it open, rushed upstairs and given this odious man the thrashing he deserved, leaving him sobbing in a bloodied heap – but there had been no gun, and no broken window.

The incident led to Hamilton embarking on a 'sex bender'. 'If his marriage had failed, then everyone else's was going to do so as well,' Diana recalled, adding how from her side of the Woodhurst fence she had watched taxi-loads of girls arriving at his flat, three of whom had discovered his bad side and attempted suicide there. Meanwhile, she and Tommy Yeardye – now listed officially on her books as her bodyguard – flew to Majorca. 'I need some sunshine,' she told reporters, 'and the way I feel right now, I might not be coming back.' She did come back, of course, and lost no time heading for her lawyer's office to instruct him to file divorce proceedings. She was advised, for her career's sake, to cite irreconcilable differences, but was having none of this: she cited mental and physical cruelty, and 'obsessive' adultery. Hamilton threatened to countersue, citing Tommy Yeardye as co-respondent, and Diana told him to go ahead. In the meantime she and Yeardye flew to Rome, where they spent a few days sightseeing before heading for Tuscany, where (her voice dubbed by an Italian actress) she was to make her first foreign language film, *La Ragazza del Palio*. This would be released in the English-speaking world as *The Love Specialist*, which was of course more befitting for its star.

In the film, Diana Dixon (Diana) is an articulate Texan who wins first prize in a television quiz show: a trip to Rome, and a Cadillac to get her there. As she approaches Sienna the car breaks

The J Arthur Rank Charm School starlet dances the jitterbug with Petula Clark in *Dance Hall* (1950).

Diana and Dennis Hamilton on their wedding day, July 1951. A heartless, maniupulating tyrant, he persistently abused her and made her life a misery.

Diana and Honor Blackman in *Diamond City* (1949).

Diana and Rod Steiger in *Unholy Wife* (1957). Her affair with married co-star Rod Steiger would bring widespread condemnation from religious groups.

As condemned to die murderess Mary Hilton in *Yield To The Night* (1956), Diana's greatest role which added weight to the campaign to abolish capital punishment in Britain.

Diana prepares for a scene in *Peeping Tom* (1963), directed by Michael Winner.

1957, en-route to Rome with lover Tommy Yeardye. While she was filming here, he would have fun at Rock Hudson's sex parties.

1957, Rome. Visiting Rock Hudson on the set of *A Farewell To Arms*, unaware that Rock was leading her 'fella' astray!

Diana with second husband, Dickie Dawson, who she married in New York in 1959.

down and she stays the night in a hotel, where she encounters a down-on-his-luck Italian prince, played by Vittorio Gassman. Assuming each other to be wealthy, they embark on an adventure which culminates at the famous Palio steeplechase, a display of machismo during which rival jockeys lash out at one another with bullwhips. The prince bribes the jockey riding the favourite to throw the race so that his own horse will win. Diana swaps places with another jockey, wins the race, and gives the prince his marching orders. Gassman (1922–2000) was one of the greatest Italian actors of his generation: equally renowned as a producer and director, he was nicknamed 'Il Mattatore' (The Spotlight Chaser) after the character he played in a television series. Three years previously, Shelley Winters (the second of his three wives) had divorced him citing serial adultery: despite the presence of Tommy Yeardye, who had a bit part in the film, Gassman made a sterling effort to seduce Diana, but failed. Italian men, she declared – though some of her colleagues might not have agreed – were only marginally sexier than Frenchmen, who she did not find sexy at all!

Rock Hudson was in Rome, shooting *A Farewell to Arms*, and when he saw Tommy Yeardye's photograph in the newspaper, arriving at the airport with Diana, he tracked him down at once. Over the next few weeks while she was filming in Sienna, and upon her insistence, Yeardye spent much of his time with Rock and Massimo, the young Italian lover he had met on the set of *Captain Lightfoot*. Rock had married Phyllis Gates the year before, a lavender union arranged by his manager Henry Willson to prevent *Confidential* and the likes of Hedda and Louella from outing him, at a time when most Americans were sufficiently naive to believe that a man could not be gay if married. In Rome, with Phyllis recovering back in Los Angeles from a bout of hepatitis almost certainly given to her by him, Rock and Massimo were having the time of their lives at the Grand Hotel with a seemingly limitless succession of hunky extras, models and rent boys. The fact that Tommy Yeardye was their guest – he shared a room with American actor Troy Donahue – leaves no doubt that he too joined in with what Hudson called their 'tarts and Romans fuckathons' where everyone camped it up in bedsheets and women's clothes. One shudders to think what Diana – who was not overkeen on homosexuals, and who hated to see men in drag – would have had to say, had she been aware what her 'Mr Muscles' had been getting up to while she had been fighting off Vittorio Gassman's unwanted advances!

When Diana and Yeardye returned to England the first person knocking on the door at the penthouse was Dennis Hamilton. His mistress had packed her bags, but he did not tell Diana this. The spiel was the same one she had heard dozens of times: he had turned over a new leaf and was on medication for his 'temper problem'. If she agreed to a reconciliation and they went back to as they had been before, with him looking after her interests, her career would reach unprecedented heights. To start with, they would fly to Hollywood and clear his name of the latest scandal invented by *Confidential.* Diana slammed the door in his face.

During Diana's absence, Hamilton had called his lawyer in Los Angeles, and added his name to the 'Trial of 100 Stars' – Hollywood's revenge on Robert Harrison, who in the July issue of *Confidential* had published 'exclusives' on Eartha Kitt ('The Man Who Sat There – All Night!') and Anthony Quinn ('Caught With A Gal In A Powder Room!'), though the most damaging exposé concerned Liberace. Under the heading, 'Why Liberace's Theme-Song Should Be Mad About The Boy', a hack using the pseudonym Hoarton Streete wrote of an incident – subsequently proved to have been true for once – where the cheesy entertainer had tried to seduce a young male press agent in his suite at an Ohio hotel. According to Streete, 'The floorshow reached its climax when Dimples, by sheer weight, pinned his victim to the mat and mewed in his face, "Gee, you're so cute when you're mad!"'

The arch-camp pianist was still reeling from an attack the previous year in the *Daily Mirror*, when columnist Cassandra had aptly denounced him as, among other things, 'A deadly, winking, sniggering, snuggling, giggling, fruit-flavoured, mincing, ice-cream covered heap of mother-love... a slag-heap of lilac-covered hokum.' Diana, who often went out of her way to poke fun at homosexuals while claiming to be gay-friendly, had called the newspaper and *demanded* the right to write a piece in defence of her friend, supporting his ridiculous theory that he was 'as manly as the next man' – only to be told that unless she 'ducked out', she ran the risk of becoming Cassandra's next victim. So far as *Confidential*'s predicted downfall was concerned, black actress Dorothy Dandridge had set the ball rolling, serving Harrison with a $2m writ for writing of her 'perverted antics' with a naturist group. Similar suits had been filed by Errol Flynn (who according to Harrison had been with another woman on his wedding night) and Maureen O'Hara – accused of having been intimate with a lover in Grauman's Theatre, she provided evidence substantiating that she had not even been in the country when the alleged incident had taken place. After this, the writs poured in thick and fast. Liberace, however, showed himself to be no less over the top when suing for libel than he was in his stage act: he hit Harrison with a whopping suit for $25m and successfully acquired an embargo prohibiting the US media from referring to the hotel incident during his lifetime.

The feature about Dennis Hamilton had been published under the heading, 'What Diana Dors Never Knew About Her Ever-Lovin' Hubby!' and was pretty tame compared to some of the exposés Harrison was used to publishing – not nearly as bad as it could have been, had his 'investigator' done a better job, though of course some of Hamilton's activities may have been too scandalous even for *Confidential* to disclose. 'There were naughty doings behind the doors of the Dors household,' the piece admonished. 'Dennis figures that faint heart ne'er won fair floosie, so while Diana snoozed upstairs, he cuddled downstairs.' Even so, Hamilton figured that he might as well jump on the bandwagon, and issued a writ for $10,000.

The trial opened in Los Angeles on 2 August 1957 and saw a mass exodus of studio employees from the film capital – from the major stars down to the extras – who might have had something to hide, no matter how trivial. Two weeks into the proceedings, one of Robert Harrison's key witnesses – Peggy Gould, a sub-editor scheduled to take the witness stand the next day – committed suicide in her hotel room. It subsequently emerged that she had been about to testify *against* Harrison, and that she had double-crossed him by supplying *Confidential*'s headlines, ahead of publication, to the district attorney. Only days later, the magazine's editor-in-chief, Howard Rushmore, shot his wife dead in the back of a New York taxi, then turned the gun on himself. Though the jury were out for 14 days before all the issues were resolved, the trial resulted in little more than a large number of out-of-court settlements, all of them considerably lower than the original writs. Liberace came off better than most, donating his $40,000 pay-off to charity, once he had discharged his legal fees, and urging everyone else to do the same. Most of them did, though few of the other settlements amounted to more than $10,000. Dennis Hamilton pocketed his $4,000. Even so, collectively the settlements were enough to force Harrison out of business and put an end to his hated publication.

Though the *Confidential* feature – along with the pool party fiasco and a whole host of other unpleasant events – had concerned Dennis Hamilton and not Diana, she was held accountable for his behaviour at the end of September when Rank invited her to a reception feting the studio's 21st anniversary. She was still under contract to them, albeit that she had not worked for them since *An Alligator Named Daisy.* Now, J. Arthur Rank personally informed her that while Hamilton was around she would never work for them again. Additionally the mogul was shocked to see her turn up on Tommy Yeardye's arm: while still married to Hamilton, she would be expected to follow the studio's strict family-values policy. The next morning, Diana called Rank and promised to cool things with Yeardye until after her divorce. On 17 October, alone, she flew to New York where two evenings later she appeared with Tony Bennett and Benny Goodman on *The Perry Como Show.* She should have appeared with ventriloquist Edgar Bergen – another breed she had always disliked – who, she was told, held a special place in the hearts of the American public. 'Any man who spends half his life with his hand up a puppet's arse can't be *that* special, believe me!' she retorted curtly.

Visiting America so soon after the pool party scandal had not been high on Diana's list of priorities. Even so, she welcomed the opportunity to put several thousand miles between herself, Dennis Hamilton and Tommy Yeardye until she had worked out her next move. Truthfully, she wanted rid of them both. Hamilton may have been a thug and all that was wrong in a man, she said, but at least he brought excitement to the proceedings. Yeardye she was beginning to find dull – considerably more interested in his barbells than he was in her. She planned writing to him from New York, rather than speaking over the telephone, to announce that it was all over between them, and to ask him to vacate the penthouse by the time she returned home. Exactly why she had given Yeardye £8,000 (or £12,000, depending on which volume of her memoirs one wishes to believe) for 'safe keeping' if she planned on never seeing him again, is equally baffling.

In New York, Diana checked in at the Plaza Hotel, where she received a call from Rod Steiger, who invited her out for old times' sake. The actor, now divorced from Sally Gracie, had recently visited England and contacted Diana there, but with Hamilton and Yeardye around she had refused to meet up with him. The meal Steiger had planned was eschewed for a night of passion in a friend's Greenwich Village apartment, but which Diana only regretted the next morning. 'I'd tried to rekindle some spark of fire from the previous year, but it was not there,' she recalled. 'I didn't understand why my heart no longer beat as fast...perhaps I was too preoccupied wondering what to do about Dennis and Tommy.' According to Diana, while in post-coital mood Steiger asked her to marry him – only to get hysterical when she rejected his proposal, and threaten to fling himself out of the window, a gesture she dismissed as little more than an extension of the Method acting at which he excelled, and which had no effect on her whatsoever. Steiger would soon forget about her: the following year he married Claire Bloom.

Much has to be said for Diana's Machiavellian tactics at this time, for no sooner had Rod Steiger walked out of her life for the last time than she returned to the Plaza – and called both Hamilton and Yeardye to explain what she had just done! Hamilton, who had arranged for the hotel florist to deliver a single red rose to her room each day, accompanied by one of his favourite poems, simply sent more – while Yeardye, having learned that his rival was thinking of joining her, made the first move by catching the next available flight to New York.

The following week, Diana celebrated her 26th birthday with Yeardye, and an appearance on *I've Got a Secret*, a CBS spin-off of Britain's *What's My Line?* where instead of guessing the guests' occupations, celebrities had to guess their 'special' secret – one which had been invented by the producers. On 9 November, against her better judgement she later said, she subjected herself to an in-depth television interview by Mike Wallace, a precursor of David Frost and Larry King who rarely minced his words. Prior to the live broadcast, she was read the riot act: no cursing or pouting at the camera, no discussing her love life and, most especially, *no* cleavage. Diana agreed – adding that Wallace must also agree *not* to refer to her as the British Monroe, otherwise she would walk whether millions of viewers were watching her or not. He introduced her as, 'A bosomy blonde bundle, with a flair for publicity that is extraordinary even by American standards', and, though few had expected her to, Diana stuck to the rules by wearing a dark pullover which covered her assets, and by confessing that the real Diana Dors was nothing like the siren constantly being misquoted by the media. There was, however, method in her madness. Only hours before the interview, she had been told by RKO's William Dozier that unless she 'pulled in her head and ditched the Hamilton creep' there was virtually no chance of her ever working in Hollywood again:

DIANA: I hate going out. I don't like going to nightclubs, I don't like going to premieres, or going around what is commonly known as the sort of smart places to be... The other side of me would rather stay at home, invite friends down, talk, swim, play tennis, generally loaf around and not have to get dressed or made up or anything.

WALLACE: What is your goal?

DIANA: My goal is to have a farm in England and settle down and raise a family and forget the whole thing!

WALLACE: Generally speaking, do you find yourself attractive?

DIANA: Oh, I wouldn't say that. I get so bored with looking at myself in the mirror every day... I try to make the most of myself, and I try to appear in the very best way possible.

WALLACE: What is it that makes you so interesting to so many of us?

DIANA: I think maybe it's because I'm representing a larger-than-life kind of character, one that is completely detached from the everyday normal kind of life that most people lead. And maybe some people have a secret yearning to do the things that I do. Maybe it's a kind of dream. I don't know.

WALLACE: Does growing old really concern you?

DIANA: No, it doesn't. I can't really imagine myself old, that's why. But in many ways, when it finally happens I'm going to rather enjoy it, because then I won't have to bother how I look any more!

Chapter Nine

Tread Softly, Stranger

Diana and Tommy Yeardye returned home, and over the next few weeks an uneasy peace was maintained at Woodhurst: she and her lover retreating to the penthouse, while Dennis Hamilton – 'separated from Mr Muscle's fists by a tall wooden fence' – entertained a succession of women in the luxury apartment Diana had paid for. Yet still she was not satisfied, calling Hamilton at all hours – sometimes to check up on him, at others to chat over old times. Shortly after separating, she had sent a Diana Dors lookalike (named in her memoirs as Jozy) through a gap in the fence just to see what would happen. Hamilton had called her bluff: Jozy had temporarily moved in with him so he could groom her for stardom, as he had Shirley Anne Field, and she was now employed as a cigarette girl at one of his favourite watering holes, London's Stork Club.

In November 1957, Hamilton attempted a truce, calling Diana and inviting her and Yeardye to dine with him at the Stork Club. Yeardye wanted nothing to do with the idea – his one ambition, he said, was to meet this odious man down some darkened alley and give him another thrashing. Diana convinced him that Hamilton really was sincere this time in wanting to bury the hatchet – and in any case he had Jozy who, rumour had it, he was thinking of marrying. By capitulating, Yeardye was effectively signing his own death warrant so far as his relationship with Diana was concerned. Providing the cabaret that evening was a handsome singer and comedian who went under the stage name of Dickie Dawson.

Like Dennis Hamilton, Dawson was an exponent of tall tales,

telling Diana that he was a Canadian Jew whose mother had recently died of cancer, and that he had an estranged father and brother living in America, though he was not sure where. Born Colin Lionel Emm in Gosport, Hampshire, in 1932 of an English mother and American father, Dawson had run away from home at 14 to join the Merchant Marine. While serving with them he had developed his skills as a boxer, but upon his discharge had chosen comedy as his profession. Though not a major name on the comedy circuit, he had developed a following with his impressions of American stars Jerry Lewis, Robert Mitchum and Dean Martin, once enjoying a brief stint at the London Palladium. For Diana, it was love at first sight: they shared the same initials, which she declared to be a lucky omen, and within minutes of being introduced she had invited him to Woodhurst for dinner. Friends such as Jon Pertwee warned her that, once again, she was falling for the wrong kind of man – that Dawson, like Dennis Hamilton, was a volatile, jealous character. Diana refused to listen, though she did not start having an affair with him just yet, preferring to keep him waiting on the sidelines until Hamilton and Tommy Yeardye were both out of her hair, she hoped for good.

Hamilton was furious, even more so when Diana accused him of only inviting her to the Stork Club anticipating that once she saw him with Jozy, Diana would be so jealous that she would make a play to get him back, and ditch Yeardye in front of everyone. Yeardye, by now little more than Diana's puppet – the 'standby fuck' when no one else was around to do the honours – may also have gone along with the ruse, well aware of what Hamilton was up to, to prove himself the better man. Certainly neither of them expected the woman they had been squabbling over for months to fall for the club comic!

Dawson turned up at Woodhurst the following Sunday – to add to the atmosphere of 'who's had who', Kim Waterfield was staying for the weekend. Kim was still on the run from the French authorities following the robbery at Jack Warner's villa, though what he had been up to since Diana had last seen him, she said, was anybody's guess. And while Diana flirted with Dawson under Yeardye's nose, Hamilton went berserk in his apartment, smashing up the furniture and shooting at the walls! 'He was just letting off a little steam, I guess,' Diana later said, when paying for the damage.

At the end of the month, Diana topped the bill on *Sunday Night at the London Palladium*, hosted by her friend Bob Monkhouse. Critics who had not seen her act prepared to lambast her, as had recently happened with Jayne Mansfield, only to be pleasantly surprised that she really could sing and dance. Monkhouse introduced her to viewers as 'The former Lady Hamilton' – she made her entrance flanked by a troupe of hunky male dancers, told a few risqué anecdotes, and closed the show with a rendition of 'I'll Take Romance', which might have given Doris Day – perhaps her closest counterpart vocally – a run for her money.

Shortly after appearing on *The Mike Wallace Show* in the States, Diana had been offered a two-shows-nightly, eight-week engagement in Las Vegas, to take place early in 1958 – an offer which she had accepted, she said, without thinking it through. (For various reasons, the engagement would not be fulfilled until much later in the year.) Now, she suddenly became paranoid about losing her voice halfway through, and elected to take singing lessons. Bernard Delfont, who had booked her for the Palladium, suggested Georges Canelli, a voice coach who ran a studio in Hampstead.

Meanwhile, there was more drama when, just days after the Palladium show, the press received a tip-off that Diana had been arrested for assault, and was being held at Hammersmith Police Station. Within minutes the place was swarming with reporters, but it was Tommy Yeardye who had been taken in for questioning, following an incident earlier in the day. Yeardye had been at the wheel of Diana's powder-blue Cadillac, with Diana sitting next to him with the poodle puppy he had just given her on her lap, when a policeman, PC Roy Anderson, had pulled him over for being about to turn the wrong way into a one-way street. Anderson had rushed up and banged on the window, then jerked open the passenger door – only to have it slammed shut by Diana, who had been terrified of her dog jumping out into the traffic. To prevent Yeardye from driving off, Anderson had stood in front of the car – and subsequently been carried 20 yards down the road, spread-eagled across the bonnet. Neither Yeardye nor Diana could deny what had happened as there had been a large number of witnesses. The Irishman was charged with reckless driving and summoned to appear at the magistrates' court the next day. Diana accompanied him: her right arm was in a pink chiffon sling having been sprained, she said, when PC Anderson had wrenched open the door. She was lucky, she added, not to have suffered more serious injury, and her lawyer had advised her to sue the police. The case was adjourned for a month, when Yeardye was fined £30 for assault and obstruction, and the judge reprimanded Anderson for being 'thoughtless and pretentious'.

The drama resumed on Boxing Day, when Diana and Yeardye threw a party at the penthouse. The guests included the Pertwees, Kim Waterfield, actress Samantha Eggar, Joan Henry and J. Lee Thompson, Patrick Holt and Sandra Dorne, Roger Moore and Dorothy Squires, Dickie Dawson, and Denis Shaw, her old friend from the Chelsea Set. The party was almost over when, at around two in the morning, several fire engines arrived, lights flashing and sirens blaring. Everyone rushed outside to see what the commotion was about, and observed the *De Bries*, Dennis Hamilton's 65-foot barge, burning at its moorings. The blaze was soon brought under control, but a subsequent inspection – which estimated the damage to be around £5,000 – declared the vessel virtually unsalvageable. Hamilton, seen earlier outside his apartment, was now nowhere to be seen.

As had happened with the earlier gun incident, there were conflicting stories over what had happened. Hamilton had called the police that afternoon: he had had a tip-off, he said, that Tommy Yeardye had threatened to damage his property, and had asked an officer to be sent around to patrol the grounds at Woodhurst. The request had been ignored: it subsequently emerged that Hamilton had made such a nuisance of himself of late, fetching the police out in the middle of the night – claiming that someone was stalking him, or that he had received yet another death threat, only for them to find him drunk when they arrived and in the middle of one of his mental 'episodes' – that they had begun ignoring him.

Diana, with her baffling tendency to defend her husband at all costs, regardless of the way he had mistreated her, only added to the confusion, telling the investigating officers that she had seen the barge alight *before* the fire engines had arrived, and that it had been set alight by a disgruntled tenant from the Woodhurst flats who she had heard bawling Hamilton out for increasing the rent.

Then she changed her mind: the culprit was a stuntman who had been present at her party, and though she refused to name him for 'personal' reasons, everyone knew she could only have been referring to Tommy Yeardye. 'She wanted him out of her life,' Dorothy Squires said, 'and rather than tell him they were through, she tried to set him up with a crime he hadn't committed!' Hamilton backed up Diana's story, and even provided a witness – Denis Shaw, who told the police that he had been sitting on a bench at the river's edge when he had seen Yeardye boarding the barge with a petrol can in his hand. It subsequently emerged that Hamilton had paid Shaw to say this.

Well aware that he had been rumbled, Hamilton dug an even deeper hole for himself the evening after the fire – sneaking out after dark, he tossed a bottle through Diana's living-room window, then called the police to say that they were both being menaced by the same 'madman'. When this did not work, he waited until she and Yeardye were out before breaking into the place and ransacking every room. The mystery was added to by the insurance company. The policy on the barge had been due to expire at midnight on 26 December, the day of the fire. Everything at Woodhurst was in Diana's name – the penthouse, the flats, the boathouse, the cars – but not the barge, which they suspected Hamilton had sabotaged to claim on the insurance. As the police were unable to prove this, however, the company paid up.

In January 1958, Diana began working on arguably her best film since *Yield to the Night* – and her first independent of Dennis Hamilton who, now that he was no longer her manager riding roughshod over Al Parker, was unable to get his hands on her £20,000 salary. *Tread Softly Stranger* was directed by Gordon Parry, who in 1951 had scored a hit with *Tom Brown's Schooldays*. Her co-star was Bulgarian-born British actor George Baker, who had recently completed his first major role in *The Moonraker*. Today he is perhaps best known for portraying Inspector Wexford in *The Ruth Rendell Mysteries*. Baker had recently had a much-publicised affair with Brigitte Bardot, and Dennis Hamilton – barred from the set, sleeping around indiscriminately and (we now know to have been) suffering from venereal disease – was loath to have him working with Diana, though he himself was no longer amorously interested in her.

One morning, Diana turned up for work limping, and with so many bruises that a sympathetic technician who had a crush on her – working on the film and involved with the London underground, he has only ever been identified as 'Max' – sent her a note. Whenever she decided that she had had enough of Hamilton knocking her around, all she had to do was place an advertisement in the *Evening Standard*, using the coded message he had provided and – for a £2,000 fee – he would ensure that her husband ended up at the bottom of the Thames wearing concrete boots. Whether she considered taking 'Max' up on his offer is not known, though she was so desperate to have this thug out of her life once and for all, anything might have been possible.

Shot at Walton Studios and on location in Halifax – the Rawborough in the story – *Tread Softly Stranger* (with a theme song performed by future *Carry On* star Jim Dale) is a classic *film noir*. Indeed, one half-expects James Cagney or Steve Cochran to burst out from behind the scenery at any moment or Joan Crawford to double for Diana while she pronounces: 'I come from a slum, from the gutter where it's quite a step up even from (sic) the pavement. I never had a home. I never had a father my mother could put a name to… I never had a thing until one day I found I was attractive to the opposite sex. I discovered my legs weren't made just to stand on. I had one talent…so I used that talent, and I got tough!'

Johnny Mansell (Baker) has gambling debts and the bookmakers' heavies are after his blood, so he ditches his latest squeeze, leaves his plush city pad, and heads north for the town of his birth, where everyone smokes a lot and speaks with dodgy on-off Yorkshire accents. 'Tell me, son,' someone asks. 'Why in heaven's name did you leave a beautiful place like London to come to this heap of cinders and clinkers?' It certainly is a grim place, not a good ad for Yorkshire at a time when the North–South divide was more pronounced than today. And not much changes when he is reunited with Dave (Terence Morgan), the brother he has not seen in 10 years and who works in the wages department at the local foundry: Johnny keeps on gambling, and falls for Dave's vampish girlfriend, Calico (Diana).

Diana makes a memorable but decidedly undignified entrance. She is exercising on the balcony of the lodging-house where

Johnny has a room and, though her face is stunning, the rest of her does not look good. Her thighs are fat, and she wears briefs which are *way* too tight – indeed, the so-called 'goat's foot' shots (another occurs later in the film) where for a few seconds we can actually see the outline of her vagina, and another where we can see *inside* her gusset, were removed from the American print, though some years later they were restored for the DVD release, ensuring healthy sales. 'You're not as feminine as you look,' Johnny tells her, desperately trying to avert his eyes. Later, she returns to the balcony to flaunt her wares, wearing a lacy camisole and diaphanous negligee – *the* classic Diana Dors pose of the late 1950s, which if anything put her ahead of her American and Continental rivals.

Cut to the nightclub (would they have had such establishments in towns like Rawborough at this time?) where Calico works as a hostess. The men scrap over her, but she only has eyes for Dave, who has been fiddling the books to keep up with her expensive tastes: now, with an audit about to take place, he needs to put back the money he swindled. 'It all went on Calico,' Johnny mocks, reminding his brother what a fool he has been. 'Her and the moonlight. Big eyes and lazy drawling voice. She's got you by the short hairs. One hand on your knee, the other in your pocket!' Johnny still hates her when they become lovers – the classic *film noir* scenario of a slap, followed by a tumble among the sheets – and never forgets to remind her that she is a 'wharf rat' and a 'tramp'.

Until now, Johnny has been content to support himself by way of the racetrack: 'I'm self-employed – I let the horses do it for me!' He has a dead cert on Moonraker – a sly plug for George Baker's recently completed film, about to be released – so while Dave is in favour of Calico's suggestion that he solve his debt problem by robbing the foundry safe, Johnny goes off to the races hoping to win enough money to prevent the robbery from taking place. Unfortunately, he gets beaten up at the meeting, and by the time he gets home Dave is already at the foundry. Johnny rushes after him to stop him, but they are rumbled and in a panic Dave shoots a security guard dead. From here, it is all downhill for the trio, though how the police and everyone else in the town *cannot* suspect Dave when he gets hysterical every time anyone looks at him is anybody's guess.

The film, as had happened with *Yield to the Night* and *The Long Haul*, was panned by some critics who preferred their Diana Dors in scatty comedies and sexy roles. By the time of its release, however, she had signed up for another dramatic role – and taken a substantial cut in salary – as a prostitute in *Passport to Shame*. The move coincided with her receiving a call from the manager of Swindon Town Football Club, who asked her to become their honorary vice-president. Diana had never forgiven the former mayor for accusing her of bringing the town into disrepute, and when she learned that he was involved with the club, she did not mince her words while turning down the offer. Later, she sounded off at a *Sunday Express* reporter when the subject was brought up, 'What has Swindon ever done for *me*? Most towns are proud of local people who achieve success. In Swindon I only ever get criticised!'

Passport to Shame was directed by Alvin Rakoff, a Canadian mostly used to working in television drama. It was promoted as a condemnation of London's low-life, with its 'firms' and prostitution rackets – referred to in the film as 'the white slave trade' – and has an opening sequence where the famed Fabian of Scotland Yard delivers a message decrying society's current lack of morals. From this point, however, titillation is high on Rakoff's agenda. Vicki (Diana) has gone 'on the game' for unselfish reasons: she is raising money to pay the hospital bills for her sister, scarred in an acid attack by sadistic gangster Nick Biaggi (Herbert Lom), who grooms girls so they can be hired and serviced by wealthy (unseen) clients. Vicki may not like her job much, but this does not prevent her from persistently parading around in basque and suspenders. Then there is Malou (Odile Versois), wanted by the French police after being framed for theft, and duped by Biaggi into marrying an inarticulate cabbie (Eddie Constantine) so that she can stay in the country and be put to work like the others.

All in all it is a sorry tale, but interesting today for 'spot-the-bit-part' enthusiasts: Jackie Collins (future novelist sister of Joan) playing a prostitute, Michael Caine as a bridegroom. The film was hammered by the critics, particularly in America – nothing to do with Diana, but on account of her American co-star. Eddie Constantine (1917–93) was a huge star in France, having arrived in Paris a few years earlier and fallen for Edith Piaf, who had put him into her stage musical, *La p'tite Lili*. Though he would eventually make it big in his own country, for the time being American critics were hostile towards him. Bosley Crowther, writing for the *New York Times*, waspishly observed, 'After seeing Mr Constantine in this latest offering, and knowing him to be a very big star in his newly acquired country, France, we can only assume that 50 million Frenchmen must be wrong.'

With her divorce from Hamilton not yet final, Diana put her penthouse on the market for £20,000. Because of its history – the violence, the rows and the sex parties – the place had developed a reputation, and there were no prospective buyers. Eventually she had to drop the price, and it was sold to an army-surplus magnate named Frank Craddock, for just £13,000. In the meantime, Diana forked out £18,000 for Palmers, a 15th-century farmhouse at Billinghurst, near Horsham, and within easy commuting distance of London. The six-bedroom property was set in 50 acres, much of it uncultivated – this suited Diana, for her grandiose plans included the addition of a swimming pool, tennis courts and a landing strip for the private plane she had dreamed of owning since the one invented by Dennis Hamilton on the eve of the Blackpool fiasco.

Palmers, Diana said, would provide her and Tommy Yeardye with the perfect dream base to start a family – though she would quickly change her mind. He too fancied himself as the gentleman farmer, though the novelty of this would soon wear off. 'Apart from the time he painted the barn door,' she recalled, 'I saw him do little except lift his barbells, sunbathe in a garden chair, or ride the horse I gave him as a present.' Amorously, she appears to have been no longer interested in him and still had her eye on Dickie Dawson. Now, Yeardye was no longer referred to as her lover, but as her business manager. He also appears to have taken a shine to Paddy, her gay, star-struck Irish butler who each morning added an elaborate floral display to the contents of her breakfast tray. Paddy, who was not averse to cross-dressing, had a fetish for Gracie Fields. 'His room was covered with photographs of her,' Diana recalled, 'and one felt that if she had reared up at any time, all the breakfasts and flowers along with the rest of it would be abandoned as he rushed headlong towards her, leaving me in the lurch.' Diana, Yeardye and Paddy posed for photographs outside

Palmers for a magazine article, and in all of them Yeardye appears much less interested in Diana than he does in the handsome butler.

It was courtesy of Jackie Collins that Diana met her variety-agent father, Joe, whose later clients would include Tom Jones and Shirley Bassey. Collins, in a one-season deal, devised for her *The Diana Dors Show*, an eight-week tour that kicked off in Coventry on 28 July and took in most of the major cities in Britain – Diana's only stipulation was that Collins should not book her at the dreaded Glasgow Empire. The tour, Diana hoped, would set her in good stead for her next trip to America, scheduled for the end of October – not to shoot a film, but to finally make her Las Vegas cabaret debut. Tired of being compared with Bardot and Monroe, she now saw herself as Britain's answer to Marlene Dietrich, arguably the most celebrated international cabaret star of all time, who since 1954 had been packing out theatres around the world with songs from her films, and *chansons réaliste* she had chosen for herself. Diana was making a big mistake, of course, by even thinking of assuming such a mantle, for she would never possess a fraction of Dietrich's appeal – much of which centred around her having been a forces heroine who had risked her life entertaining soldiers at the front during World War II. Diana's Darnell gowns, on the other hand, were as sensational as the ones Jean-Louis had designed for Dietrich, and included a scarlet creation – at a time when the colour was taboo – slit to the thigh, and which literally struggled to contain her breasts. The first time she wore it for her curtain call, the males in the audience wolf-whistled all the way through the song.

This time around, Diana's act was more compact: a 45-minute spot which, like Dietrich's shows, never varied in its content – from the 'I've Got the World on a String' opener to the autobiographical 'Too Young', by way of a clutch of old favourites, and the Miss Muffet routine from *Rendezvous*. Her stooge and MC was none other than Dickie Dawson, with whom she enjoyed a friendly on-stage banter. The jokes were corny and ancient: 'I say, Dickie. My dog has no nose!' 'That's awful, Diana. How *does* he smell?' To which the audience joined in with the response, 'Terrible!' The first shows played to 70 per cent capacity audiences, there mostly out of curiosity, but when word got around that

Diana really could sing, there were house-full notices all along the circuit, and scalpers were selling tickets at 10 times the regular purchase price.

At the end of August 1958, between venues, Diana and Tommy Yeardye attended the funeral of Bonar Colleano, who had died in a car crash outside Birkenhead, aged 34. For years, Colleano had been swindling the taxman, buying property and cars, then signing them over to his wife – Susan Shaw, who had appeared alongside Diana in the *Huggetts* films. Over the course of the next 20 years, Shaw would spend that money slowly drinking herself to death. Diana monopolised the ceremony just by being there, and some of her comments – such as how clever Colleano had been to outwit the system – got back to the Inland Revenue, who investigated her for a third time. A few minor discrepancies were found, but the officials never discovered her 'secret stash'. Whenever she had been able to get away with it, Diana had asked some theatres to pay her cash in hand, and a large part of these undisclosed earnings had been paid into a safety-deposit box at Harrod's.

Halfway through the tour, Diana informed Tommy Yeardye that she had fallen in love with Dickie Dawson: they had not yet slept together, she added, though it was but a matter of time before they did, and she did not wish to hurt Yeardye's feelings by cheating on him. A mutual if not bizarre decision was reached: Yeardye would return to Palmers, where he would stay until Diana had finished the tour, before moving on. No sooner had he left than Joe Collins contacted her: due to public demand the tour had been extended by four weeks. This meant postponing her Las Vegas season, which she had never been bothered about in the first place. In the middle of September, she played a week at the Liverpool Empire, and while there she received word that Dennis Hamilton had been admitted to the London Clinic and was seriously ill. When Diana called the hospital, the switchboard operator informed her that he had specifically asked that no calls should be put through to his room – more than this, neither she nor the press were to be told what was wrong with him.

The tour ended on 7 October with an extended show at London's Finsbury Park Empire. The next morning, Diana headed for the London Clinic, where she bribed one of the nurses into letting her see her husband. She subsequently confessed that though she had been shocked at his frailty, she had felt no pity whatsoever for this man who had brought her nothing but misery. The purpose of her visit was to inform him to his face that she had amended her divorce petition: Shirley Anne Field's lawyer had been in touch to say that his client was considering taking legal action if Diana persisted in citing her as 'the other woman', therefore she had had her name removed from the document. Hamilton may have looked weak, but this was not the case a few days later when he discharged himself from the clinic, claiming that he had an important business matter to deal with. This involved an after-hours visit to El Dors, where he accused the manager of fiddling the books – and gave him a good hiding. The same day, Diana was taken ill with what she thought was food poisoning. Her doctor diagnosed pancreatitis and prescribed morphine. Later she would learn that it was something much more serious.

Two weeks later, Diana was seen entering Chelsea police station, and within minutes the place was swarming with press. That morning, she had opened her Harrod's safety-deposit box and, according to her statement, discovered that £18,000 of her savings was missing. The thief, she said, could only have been Tommy Yeardye, because there were just two keys to the box – the one she had given him, and the one she carried on her person at all times. She had given him the key, she added, in case he needed emergency funds while she was touring towards the upkeep of the farm. A warrant was put out for Yeardye's arrest, but the police were unable to act on this because he was holidaying in the South of France, allegedly with his new girlfriend. The incident made the papers, and resulted in Diana receiving a visit from tax officials who wanted to know why she had secreted such a large amount – quite obviously undeclared earnings – into a safety-deposit box. This question was answered by Yeardye himself later in the week when he returned to London. Acting in the capacity of Diana's business manager he *had* taken the money – but only £11,000 – and transferred it to Diana's bank account. A member of staff had witnessed him doing this, and he also had a receipt from the bank to prove that the transaction had taken place. Diana had hiked up the missing amount, he added, to make him feel bad because they were no longer lovers and she was jealous that he had someone else.

The investigation was dropped when Diana apologised for the mix-up. Her husband was seriously ill, she explained, and in her confusion she had made a mistake that any worried wife might have made. She now conveniently remembered that there *had* only been £11,000 in the safety-deposit box, and recalled phoning Yeardye and asking him to put the money in the bank – a story she had made up, now she had been rumbled. Almost certainly, if there had been another £7,000 in the box, Diana had removed it herself and pinned the blame on Yeardye as an act of revenge for 'cheating' on her with this mysterious woman in France – forgetting, of course, that she had cheated on *him* with Dickie Dawson!

That same evening Diana and Yeardye went out to dinner as if nothing had happened. And after they had gone 'Dutch' over the bill, the pair mutually decided that it might be for the best if they never saw each other again.

Chapter Ten

Death of a Tyrant

Little is known of Diana's December 1958 tour of South Africa, save that it was put together at the last minute and, in common with many celebrity trips to this part of the world at the time, ended badly.

One of the first British stars to visit the country when apartheid was starting to have its grip had been George Formby in 1946. Accompanied by his fearsome wife-manager, Beryl – from a business stance almost the female equivalent of Dennis Hamilton, minus all the unsavoury traits – Formby had refused to perform for segregated audiences and, when threatened with expulsion from the country, had taken the very daring step of performing *only* in black-township theatres. Subsequently, he and Beryl had been escorted back to the airport by machine-gun-toting policemen. A few years after Diana, Dusty Springfield would evoke a similar controversy.

Diana claimed to have been totally unaware of South Africa's political unrest, which one finds hard to believe. Unlike the Formbys and Dusty, who toured the whole country, she was booked for cabaret appearances in just two cities – a week each in Durban and Johannesburg. The managers of both venues ordered her to wear dresses buttoned up to the throat, which did not go down well with her. Also, she was displeased that she and Dickie Dawson would have to adhere to the country's 'family policy' and sleep in separate rooms. 'What a place,' she told journalists. 'It's bad enough they have to split the audience in two, without having to segregate us as well!'

During her shows she was further instructed to remain in the middle of the stage behind the microphone – if she did find it necessary to move around while singing, then she should move only to the side of the stage which faced the white section of the audience. Diana did exactly the opposite, and further enraged the promoter by refusing to attend any functions where black people were excluded. When it was all over and a reporter asked her at the airport if she had enjoyed her South African experience, her curt response was, 'Never again, sunshine!'

Diana returned to England on 20 December, and to more drama. A feature had appeared in the *National Enquirer* (since the demise of *Confidential* the undisputed doyenne of American trash-mags) alleging that she had recently attended a private party in Hyde Park's Rotten Row, during which she had whipped off her blouse and danced bare-breasted atop a table. The story was pure fabrication: there were *no* houses in Rotten Row, and she had been in Johannesburg when the supposed event had taken place. Even so, Diana received an angry call from William Dozier, informing her that RKO had now officially terminated her contract – not that she had ever expected to work for the studio again, in any case.

Unperturbed, Diana spent the festive season of 1958 at Palmers with Dickie Dawson. On 2 January she visited Hamilton – now recuperating at a rented house in Belgravia with his latest squeeze, an actress named Vera Day. He was in a morose mood and when Diana informed him that she was going to America for a month, his response was that he would not be alive when she returned. 'Dennis made a habit of telephoning his friends every day, sobbing that he was dying or that the doctors didn't know what they were doing,' she recalled, adding that she had merely shrugged her shoulders and assumed that he was in another of his 'playing for sympathy' moods.

The next day, Diana and Dawson flew to New York – where for a cool $40,000 she had been booked for guest slots on *Phil Silvers' Pontiac Special* and *The Steve Allen Show*. The latter saw her performing with Les Brown and his Orchestra, famed for his earlier appearances with another famous DD – Doris Day.

In the television studios, she bumped into Dorothy Squires, who she and Dennis Hamilton had first met in 1952. Dorothy invited her and Dawson to spend a few days at the Hollywood home she shared with actor Roger Moore. One of Britain's biggest recording stars of the 1940s and 1950s, and a cult concert star in the decades which followed, Dorothy had moved to America with Moore, whose career had reached new heights since appearing with Elizabeth Taylor in *The Last Time I Saw Paris*. It was Dorothy, whose own marriage was no bed of roses by this time, who took the call from England on 31 January reporting that Dennis Hamilton had died. Hospitalised shortly after Diana had left for New York, he had succumbed to a heart attack. Dorothy told me:

> If I'd have been married to that man, I would have put poison in his tea. He was a louse, through and through. He treated Diana like something you'd scrape off the bottom of your shoe, yet she had nothing but praise for him after he died. It really was a case of good riddance to bad rubbish. Dennis Hamilton would sleep with anyone – male or female – next door's cat if it stood still long enough.
>
> I took the call. Diana thought it was him again – he'd been pestering her nonstop for two days – and she ran out of the room screaming she never wanted to talk to him again. I followed her upstairs and told her what happened, and she went to pieces. All of a sudden, the man she'd just called the most evil bastard in the world had become her lost knight in shining armour. She kept sobbing how Dennis was the only man she had ever loved – all very disconcerting for Dickie Dawson, who was standing next to her wondering what to do. But *he* was another story...

Diana was still married to Hamilton, and therefore entitled to have the last word in his funeral arrangements. She wanted him buried in the picturesque churchyard at Bray, but when she arrived home learned that matters had been taken out of her hands.

While in hospital the first time, Hamilton had refused to see Diana because he had not wanted her to find out that he had converted to Catholicism, a religion he had always professed to hate. 'Wheeling and dealing to the end,' she recalled, 'Dennis had tried to buy a fast ticket to heaven by turning Catholic before he met his Maker.'

Hamilton, aware that the end had been near, had stipulated that should anything happen to him, Diana should be excluded from having anything to do with his funeral, which took place on 3 February. His parents certainly could not bar her from the service, which was conducted at St James' Roman Catholic Church in Spanish Place, at which she said she had felt like a stranger gate-crashing a party. A 1,000-strong crowd had gathered there, along with dozens of journalists and photographers, few of them interested in Hamilton – only in the black-clad widow, wearing the diamond engagement ring given to her by Dickie Dawson the previous Christmas. She was escorted into the church by Jon Pertwee, one of the few friends Hamilton had had left.

The media also had a field day trying to work out the identities of the 30 or so young women who walked up to the altar and kissed the coffin – Hamilton's mistresses and girlfriends, with the most recent one, Vera Day, leading the parade. Half a dozen young men paid similar homage, but nothing was said about this. Among the wreaths was one from Jennifer, Teasy-Weasy's wife, who had also had an affair with Hamilton and was currently involved in a costly, messy public divorce from her crimper husband.

Diana wept quietly throughout the prayers and lessons, until there was a commotion at the back of the church: dozens of yelling fans, clutching autograph books and pens, who now clambered over the pews to get to Diana. Four photographers, taking advantage of the situation, shouldered their way through the mourners who had suddenly jumped up to protect her – when these tried to snap her wiping the tears from her eyes, security men manhandled them out of the church. A few minutes later, suitably composed, Diana left the building via a side door to where Dickie Dawson was waiting to drive her back to Palmers. Hamilton's parents had made it clear that they did not want her at the graveside in Westminster Cemetery.

Immediately after Dennis Hamilton's death, Diana was presented with a conundrum, which was never really solved. Firstly she was informed by Jon Pertwee that Hamilton had not died of heart disease, but of tertiary syphilis. According to Pertwee, this information had come from a doctor friend at the London Clinic. On closer examination of the facts, and taking into account Hamilton's character, the story is not as ridiculous as it initially seems. He had asked the doctors to let her know that he had been *admitted* to the clinic, for no other reason than to worry and upset her – once this had happened, instructions had been given not to let her see him. Then, knowing that she *would* make a point of seeing him, he had added to her anxiety, telling her that he would be dead before she returned home from New York.

This attempt to make Diana feel guilty had failed. Indeed, she had nothing to feel guilty about. She may have cheated on him with Rod Steiger, Kim Waterfield, Tommy Yeardye and Dickie Dawson, to mention just the ones we know about, but their marriage had been little more than a sham, and she had been looking for a shoulder to cry on after the abysmal way he had treated her right from the day she had married him. Now, from beyond the grave, he had exacted his revenge. Diana went to see the doctors at the clinic, who initially were reluctant to reveal the details of her husband's illness. But of one thing she was certain. If Hamilton *had* been suffering from the disease, with his promiscuity it must have given him enormous sardonic pleasure to know that he could be leaving behind him a legacy of potential misery and suffering.

Tertiary syphilis most often occurs between one and ten years after initial infection, which means that Hamilton could have been harbouring the disease *before* meeting Diana – who similarly could have been a carrier, and naturally unaware of the fact, for almost eight years. If this was the case, it could have been passed on not just to their own partners during these years, but their partners' partners, and have reached almost epic proportions without anyone being the wiser, unless the symptoms had shown up at once (which, according to the experts, would have been unlikely).

It is not known if Diana was actually tested for syphilis, a dirty word in those days, whose very mention might have seriously compromised if not ended her career – particularly in addition to the stories circulating about the sex parties and other goings-on at the various Hamilton homes. Diana complicated matters by telling the press that her late husband had never had a day's illness in his life. Therefore, she posed, how could he possibly have had a life-threatening heart condition and no one known about this? More importantly, she wanted to know, why had there been no post mortem?

Diana could have answered this one herself. When informed of Hamilton's death, she had called the London Clinic and specifically asked for there *not* to be an autopsy, declaring that 'poor Dennis' had suffered enough without being subjected to the indignity of being 'dissected'. The fact that she had been adamant about this might suggest that she knew precisely what had been wrong with him, all the more reason for her wishing to contest the will. Despite sponging off her for years and using her money to finance his scams, Hamilton had left her nothing, and Diana was told by her lawyer that there was every chance of the will being declared invalid because he had not been of sound mind when signing the document.

In *Dors By Dors*, written 20 years after his death, Diana still feigned ignorance of Hamilton's condition when he died. Amending the facts, she claimed that doctors at the London Clinic had informed her that Hamilton had contracted syphilis *17* years earlier, clearly so that her readers would not assume that he had caught it from her. Then she almost contradicted herself by concluding that the diagnosis had come as no surprise, for reading about the disease in a medical book had been like reading Hamilton's biography:

> Brainstorms, emotional neurosis, persecution complexes, delusions of grandeur – the ornate furnishings and attempts to buy a Welsh castle and Fort Belvedere. Sexual aberrations and disturbance of conduct that might necessitate bringing in the police, writing large cheques, schizophrenia, completely demented behaviour. Now at last I knew what had been wrong with the man I married.

Others had, of course, for years been witness to Hamilton's antisocial behaviour, but until now had never even thought of attributing the symptoms to venereal disease: the periods of hyperactivity which had alternated with episodes of self-loathing, the mood swings, the violence towards Diana and others, and now the doctors at the London Clinic were admitting that he *had* died of heart failure, but brought about as a result of aortic regurgitation linked to his syphilis. Her solicitor warned her again of the repercussions of her contesting the will and this becoming public knowledge. Diana did not want this – and in any case, while investigating Hamilton's finances it emerged that there was very little money to fight for, and no property. Only weeks before his death, Hamilton had sold his interests in Woodhurst – it is believed to fellow crook Peter Rachman – along with the nightclub and coffee bar in Maidenhead, to prevent Diana from getting her hands on them after their divorce. What he had done with the proceeds was not known, though Diana believed they might have been stashed away in a secret overseas bank account.

Having therefore opted to let sleeping dogs lie, Diana concluded that Dennis Hamilton had died at exactly the right time. So too did Dickie Dawson, who 10 days after Hamilton's funeral – leaving Diana at home to milk as much out of her ersatz widow status as she could – flew to New York to negotiate television and variety appearances for them both. Within 24 hours of him leaving, Diana ditched the mourning apparel: speaking to reporters she declared that she was the happiest she had been in her entire life.

In New York, Dawson met up with several RKO representatives. Though the studio was no longer interested in having Diana work for them, two films remained to be made under the terms of the contract she had signed with them in August 1956, prior to the notorious pool party, and she was now suing them for $250,000 in lost earnings. She had, of course, contravened that all-important 'moral turpitude' clause by having the affair with Rod Steiger, therefore the studio had been legally entitled to drop her. When Dawson was reminded of this and relayed the tidings to Diana, she did not see things this way. All Hollywood stars had affairs. In her opinion, RKO had deliberately set out to double-cross her.

Dawson flew back to London and, now officially a couple, he and Diana set about making their relationship permanent. Her wedding to Dennis Hamilton had been a rushed affair, and this time around she wanted to do things properly – a summer ceremony close to her home, or maybe in London, so that all her friends and family could be there. Dawson had other ideas. Upon her insistence he had legally changed his name to Dickie Dawson, so that she would not have to 'suffer the indignity' of being officially listed as Diana Mary Emm – this way, she would also retain those famous DD initials. Therefore, she owed *him* a favour. Dawson may not have been quite so manipulative as Hamilton, but he clearly regarded her as a meal ticket, hence his insistence that they marry in America, where the resultant publicity would hopefully kick-start the career he was hoping for there. He had already appeared in cabaret with Diana, where his impersonations of American comics and actors had been well received. Now he wanted to repeat the process on their territory.

Since dropping Louis Shurr, Diana had a new American agent, Harry Steinman, and the seven-minute ceremony took place in New York at his Riverside Drive apartment on 12 April 1959— two hours after Diana had performed 'Love' on *The Steve Allen Show*. The celebrant was a Jewish judge brought in at the last minute: the witnesses were Diana's actress friend Jean Marsh, now separated from Jon Pertwee, and her current (unnamed) lover. Afterwards, there was a reception at the exclusive Harwyn Club. 'The bride wore gold lamé,' observed one of the New York papers the next day.

As had happened with Dennis Hamilton, everything changed once the rings were exchanged. 'Gone was the man who made me laugh all the time,' she recalled. 'Gone were the hilarious sketches before breakfast. Now I found myself living with a man who could not be spoken to until well after noon, who stopped amusing me unless there was an audience of fans to impress.'

On 17 April, the Dawsons flew home, and no sooner had they slept off their jet lag than Diana was repeating to reporters what she had said when first taking up with Tommy Yeardye: she wanted to start a family, and was seriously considering retiring from show business to devote more time to being a wife and mother. The last thing she wanted, she said, was to end up an ageing joke like Mae West. First, though, there would be a movie swan song, followed by a farewell tour comprising various variety engagements on both sides of the Atlantic.

Taking Dawson's advice, she had signed up for a 39-episode Stateside television series, which she would begin taping in the late summer. In the meantime, she taped *The Diana Dors Show* for ATV: Dawson had part-written the script. The show, which aired at the end of May, saw her adding Marlene Dietrich, Eartha Kitt, Clara Bow and Marilyn Monroe to her roster of impersonations.

Her 'final' film, shot on location in Spain, was a stinker in more ways than one. *The Scent of Mystery*, produced by Mike Todd Jr and directed by Jack Cardiff, who had photographed *Black Narcissus* so brilliantly, was an oddity filmed in Smell-O-Vision. The tagline itself was enough to put cinemagoers off: 'First They Moved (1895)! Then They Talked (1927)! Now They Smell!' With such a gimmick at its centre, and despite the presence of Todd's former stepmother Elizabeth Taylor, the film had a limited release and was thankfully soon forgotten. It told the story of Englishman abroad Denholm Elliott and his attempts to save wealthy heiress Taylor from being murdered, and saw fans choking on the stench of food and perfume as this was pumped through theatres' air-conditioning systems.

The retirement plan looked like becoming reality this time when, during the first week of August and halfway through rehearsals for a second television spectacular for ATV, Diana announced that she was pregnant. Cynics – and even some of her friends – were surprised when she did not make immediate plans to have an abortion, as had happened three times before. Next, she decided she did not want her child growing up on a farm in the middle of nowhere, and promptly put Palmers on the market for £25,000. The place, she said, also held bad memories of her time with Tommy Yeardye: she needed to wipe the slate clean and start over with her new husband in a new home which did not come with excess baggage.

The couple bought Springwoods, a five-bedroom modern property in Virginia Water, Surrey. The property was very basic, she told the press – why, it did not even have a swimming pool! – but she preferred things that way because customising the house and turning it into their very own little family nest would be that much more rewarding. The first room to be worked on was the nursery: this she had done out in lemon and white so that it would not matter if the baby was a boy or girl.

While the decorators were in, and suffering terribly from morning sickness, Diana embarked on a brief tour of Europe with Dawson, performing in selected venues in Cannes, Rome and Madrid. Returning to London, and refusing to take a break, Diana set about recording her first (and, it would turn out, only) album of love songs, for which she had chosen the title *Swingin' Dors*.

The idea was the brainchild of music publisher David Platz (1929–94), the German-born former Tin Pan Alley office boy who would later produce artistes as diverse as Anthony Newley, Johnny Dankworth, and the Rolling Stones. Diana herself suggested the artwork: the record would be of red vinyl to match her infamous 'Victory Red' pout, housed in a gatefold sleeve which would swing open to reveal her wearing one of her Darnell gowns and posed provocatively as if on stage. For the orchestrations, Platz brought in Wally Stott (1924–2009), whose arrangement of 'As I Love You' would soon rocket Shirley Bassey to the top of the British charts. Retrospectively, Platz could not have chosen a more apt and controversial figure – some years later, Stott would undergo a sex-change operation and become known as Angela Morley.

Diana completed the album in just two weeks. Everyone had forgotten the single she had released a few years earlier, so it came as a surprise for those who had not seen her stage act that she could actually sing – not only this, but sing inordinately well in a relaxed, controlled, jazzy style not unlike Julie London. It was only when the master tape had been assembled that David Platz set about finding a record company to release it – effectively, the highest bidder, Pye, who chose a date which would coincide with the birth of Diana's baby.

Platz and Wally Stott had allowed Diana full rein over her choice of material. Most of the songs, though not written for her, were selected because the lyrics appertained to certain episodes in her colourful life – if they did not, she added a few lines of her own.

Opening the proceedings was 'The Point of No Return' – not the emotive song with the same title penned by Dorothy Squires, but a big-band number she had recently performed in ITV's

Armchair Theatre production of 'The Innocent': aired on 8 May, this saw Diana playing a chanteuse accused of murdering her lover, and saw her working with Ian Hunter and Patrick Macnee. Whereas Dot's song signified the break of her relationship with Roger Moore, Diana's applies to the start of hers with Dickie Dawson, which she gives every impression of being reluctant to enter into. 'You fight the feeling that keeps stealing up your spine,' she sings, confessing that though she is hooked on her new man, she may not wish to admit that she is in love.

Next up is Johnny Mercer's 'Namely You', from *Li'l Abner*. 'You deserve a girl that's willing...one who's willing to raise your children,' she sings, obviously with Dawson in mind.

Jay Livingston's 'That's How It Is' is the first of several standards on the album. Sounding very much like Doris Day, she informs us that love is a lottery – some you win, some you lose. Directly referring to Dawson, she sneaks in the observation, 'I didn't make the rules... All of those who claim love's just a game are comedians and fools,' but concludes that, when all is said and done, the gamble is worth it.

'Let There Be Love' is the Nat King Cole favourite which sees Diana adding a few embellishments of her own: 'Let there be sports cars and wonderful clothes... Let there be moons circling in space... Let there be movies, and Princess Grace!' Then, after Jimmy Van Heusen's classic 'Imagination', famously performed by Ella Fitzgerald and Kate Smith, side one closes with 'Roller Coaster Blues', a late-night smoochy piece, obviously aimed at Dennis Hamilton, the Janus figure who is 'tender as the inside of a caterpillar's thigh', but whose air of danger cannot help but excite her. 'Your mouth's a roller coaster,' she croons, 'Baby, I want to take a ride!'

Side two of *Swingin' Dors* opens with Rodgers and Hammerstein's 'The Gentleman Is a Dope', a US chart hit for Jo Stafford in 1947. In this one, the lover she is thinking of is Tommy Yeardye, 'A clumsy Joe who wouldn't know a Rumba from a Waltz'. The man does not really belong to her and she cries her eyes out because she wants him, then changes her mind and opines that the woman who has him right now is welcome to him! Exactly who Yeardye's mystery woman – or man – was, or if indeed there was one, is not known.

Next up is 'April Heart', another song that refers to Dennis Hamilton, which juxtaposes their relationship with extremes in the weather. 'The temperature drops and your eyes say stormy, Up the mercury pops and they're shining for me,' she sings, before concluding of his adulterous ways, 'But half a love's worth more than none!' Then she completely confounds the issue with the next number – for having debunked Hamilton and Yeardye she proclaims, 'I'm in Love for the Very First Time'. The song, from *An Alligator Named Daisy*, had won Paddy Roberts an Ivor Novello Award in 1955.

Diana next tackles a Billie Holiday standard, Carl Sigman and Bob Russell's 'Crazy He Calls Me', and again the mood is optimistic: she will move mountains and go through fire for the man she loves. 'Come By Sunday' had been written for big-voiced jazz singer Sallie Blair in 1957, one of her few hits: Diana had also performed her 'Squeeze Me', a sultry number composed by Fats Waller. Here, she coquettishly invites her lover to drop in on her unannounced – but only on Sunday, after three, because the rest of the week her social calendar is full! The album ends, sadly, on a weak note: Stalter and Gottlied's 'Tired of Love', which has Diana duetting – wearily – with an uncredited male singer.

The album did not chart on either side of the Atlantic – no one really expected it to, and for years it was regarded as something of a novelty, but since 1960 it has managed to shift almost a million copies.

Though she had promised to retire, it was almost certainly Diana's idea to fill her diary with engagements – the first to take place almost immediately after the expected birth of their child. Diana recalled in her memoirs that she desperately needed the money, that Dennis Hamilton's sudden death had saddled her with a huge tax demand she had been previously unaware of. This was not true. Though Hamilton had 'sidelined' sizeable portions of her earnings into his business ventures, and though these had rarely been above board, his only 'crime' so far as the taxman had been concerned had been to inflate the amount of her earnings as a means of increasing her market value to prospective producers. Neither was she greedy for money. The real reason Diana hated taking time off, pure and simple, was she had become so accustomed to being in the spotlight that she would never have

coped away from it. The fans needed her, and she needed them –
her lifeblood – more than they would ever realise. She had already
come to the conclusion that this marriage would end in disaster
like her first.

Chapter Eleven

Roller-Coaster Blues

In January 1960, Diana called her American agent, Harry Steinman, and asked him to renegotiate with the management of Las Vegas's Dunes Hotel, where she should have performed the previous October. She was snapped up in an instant, and Steinman also booked her for a season at the Chi-Chi Club, in Palm Springs. There would also be numerous television appearances.

In England, she was offered the part of Brenda, the female lead in the screen adaptation of Alan Sillitoe's controversial bestselling novel, *Saturday Night and Sunday Morning*, opposite a then little-known Albert Finney. The gritty Northern drama would have suited her well, and Diana accepted the part without reading the script – she had read the book, she said, and loved it. Moreover, her friend Hylda Baker would be playing one of the leads, and she had always wanted to work with director Carl Reisz, whose recent television documentary, *We Are the Lambeth Boys*, she had admired. Then she just as suddenly changed her mind, her official reason being that she no longer felt comfortable – bearing in mind her own experiences – playing a character who has an abortion. The real reason, however, was that Reisz had also cast Shirley Anne Field in the film. Reisz subsequently replaced Diana with Rachel Roberts.

Meanwhile, on 4 February, and at the London Clinic – in the very room where Dennis Hamilton had died, almost exactly a year before – Diana gave birth to her first son, Mark Richard Dawson. As had happened with her own birth, the labour was an exceedingly difficult one – 27 hours – before the seven-pound baby, subsequently nicknamed 'The Cabaret Orphan' by the tabloids, entered the world.

Diana was attacked by religious and moral groups for returning to work immediately after leaving the clinic. Baroness Mary Stokes, a precursor of clean-up campaigner Mary Whitehouse and an outspoken member of the BBC's Advisory Council, laid into her during a live radio debate on *Any Questions?* When asked what advice she might offer Diana regarding the subject of motherhood, Stokes shot back, 'My advice is that she should get it adopted.' Diana's response to this remains unprintable. Diana also propelled herself from the frying pan and into the fire at this time by selling 'The True Story of Diana Dors' to the doyenne of British tabloids, the *News of the World*.

Diana's four subsequent volumes of memoirs would be penned by her, and edited to remove any libellous content or remarks about others considered by the publishers to be too over the top – but without sacrificing any of the innate wit which almost puts her on a par with a Molly Weir or a David Niven. Having her story ghostwritten by a tabloid journalist, however, who was interested in 'the mucky bits' and in making his subject read like some kind of sex-obsessed madam was a massive mistake for Diana to make. The newspaper paid her £35,000 – only £1,000 less, she said with pride, than a rival publication had forked out to serialise Errol Flynn's even more scandalous posthumously published autobiography, *My Wicked, Wicked Ways* – a vast amount at the time. Everything was here which had appertained to her 'seedy' life with Dennis Hamilton: the sex parties and two-way mirrors, Diana's admission that he taped guests having sex, then played the tape back to the entire household over breakfast, the episodes of violence, the scams. Each episode was reeled out unflinchingly by Diana who, horrified as she claimed to be by being forced to confess her late husband's sins from beyond the grave, was only doing so now because she was desperate to bury her past with him so she could settle down to the kind of family life she had only ever dreamed of with a new, genuinely loving husband and a son they both doted on.

Leading the attack this time was someone much more vocal and powerful than Baroness Stokes – Geoffrey Fisher, the Archbishop of Canterbury, who during his Sunday sermon denounced Diana from the pulpit as 'a wanton hussy'. Fisher reported the *News of the World* to the Press Council, who further denounced her as 'lewd and an insult to every decent man, woman and child in Britain'. 'Diana hit the roof over that one,' Dorothy Squires said. 'Henceforth, whenever she referred to him it was as the Archbishop of *Cunt*erbury!' The Mayor of Swindon further accused her of bringing shame on the town, and claimed to be speaking on behalf of everyone there by requesting that she never set foot in the place again. Diana's response to this was that they need not hold their breath.

Diana then made matters worse, if such a thing was possible, by changing her story about how the *News of the World* had acquired the rights to the serialisation. Three years previously, she claimed, a journalist from the paper had visited them in Hollywood, as a result of which Hamilton had written the script, which she had not bothered reading because the deal had fallen through. The same journalist had contacted her shortly before Christmas, she added, at a time when she had been heavily pregnant, unwell, and not in a position to check the copy – therefore she had given the journalist permission to lend her name to it, and publish the piece as it stood.

Naturally, no one believed her. She was partly defended by Thomas Wiseman of the *Evening Standard* – Wiseman wrote in his piece, 'The Far From Shocking News About Diana Dors', that the offensive elements of her story referred not to Diana's sordid activities, but those of her late husband. Then, to assure his readers he was not taking sides, he suggested that she was kidding no one if she was expecting her fans to believe that she had been shocked to learn that Hamilton had installed two-way mirrors in their home. 'Diana Dors doesn't take sex *that* seriously,' Wiseman admonished. 'Her whole exaggerated personality is a parody of sex – the movement of her hips, the flutter of her eyelashes...they all suggest the downright absurdity of sex.' In years to come, Diana would similarly feign shock and even disgust at the 'homosexual acts' that had taken place under her roof, and that members of the clergy had also attended Hamilton's parties. Yet she had been well aware of them, and uncomplaining then.

There were several codas to this latest scandal. Friends of the Hamiltons, some of who had participated in the sexual shenanigans at Woodhurst, proffered exposés of their own to the tabloids – as did Tommy Yeardye, never less than eager to earn an easy buck at her expense. Then, at the end of April, Diana received an anonymous letter, the sender of which threatened to kill her husband and baby unless she deposited £2,500 at a specified spot on the driveway to her home. She contacted the police, who instructed her to make the drop. The would-be assassin, a teenage naval cadet, was subsequently apprehended and claimed that he was only the 'middle man' who had been paid 'just a quid' to pick up the cash for a man he refused to name. The police did not believe his story, and during the hearing at Chertsey Juvenile Court he pleaded guilty, confessing that he had been about to take his driving test and needed the money to buy a sports car like his idol! Diana was rather hoping that the magistrate would throw the book at him on account of the stress he had caused her, but the boy was fined just £10 and ordered to make a public apology. The press gave every impression of being on his side: in their opinion, Diana Dors had more money than she sensibly knew what to do with and, in the wake of the recent serialisation of her 'dirty' life story, not always honourably earned.

The next 'mini-scandal' was as a result of Diana's name being added to the line-up of that year's *Royal Variety Show*, to be held on 16 May at the Victoria Palace. Headlining would be Sammy Davis Jr, Nat King Cole and king of camp Liberace. What worried the so-called watchdogs was that the show was being televised for the first time, and the Archbishop of Canterbury – this time supported by Randolph Churchill, a hypocrite if ever there was one who had denounced Diana as 'a tart', but only after going to see her stage show five times before coming to this conclusion – was worried about her shocking the royals by appearing in one of the Darnell gowns which, he claimed, were as immoral as she was. Churchill contacted Buckingham Palace. 'Did the Queen and Prince Philip *really* want to see this reprehensible woman?' he demanded. The answer was a resounding yes. 'Obviously, the Royals were not the prim and proper fuddy-duddies the newspapers often made them out to be, and certainly had a much less narrow outlook than the Archbishop,' Diana later recalled with great satisfaction.

At the end of May, while the *News of the World* debacle raged on, Diana and Dickie Dawson jetted off to New York to prepare for her Las Vegas debut the following month, leaving baby Mark in the (incapable, it would come to be seen) hands of his nanny, Amy Baker. How Diana had come to hire her is not known, and what is strange is that she appears to have distrusted her from the start: Baker claimed to be psychic, and was certainly unhinged to the extent that within days of taking up her position, she was telling everyone that Mark was her own. Had the press known this at the time, there is little doubt that social services would have moved in during his parents' absence and taken the child into care.

Diana and Dawson lingered in New York long enough to collect the musical director for her show, then headed for Los Angeles, where rehearsals took place at Liberace's palatial home on Sherman Drive. The Dunes Hotel was paying Diana a staggering $7,000 a week, but she was made to work for it. Her act now ran to 50 minutes, from the big-band 'How Long Is This Going On?' to the 'Love' finale which saw her emerging from pink smoke, flanked by a quartet of muscular male dancers and delivering a stunning impersonation of Lena Horne. However, there were to be three shows nightly: the first at 8pm while the audience were dining, the second at midnight, and the third at 4am, by which time she was sometimes scarcely able to stay on her feet. Neither did she see much of her husband, extant of the show. Dawson, who was hoping to fashion an international career of his own as opposed to being his wife's opening act and MC, could not believe his luck at being in an environment where he could meet and mix with the very stars and comedians he had been emulating for years. Dawson had also developed a passion for gambling and, according to Diana, an unhealthy interest in gangsters.

Owing to extreme fatigue, Diana missed several of her 4am performances, though the venue's management was so pleased with the returns – every show was a sell-out – that halfway through the four-week run they upped her salary to $10,000 and asked her to stay on for another month. She politely turned the offer down, explaining that she was missing her son and needed to get back home. Two days later, while they were driving back to their hotel, Dawson announced that he had good news for her – he had lined up a tough-talking lawyer, the best in the city, who would take on RKO and get back the money they owed her, and this man was waiting to see her in their suite. The 'lawyer' turned out to be Amy Baker, who had arrived that afternoon from England with baby Mark!

Dawson's trick had worked. Diana agreed to stay on in Las Vegas for another month, and the next morning she realised that her husband had not been joking about the lawyer. One week later, this man forced a settlement with RKO, who not only paid her the $250,000 she had sued them for, but offered her an apology for the offensive remarks they had made in the wake of the pool party! Like a great portion of Diana's earnings, this payout seemed to simply disappear.

Diana closed at the Dunes Hotel on 4 August. She was pining for England, and wanted to see how the renovations were coming along at Virginia Water – particularly the swimming pool she had commissioned. Dickie Dawson had other ideas. Despite Diana's success, the career he had been hoping for had not taken off and he needed more time – and of course her financial support – to have one more stab at the big time. Like Dennis Hamilton, he was blessed with the 'gift of the gab', and thought he knew precisely what was best for her so long as this was to his advantage. Therefore he secured them a two-week, $24,000 stint at Lake Tahoe, to be followed by a two-week engagement on a slightly smaller salary at Ciro's in Los Angeles – where, she claimed, from the stage she had seen Bobby Kennedy's latest mistress slide under the table and administer a blow job to the tragic senator.

While Diana was wooing the snooty audiences at the then most prestigious club on Sunset Strip, she was approached by Ken Hughes, who had directed her in *The Long Haul*. Hughes had recently triumphed with *The Trials of Oscar Wilde*, starring a woefully miscast Peter Finch – in a scenario so hackneyed to placate the censor that it bore little resemblance to the real story of Victorian England's most celebrated genius. And now, Hughes wanted Diana to portray herself in *The Diana Dors Story* – based on her memoirs recently serialised in the *News of the World*. In no uncertain terms she informed him that she was not interested.

While in Hollywood this time around, the Dawsons had taken out a short lease on Greta Garbo's former home, which Diana claimed had brought her luck when she was offered a part in Jerry Lewis's next film, *Ladies' Man*, which the zany comic was producing and directing. She and manager Harry Steinman met Lewis – one of the most egotistical figures in US show business – at Paramount Studios, where the walls of the corridor leading to his private office were plastered in photographs of the comic, all placed there by himself. Lewis's agent had told Steinman that Diana would be paid $5,000 for her part in the film, not a very large one, but Steinman decided to ask Lewis personally for $7,000. Lewis shook his head, and after a lengthy and embarrassing pause declared that he *would* however pay her $10,000. The deal was secured with a handshake, and Diana was informed that shooting would begin in three months' time.

In the meantime, Steinman put Diana into *On the Double*, starring Danny Kaye – a comedian she had never been overly fond of since seeing him at the London Palladium back in 1951. In the film, set during World War II, Kaye plays a wimpish GI, a master of disguise who is mistaken for a brave English colonel – and asked to impersonate him so the colonel can sneak out of the country on a secret mission. It was a daft comedy, but Diana acquitted herself well as a sexy woman sergeant. Working with such a big star, however, along with the proposed film with Jerry Lewis, was enough to convince her that Hollywood had given her another chance. She was even willing to sacrifice one of her most celebrated assets – her lovely long blonde hair. She had refused to dye it for Bob Hope when ordered to do so, but when Kaye's director *suggested* that she might look better with it cut shorter, as Doris Day and Jayne Mansfield had done, she complied. She was almost 30, she said, and was preparing to leave her 'sex bomb' days behind in the hope of finding better roles.

Jerry Lewis, however, took umbrage against Diana working with Danny Kaye before him. 'I suppose he looked upon him as a rival,' she recalled, 'though I find it hard to believe with his enormous ego that he ever truly regarded anyone as that!' Lewis unceremoniously dropped her from his film and replaced her with Broadway actress Hope Holiday, who had recently partnered Jack Lemmon in Billy Wilder's *The Apartment*. Diana was livid. To her way of thinking, a gentleman's handshake was just as binding as a signature on a contract, and when she visited Paramount again only to have Lewis walk straight past her and ignore her, she collared him and gave him a piece of her mind. A few days later,

Harry Steinman received a cheque for $5,000, her original fee for the film.

Diana's next film was as a gangster's moll in *King of the Roaring Twenties*, the story of flamboyant Jewish mobster and bootlegger Arnold Rothstein, portrayed by David Janssen. Though set in Chicago, the locations were shot in London, and before boarding the plane Diana announced that this would be her last visit to England for a while – maybe even her very last, because she had decided that it was time to put down roots in Hollywood again. This would mean selling the property in Surrey – good news for Dickie Dawson, who stayed on once the film had wrapped to supervise the sale of the house and its contents. In the meantime, Diana put in an offer – a whopping $150,000 – for a mansion on Angelo Drive, which was actually on the market for $175,000. The vendor refused to drop the price, so Diana paid a deposit and took out a hefty mortgage she could ill afford. No problem, she told reporters – she would just have to work that little bit harder!

Being seen to be married to a man clearly much more stable and level-headed than his predecessor had helped repair Diana's reputation. She was, however, desperately unhappy and unfulfilled in her marriage, and almost incapable of coping with Dickie Dawson's moods. With Dennis Hamilton, she said, she had known the score – a sudden explosion, followed by a slap or a punch, and things had returned to normal. Dawson offered her the 'cold war' treatment after an argument, retreating to his room and sulking for hours, sometimes days on end. He had also begun criticising the way she dressed: Hamilton had called her a whore for displaying too much décolletage, whereas Dawson more politely denounced her as 'looking like a tart'! Amy Baker would invariably add to the couple's problems by taking his side. Sometimes, Diana said, she would arrive home from an engagement and head straight for bed, her only way of avoiding them both for fear of one of them throwing a tantrum. When asked why she did not just fire the troublesome nanny and have done with it, her response was that Mark would have never accepted anyone else looking after him – not even his own mother.

The next three months of Diana's life were an absolute whirligig of work, emotions and drama. 'When a man treats a woman with disdain, especially when she's paying the bills,' she later observed, 'another man will come along and give her the attention she craves.' Such a solution – though not necessarily the right one – occurred in August 1961 when she was offered a part in 'The Sportscar Breed', an episode of ABC television's weekly motor-racing drama series, *Straightaway*. This starred Kansas-born John Ashley (1934–97), the darling of America's closeted gay teenage fraternity who appeared in such camp classics as *High School Caesar*, *Motorcycle Gang* and *Dragstrip Girl*. Ashley's infamous 'bubble butt', effected by his not wearing anything under his skintight trousers – and the fact that he always seemed more interested in the males in his films than the females forever flinging themselves at him – saw some parents protesting outside cinemas. His on-screen 'gyrations' were also considered immoral by some religious groups, in much the same way as Elvis Presley's movements saw him filmed from the waist up in television shows around the same time. In *Straightaway*, Ashley plays the central character of Clipper Hamilton, a name that naturally intrigued Diana. Despite the fact that Ashley was gay (he married very briefly not long afterwards), she managed to entice him into having an affair with her while shooting the locations in Miami.

Ashley was sufficiently enamoured of Diana – or maybe afraid of being 'outed' by the tabloids – to ask her to marry him, and even persuaded her to consider filing for divorce from Dickie Dawson. The lawyer assigned to handle the petition was Sam Brody, who became Jayne Mansfield's lover and died in the same car crash that killed her. Brody advised Diana that such a divorce would cost her dearly. Dawson did not have much money of his own, he had remained faithful to her throughout their marriage, and almost certainly – given her reputation – he would be granted custody of their son once he had taken her to the cleaners.

In her memoirs, Diana says nothing about this, preferring to feign concern over how Dawson would have coped without her, though he too was clearly disappointed with their marriage. Of course, had she been truly concerned for her husband, she would not have made so sterling an effort to cheat on him in the first place. In time, Dawson would become a big name in America. But this would be years into the future – right now, no one seemed to be bothered about helping him with his predicament; the fact that he was suffering from what appears to have been acute clinical depression on account of his persistently being forced to walk in the shadow of his wife's sun. No matter how hard he tried to forge ahead with his own career, there would always be someone close at hand to remind him that there was every chance of his never being regarded as anything more than 'Mr Dors'. Dennis Hamilton had relished such a position: Dawson hated it.

The almost certainly 'lavender' affair with John Ashley was still ongoing when Dawson returned to Hollywood, a week earlier than expected. Amy Baker had called him, relaying all the latest gossip and complaining that Diana was spending virtually no time at all with Mark. Dawson also learned that Diana had removed her wedding ring, and that she had given Ashley the gold bracelet *he* had given her: this Ashley had attached to the exhaust of his Porsche, his way of letting all of Hollywood know that he was madly in love with Diana Dors. Dawson had only half-believed the story, but when Diana and Ashley walked into the living room – holding hands and giggling like teenagers after a night on the town – to find Dawson waiting for them, there was an almighty row and the two men almost came to blows.

For a little while, Diana moved into John Ashley's apartment. Harry Steinman had booked her on a 21-venue tour of South America, which saw her performing in Brazil, Chile, Bolivia, Venezuela and Peru. She left without even seeing her husband and son, refused to allow Ashley to accompany her, and while away is said to have received a call from Dawson – as Sam Brody had predicted, asking for a divorce and full custody of Mark. This appears to have brought her to her senses. Upon her return to Hollywood, Dawson and Mark were waiting in the airport lounge. That evening, she said, the two of them talked things through. Dawson had been to see Ashley, and informed him that he would be willing to grant Diana a divorce, on her terms, but she would have to prove how much she truly loved Ashley by promising not to see him for a whole year!

The next day, John Ashley was given his marching orders, and the Dawsons went back to playing happy families. Taking Mark and his nanny with them, they flew to England, where Diana topped the bill on *Sunday Night at the London Palladium*. Then, accompanied by Amy Baker and Mark, on she flew to Spain, where she was scheduled to begin shooting *Encontra A Mallorca* for

José Maria Ochia, who had recently worked as assistant director on *King of Kings*. Only days into the schedule, Ochia pulled the plug on the production upon hearing that one of the sponsors was experiencing financial difficulties: Diana had been promised $75,000 for the film, but subsequently only received a fraction of this. There was, however, some compensation when her friend Lionel Jeffries put in a good word for her and she began working at once in his new film, *Mrs Gibbon's Boys*. Directed by Max Varnel and co-starring her old friend Kathleen Harrison from the *Huggets* series, the story centred around the dotty mother of three delinquent youths recently released from prison.

Then, early in November, Diana discovered she was two months pregnant. For some reason, she relayed the news to her friend Dorothy Squires before telling her husband. 'Obviously she was unsure who the father was,' Dorothy said. 'It didn't take a mathematician to work out that the baby had been conceived at around the time of her affair with John Ashley.'

The news coincided with Diana, but not Dawson, being invited to a Guy Fawkes Night party at the Buckinghamshire home of Tommy Steele's manager, John Kennedy. In fact, there was a sound reason for his not being there, for among the celebrity guests was Diana's old flame, Tommy Yeardye. She later said that finding him there had come as a big surprise, but it has been suggested that Yeardye had been seriously thinking of getting back with her, until she told him about the baby. Even so, the pair spent much of the evening huddled in a corner, reminiscing over old times, until events took a tragic turn and someone tossed a firework into the living room. This landed next to a box containing hundreds of others waiting to be set off in the garden. Within minutes, in an attack which appears to have been deliberate, the place was ablaze. The actress Sara Leighton told the subsequent inquest: 'I looked up and saw the shape of a man standing in the doorway. He threw what I can only describe as a Roman Candle. It hit the floor and a shower of very pretty pink sparks went up. By the time [Yeardye] got me into the garden, Miss Diana Dors came out through the window, and he was only just in time to get back and catch her.'

Diana's unborn baby was unharmed, and her only injury was a gash to her leg. Others were not so lucky: a young male model and his friend died of smoke inhalation, while another guest managed to get outside only to suffer a fatal heart attack on the path.

Scarcely recovered from her ordeal, Diana played a short but lucrative season at the Bal Tabarin, sex-club supremo Paul Raymond's newest but short-lived venture (it closed six months later) in Mayfair. On 14 February 1962, £6,000 richer, the Dawsons and their nanny returned to Los Angeles. 'Valentine's Day,' she told reporters at the airport, 'Love is in the air, and I won't be back to this cold place in a hurry. This baby's going to be born in the California sunshine!'

In Hollywood, Diana spent much of the next four months resting in the garden of her Angelo Drive home, while Dickie Dawson played the odd engagement. In March she taped an episode of *Alfred Hitchcock Presents*, which, through no fault of her own, resulted in a complaint being lodged on behalf of the Women's Catholic Guild. 'The Sorcerer's Apprentice' saw her working opposite former child star Brandon De Wilde. In a story by horror maestro Robert Bloch, of *Psycho* fame, Diana played the wife of a circus illusionist who comes to a sticky end when she tries to manipulate De Wilde into murdering her husband. The Guild made such a fuss – did Middle America really want to watch a heavily pregnant woman being hacked to death by a buzz saw in a magic trick that goes wrong? – that two days before it was scheduled to be aired, the episode was pulled. For many years, until being rediscovered in a studio vault, it was believed lost. Seeing it today, however, makes one wonder what all the fuss was about.

On 27 June 1962, at the Cedars of Lebanon Hospital, and this time after an easy labour despite his tipping the scales at over 10 pounds, Diana gave birth to her second son, Gary. This time the godparents were Hollywood A-listers: Liberace, Steve Allen, Terry-Thomas, and Pamela Mason – socialite wife of actor James. Having a new baby, and a two-year old who insisted upon calling his nanny 'Mom', did not however curb Diana's enthusiasm to return to work – besides which, with Dickie Dawson earning so little, she needed the money to keep up with the mortgage payments – and five weeks after giving birth she opened a new cabaret season in Las Vegas.

It was here, during the evening of 4 August, that Diana and Hollywood legend Betty Grable, who had befriended her during her first visit to the town, were involved in an unpleasant incident at the Thunderbird Hotel. Since quitting the movies in 1955, Grable – whose fabulous legs were still insured by Lloyds of London for $1m – had also enjoyed great success on the cabaret circuit. On one of their evenings off, Diana and Grable hit the clubs with a couple of male dancers, and wound up at Frances Faye's show at the Thunderbird. Here, a drunken customer asked Grable for a dance and when she refused began making homophobic comments about her escort, a man Diana subsequently named as Steve. Naturally, Steve had taken exception to this: there had been a confrontation, as a result of which he had ended up with a broken nose. The story almost certainly would have made the next day's headlines, had it not been for the singular event which occurred mere hours later: the death of 36-year-old Marilyn Monroe.

Cynics have said that Diana was completely unmoved by the tragic news, and one can understand this. Since first setting foot in America she had been regarded by many as a second-rate Monroe. Her only statement to the press came with a shrug of the shoulder: 'If she'd have had children, she wouldn't have killed herself.' Suicide, of course, would be but one of several theories applied to Marilyn's demise, though at the time it was the only one. But of one thing Diana was certain: now, Jayne Mansfield and a handful of inconsequential rivals aside, for a little while at least she would have the whole blonde bombshell arena to herself.

Chapter Twelve

A Conveyor Belt of Men

In January 1963, following a hugely successful tour of the North American cabaret circuit which had amassed Diana a small fortune, the Dawsons accompanied by Amy Baker and the children breezed into London, where Diana was to shoot *West 11* for maverick director Michael Winner. On account of a blizzard, the flight had been diverted to Manchester and, not wishing to stay there, Diana had insisted on taking the crowded overnight train to London, which had put her in a bad mood. When a reporter asked her if, as a mother of two, she still enjoyed being thought of as a sex symbol, she snapped back, 'I hate it. But it brings the money in, so who am I to complain?'

Later in the day, after she had rested, Diana apologised for having been so grumpy. When asked to define herself, she told a journalist from the *Evening Standard* that she felt she belonged in the same category as Joan Crawford, as opposed to the one occupied by Marilyn Monroe and the other 'dumb' blondes. Crawford, she said, had during her formative years been the darling of factory workers and shop girls: ordinary women who had seen her slogging it out in films such as *Mildred Pierce* and seen a way forward for themselves. America, she added, was different from Britain in that the majority of her fans were working-class females, whereas in Britain she seemed to attract only frustrated youths and dirty old men more interested in ogling her assets than her acting.

West 11, a rarely seen gem of a film, must have brought back bad memories for Diana, for it is set in Notting Hill at the time when Peter Rachman was inflicting misery on the mansion- block population – and, if this were not enough, the Rachmanesque crook at its centre is played by Dennis Hamilton's former sugar daddy, Eric Portman. Alfred Lynch plays an otherwise decent young drifter who, desperately short of money, ends up working for conman Portman, who commissions him to murder his wealthy elderly aunt. Diana, caught up in the transition between blonde bombshell and character actress par excellence, plays the bad mother who hangs around with a younger crowd she dislikes, simply because she is afraid of growing old. What we see is not always pleasant, but a deadly accurate exposé of this reprehensible man.

No sooner had shooting wrapped than the Dawsons returned to Hollywood, where Diana played a blackmailing 'boomerang baby' lounge singer, opposite John Gavin and Scott Brady in another episode of *Alfred Hitchcock Presents*. Off the set, she made a play for the dashing Brady, who she had admired as Joan Crawford's hard-bitten would-be lover in *Johnny Guitar* (1954). Sadly for her, Brady was not interested – unlike John Ashley, this was one gay man she would not turn 'the other way'.

While in England, Diana had called Dickie Dawson's (he said) only relatives, the aunt and uncle who lived in Lancashire, and talked them into flying to Los Angeles, where for a 'generous' allowance they agreed to house-sit and keep an eye on Amy Baker. Diana was hoping that the Emms would see the troublesome, tale-telling nanny in the same light as she did, and talk their nephew into getting rid of her. Now, upon meeting the Emms for the first time, she was shocked to learn that her husband had lied about his mother dying of cancer and his father absconding to America – his aunt and uncle were actually his parents! Neither was Dawson a Jew: he had 'had the operation', he now confessed, to make him more American and *appear* Jewish because all the great American comics he worshipped belonged to the faith!

No sooner had Diana taken this in and set off with Dawson on yet another cabaret tour than she received more bad news. She had just come off stage at New York's plush International Club when she received a call from Steinman, who that evening had received a cable from England. Albert Fluck had died in his sleep the previous day, aged 69.

Diana had been devastated by her mother's death, even though they had drifted apart – victims of the career Mary Fluck had strived so hard to make happen for her daughter. For her father – if indeed Bert *was* her real father – she felt almost nothing. The last time she had seen him had been during a weekend visit to Swindon while she had been shooting *King of the Roaring Twenties*. Bert had taken such a dislike to Amy Baker that he had told Diana never to bring her to his house again – and as he had also insisted that *she* never come to see him without the children, and as Dickie Dawson had refused to fire the nanny, Diana had opted to give Swindon a miss during her subsequent visits to England, something she would deeply regret for many years to come.

Diana was only lightly touched by the events of the summer of 1963 and the so-called Profumo Affair. Had she been in England when the scandal broke, if only by association, her name would almost certainly have been dragged into the drama generally credited with paving the way for the colourful and frequently hedonistic period in British history known as the Swinging Sixties.

John Profumo was Secretary of State for War under Prime Minister Harold Macmillan: earlier in the year, he had been subjected to rumours that he was having an affair with a 21-year-old model and alleged call girl named Christine Keeler – who was also reputedly the mistress of Yevgeny Ivanov, a naval attaché at the Soviet Embassy in London and a known spy. On 5 June, the rumour was shown to be true, and Profumo resigned his post. The damage to the government proved irreparable – soon afterwards, Macmillan also resigned, citing ill health. Only days after Profumo stepped down, 50-year-old Stephen Ward – the doctor who had befriended Diana while she had been shooting *Lady Godiva Rides Again* and a long-standing acquaintance of Keeler – was charged with living off the immoral earnings of prostitutes (the word 'pimp' was never used during his trial) while living at Bryanston Mews, a property he had bought from Dennis Hamilton's partner-in-crime Peter Rachman, who had died the previous November.

Stephen Ward had been supplying well-heeled friends with call girls for years – Ruth Ellis had been one – and another of his protégées was an 18-year-old Birmingham model named Mandy Rice-Davies. Both she and Keeler had also served time as Rachman's mistresses, and therefore had almost certainly known

Dennis Hamilton and maybe even Diana. Ward was refused bail, and held in custody for two weeks while the police investigated further charges against him, including one for procuring an illegal abortion. For weeks, the tabloids ran heavily censored stories of how the other half lived: drink- and drugs-fuelled orgies, vast amounts of money exchanging hands for sex, pool parties and episodes with two-way mirrors. Ward was eventually granted bail pending his trial, but evaded sentencing by taking an overdose of Nembutal. After spending several days in a coma, he died on 3 August 1963 – some tabloids noting that this was almost the first anniversary of Marilyn Monroe. Later, as with Marilyn, stories would circulate (one theory coming from entertainer Michael Bentine, a former M19 intelligence officer who had operated during World War II) that Ward had been silenced by one of Rachman's underground connections, who had sneaked into his hospital room and injected air into his veins.

Diana was lucky not to have been mentioned during the trial, save indirectly when Mandy Rice-Davies had referred to herself as 'the new Lady Hamilton'. This had been in reference to the riches she had acquired while under Ward's tutelage, a quip which went over the journalists' heads and could just as easily have been interpreted as her confessing to having been one of Dennis Hamilton's many mistresses. And of course, though Diana personally had nothing to do with the scandal, the British press – had they investigated just a little further – would have delighted in reporting that she had known at least two of the protagonists, albeit that she had loathed them both.

In Hollywood, meanwhile, Diana was enjoying a little hedonism of her own. Early in August, while Stephen Ward's suicide was making the headlines in England, she appeared with Gene Barry in an episode of *Burke's Law*. Not long afterwards she earned rave reviews as Babe Williams in New Jersey's Meadowbrook Theatre production of *The Pyjama Game*: sadly, though she often performed it on stage, she never got around to recording the show's most famous song, 'Hey There'. En route to New Jersey, she checked into New York's Plaza Hotel and decided that it would best serve as a base for the play's two-month run, being just a half-hour journey from the venue. After checking in, she told reporters in the foyer that she had decided to give her marriage another go and, as Dickie Dawson was not working much these days, she had arranged for her salary to be paid directly to him. The 'giving it a go' lasted all of 48 hours until she met a young Italian-American actor-singer-playboy named Frank Jacklone in the Plaza bar.

Jacklone was well-heeled and spoiled. His father had bought him his own nightclub so he could sing whenever the mood took his fancy, and not worry too much if the customers disliked him. Jacklone was divorced, and had weekend custody of his small son, who was frequently mistaken for Diana's whenever they went out *en famille*. He was also an alcoholic, and Diana's initial way of dealing with this was to match him glass for glass. Most days, Jacklone travelled with her to New Jersey for the show, and she appeared with him each night at his club. Within two weeks, Jackone was proposing marriage, and it was at this stage that Diana developed cold feet. One husband had treated her like dirt, she told him, while another did nothing all day but sit around the house feeling sorry for himself – the last thing she wanted was a husband who was slowly drinking himself to death. When Jacklone promised to give up the bottle and seek professional help, her excuse was that she did not want to live in New York. This presented no problem for Jacklone: he hated the hustle-bustle of the city, he said, and had been thinking of relocating to Hollywood for some time.

Diana's response was that she needed a little time away from him to think things through, though of one thing she was absolutely certain – her marriage was over. She then returned to Angelo Drive, and the very next day she, Dawson, Amy Baker and the children flew to Hawaii for a family holiday she later described as the most exciting she had ever had! And each day she called Frank Jacklone in New York, telling him how much she was missing him, that she lived only for the day when they would be together for ever!

Jacklone took her at her word, and when she returned home, Diana learned that he had rented a house just a few doors from her own on Angelo Drive – moreover, that he wanted her to move in with him. 'My summer flirtation had quickly turned into a Mafia-style drama,' she recalled. Jacklone was now accused of stalking her – and yet, when she learned a few days later that she had been booked for a tour of Australia, she called the promoter, Jack Neary, and informed him that Jacklone would be accompanying her on the trip, and not Dickie Dawson! Journalists reporting her complicated helter-skelter love life no longer knew what to make of her. Fearful that he might be cited as co-respondent, Jacklone dropped out of the tour and returned to New York.

Terrified of the prospect of having to endure the 18-hour flight on her own, and to a country that had never interested her, Diana begged her husband to travel with her. Dawson refused, it is believed because he felt the Australians might not appreciate his Jack Benny-style humour. Instead, he arranged for her to travel with an English guitarist friend, Les Bennetts, who among other things played skiffle with Lonnie Donegan, and who would accompany Diana while she was touring down under.

Diana and Bennetts arrived in Sydney, then flew on to Perth where she had been booked for a week at one of the city's leading theatres. The Australians had heard rumours of her fondness for men in uniform, and she was greeted by a military brass band and a regiment of soldiers that saluted as she strolled across the tarmac – after which she was escorted to her hotel by a motorcycle cavalcade. She later said that she had loathed the whole experience, but truthfully she loved every minute of it.

Speaking to reporters in the lobby, Diana confessed that she had dreaded coming there – not just the long flight, but the prospect of long, lonely nights in a hotel so far from home. Not that she stayed lonely for long once Jack Neary introduced her to the man who would be opening the show while they were in Perth. Darryl Stewart was a handsome band singer of around Diana's age. He was also married.

Diana would recall how Australia had seen the start of her five-year descent into madness and deepest despair – a period which, she said, would make her troubled past appear almost blissful. It is an undeniable fact, of course, that Diana had always been the sole orchestrator of her countless dilemmas, personal and professional, a situation that would never change. Within hours of meeting Darryl Stewart, the two were sleeping together and she knew all there was to know about his private life, gleaned from post-coital conversation. As had happened before, she coped with cheating on her husband by feigning guilt – Stewart was, she said, her first married man since Guy Rolfe, which in her eyes made everything all right, though this was not true. She had clearly forgotten about Rod Steiger, and one or two others.

After Perth, Diana and Stewart flew to Sydney together, separating at the airport – Stewart had engagements elsewhere in the city, though over the coming weeks they would not be apart for more than a few hours and, once Diana hit the circuit, taking in Melbourne and Brisbane, Stewart would tag along. In the meantime she received a call from Frank Jacklone, who had called her earlier in Perth where, instead of telling him she wanted nothing more to do with him, Diana had promised to make arrangements for him to join her in Sydney. Clearly she had not expected her fling with Stewart to last beyond that first week. Now, Jacklone was fobbed off with the story that Dickie Dawson was flying out to Australia with the children, while Diana crossed her fingers that the press would not get hold of a story which might result in a messy confrontation between her husband and *both* of her lovers!

There seemed every chance of this happening, especially when news of Diana's and Stewart's all-night parties began appearing in the US press – at one of which, the Australian had asked her to marry him – mindless of the fact that he was married already, and that his wife was only eight weeks off having their baby.

Sure enough: the tour ended, and Darryl Stewart announced his plans for the future, which did not appear to include his family. Within the past year he had worked in Las Vegas, as a result of which he was in possession of a 12-month US resident's card which he would not have to re-apply for, but just renew, if he returned there now. When asked by reporters if Stewart was her lover – a question they already knew the answer to – and how she felt about him 'dumping' his loved ones to go off in search of fame and fortune with her, Diana laughed. Stewart, she explained, was *not* deserting his family – he was merely heading back to Las Vegas to pick up where he had left off, and once he was settled his wife and children would be flying out to join him. In fact, virtually no one involved with the cabaret scene there had even heard of him. Then, to compound the charade and prove that she had indeed been spinning another of her tall tales, instead of boarding the plane for Los Angeles, Diana and her 'fellas' caught the next flight to Honolulu – with her footing the bill – where they frolicked for two weeks, firmly putting their respective families to the back of their minds. Then, leaving the two men with enough money to last them through the festive season – and, it would appear, hoping to give everyone the impression that *they* may have been an item, and not she and Stewart – Diana returned to Los Angeles. Her closest confidante there, Pamela Mason – separated from James and about to file for divorce – certainly seems to have attempted to add to the rumour by finding Stewart and Les Bennetts an apartment, off Sunset Boulevard. Again, Diana picked up the tab.

Diana was, of course, deluding herself by thinking that she would keep her affair with Stewart a secret for much longer – and if she was hoping to throw the heat off them by suggesting that her lover may have been gay, she was on to a loser. Stewart was not gay, but even if he and Bennetts *had* been in a relationship, few would have believed it. Middle America was still caught up in an age where it was generally believed that a man could not be gay *and* married – as in the case of known (to their colleagues) gay stars like Rock Hudson, Cary Grant and Troy Donahue, once they had walked their bride down the aisle, the rumours stopped at once. And Stewart had the added advantage that in those days made a man 100 per cent heterosexual – he had children!

Effectively, Diana and Stewart's affair was exposed not by the gossip columnists, but by his wife, who wrote to Dickie Dawson informing him and added that they had something else in common other than sex – both were pretty adept at neglecting their children. By now, Stewart had begun socialising with the Dawsons, who until receiving Mrs Stewart's letter appears to have believed Diana's story that Stewart and Bennetts were an item, particularly as they were living together. Now, rather than confront them publicly, Dawson followed them in his car to Stewart's apartment, where there was almost a punch-up in the street. Diana confessed to being the Australian's lover, but initially denied knowing he was married, let alone that his wife was about to have their third child. Stewart had lied to her, she sobbed, and she would never trust him or another man again, other than the husband she loved more than life itself! Dawson was not buying: returning to Angelo Drive, he packed two suitcases with Diana's clothes and when she arrived home later that day, she was given two hours to leave 'his' house and just two days to send for the rest of her possessions – otherwise he would personally drag everything she owned into the back yard and treat the neighbours to the biggest bonfire Hollywood had ever seen!

As had happened with John Ashley, Diana moved in with her lover – the press were told that her marriage had broken down and that she was staying with Pamela Mason. And, as before, she behaved like the wronged wife. She would divorce Dawson, she said, and marry her handsome Australian. Ashley had got her to consult Sam Brody, but Pamela Mason decided her friend needed a much more powerful ally, and fixed her an appointment with Marvin Mitchelson, considered by many to have been the best – and most expensive – divorce lawyer in America. Mitchelson (1928–2004) was just starting out in his career and would soon win Mason an unprecedented $2m settlement from actor James. In his heyday he lived in a 38-room Beverly Hills mansion and owned four Rolls-Royces. His cocaine addiction and tax fiddles were more or less open secrets in Hollywood – in 1993, when the authorities finally caught up with him, he would be found guilty of fraud and sentenced to 30 months in jail.

On 17 January 1964, Diana filed a petition with the Los Angeles Superior Court for a quickie divorce, with Mitchelson promising that it would all be over by the end of March. She later claimed to have felt disgusted with herself for the misery she had caused, though this did not prevent her from blaming Dawson for the whole fiasco, citing cruelty and accusing him of holding her a prisoner in her own home. Just what kind of cruelty she was referring to is not known. There was certainly never any evidence of physical abuse, as had happened with Dennis Hamilton – and she could hardly accuse Dawson of keeping her prisoner, for she was hardly ever home. Acting on Mitchelson's advice, Diana withdrew all the money from their joint bank account, served Dawson with an eviction order, and filed for custody of their children – the court giving him just 14 days to file a counterclaim.

It was the thought of losing his sons that spurred Dawson into action. Diana's persistent claims of how guilty she felt not spending enough time with her sons, but that she had to spend so much time away from home working to put food on the table and pay the bills, were starting to wear thin. She was of course no different from most Hollywood mothers, but Dawson's argument was that while they spent time away from their offspring furthering their careers, Diana's time of late had been spent equally on work and pleasure-seeking. It had been necessary for her to go to Australia. But, he wanted to know, had it been necessary for her to spend two weeks in Hawaii with her lover before getting back to the children? Dawson therefore filed for *full* custody of Mark and Gary, and when Mitchelson informed Diana that there was every chance of her sons being taken away from her if the law came down on his side, Diana changed her mind and on 1 February instructed Mitchelson to cancel the divorce petition. All of a sudden, the alleged brute who had made life at Angelo Drive a living hell was being described as 'a very gentle kind of man...one who would never dream of hurting a fly'!

Diana moved back into the family home, though the affair with Darryl Stewart was far from over. She flew to England – alone – for a series of cabaret engagements in Manchester, Selby and Newcastle. She also appeared in another *Armchair Theatre* production, *A Nice Little Business*, and topped the bill on ABC Television's *Big Night Out*. When asked if she was still happily married, she pointed to the new 'companion' that accompanied her everywhere – the silver mink which she said had cost her husband an arm and a leg, proof of how much he truly loved her. In fact, she had bought the coat herself.

Diana's subsequent return to Los Angeles was brief. She spent just one week with her husband and children before dashing off to Chicago for a four-week stint in the stage version of *Miranda*– the story of the mermaid made famous in the film by Glynis Johns. She was joined here by Darryl Stewart, who stayed with her until the play closed, before jetting back to his family in Australia. The reunion again caused her to cast doubts on her marriage. Dickie Dawson was the kindest man in the world, she said – obviously she had forgotten that, only weeks ago, he had been akin to the devil incarnate – and though she loved him dearly, she hated the way that each time she returned home after a trip, he had transformed their home that much more into a 'Blackpool amusement arcade'. For while other children had toys and games, or were taken to the movies or fairground, her sons had their very own indoor funfair which was starting to take over the entire house: pinball and slot machines, a bowling alley, billiard tables and a rifle range, coconut shies and other paraphernalia – all commissioned, at phenomenal cost, in his favourite colours of yellow and red. She had never really liked Hollywood, she told David English of the *Daily Express*, but she had coped until now with its artificial glamour because each time she had gone home, it had been to a little corner of England. Dawson had ruined this. But, what could she do?

What she could do, of course, was move *back* to England, which she seriously considered when she flew back for another batch of club appearances, and to film *Allez France!* – a daft comedy about a bunch of rowdy footballers en route to a match in the French capital – at Shepperton Studios and on location in Paris. All her life, she said, she had been supporting scroungers and leeches – husbands, lovers and friends – but from now on she would be living for herself. She had taken out a six-month lease on a cottage in Chelsea, not far from where she had lived when part of the Chelsea Set, since which time she had never been truly happy. She would live here until she had sold her Hollywood home, and then find a bigger place for herself and the children. Dickie Dawson, she concluded, was no longer part of the equation. To prove the point, Diana called Darryl Stewart in Sydney and asked him to fly over and move in with her. His new baby was due any day now, and when he deliberated, she offered him an ultimatum: unless he joined her immediately, they were through. Stewart called her bluff and put the phone down. In her memoirs Diana would claim that *she* had dumped *him* by letter, and revise her opinion of Australian men. In 1964 she had found them 'hot and sexy'. Twenty years later, she would observe, 'Only a woman with masochistic tendencies could fall in love with some of these rough, beer-swilling men whose manners are fit only for the outback, and whose coarse humour belongs to the lowest type of stag night imaginable.' Yet *she* had fallen for one, and in a big way!

Once again, Diana was alone – but not for long. One of the first visitors to the new abode was Kim Waterfield, who since last seeing Diana had had his own share of self-inflicted drama. In January 1960, the French police had finally caught up with him for the robbery at Jack Warner's villa, and he had subsequently been extradited – after spending 16 months in prison the authorities had allowed him to 'buy off' the rest of his three-year sentence for 100,000 *ancien francs*. Two days after breaking up with Darryl Stewart, and to welcome Kim back into the fold, Diana threw a party at the cottage, where the guests included Shirley Bassey and Philip Jones, the producer of television's long-running music magazine, *Thank Your Lucky Stars*, who was asked to bring along as many 'bright and breezy' pop stars as he could muster at such short notice.

England was in the grip of Merseymania, and Diana had already met the Beatles and some of the other big names currently riding high in the charts: she had also signed a deal with Fontana to bring out a single which she hoped would give the likes of Dusty Springfield and new-kid-on-the-block Cilla Black a run for their money. Jones had promised her a spot on his show, but as yet she had to decide on the song that would launch her pop career. Hopefully someone at the party would offer her one! Also, she told *Melody Maker*, like her character in *West 11*, she loved being around young people. And, the young woman asked her, did she as part of the 'older' generation, find long-haired men effeminate? 'Not at all,' she replied. 'If anything, they're even sexier than the regular kind. Who knows, one day soon I may find my very own long-haired lover from Liverpool!' At the party, Diana half-realised her ambition – the lover was long-haired, Welsh and spoke with a Cockney accent! – when she was introduced to 27-year-old Troy Dante (Noel Frederickson), who with his group the Infernos had recently had a minor hit with 'Tell Me', also on the Fontana label. He was also married.

As an artiste, Troy Dante is largely forgotten today. He was not a bad singer – certainly no less talented than most of his rivals and contemporaries – but sadly never had luck on his side. Diana was so enamoured of him that when she left for Paris to film the locations for *Allez France!* less than a week after meeting him, she gave him the key to her cottage and asked him to look after the place while he was away, with a view to moving in permanently. And yet, like all the other men in her life, she already suspected that Dante was only using her for his own aims:

Troy had found my Achilles heel, making me laugh all the time.

I didn't stop to think what his reasons might be for making an all-out play for me. In a vain, feminine way I chose to believe he found me attractive... Troy brought out the worst in me, and there was no doubt I did the same for him.

Though there were only six years between them, Diana was initially worried about being accused of 'cradle-snatching', and so as far as the press were concerned, she was Troy Dante's manager: now that Dickie Dawson was out of the picture, he and his group would be opening her shows – and if the managers of some of the 'non-pop' clubs who had hired her during her next tour did not like this kind of music, *she* would not be working for them either. Dante introduced her to the then elite of what then passed for Brit-Pop: Kenny Lynch, Leapy Lea and Jess Conrad all became close friends, and she promised them all a spot in the show. *Because* she was working with a pop group – which she considered beneath her – and because she needed the money to continue supporting a family she rarely saw *and* a lover, Diana often found herself performing in establishments which, a few years ago, she would never have set foot in: gay bars, and rough-and-ready working men's clubs where her spot was often secondary to the bingo. Even so, she handled herself well in every situation. In Hull, when a heckler yelled, 'Show us your tits, Diana!' she shouted back, 'I will, if you show me yours first!' Later she joked, 'I wondered how Frank Sinatra's act would have gone at Doncaster, with one dodgy organist and two neon lights?' – though at the time it was no laughing matter.

Diana also promoted her single, 'So Little Time', an English adaptation of a German song ('So Wenig Zeit') on television's *Ready! Steady! Go!* This was a fine, Kathy Kirby-style number, which sadly did not chart. Some 40 years later, Morrissey, one of Diana's biggest fans who frequently performed in front of an enormous backdrop depicting her in *Yield to the Night*, would reintroduce the song on *Under the Influence*, a compilation album featuring singers who had made an impression on him during his formative years. Also appearing on the show was Tom Jones, described by Diana in her memoirs as 'The sexiest singer ever to come out of Wales...not too much of an intellect, with a rather limited sense of humour, but a straightforward, natural person.'

Diana and Jones were obviously attracted towards each other, and she later invited him to a party at her place. Jones was married and, she said, Troy Dante was watching her like a hawk, so despite making a play for him nothing happened that night. She therefore set out to seduce him at jazz-singer Annie Ross's club in London: this time, they got as far as holding hands under the table, and smooched on the dance floor. Diana later said that Jones had told her how he had *wanted* to make love to her, but that he had been afraid of her laughing at him if he tried. 'My sense of humour and ability to laugh at almost anything had given one of the world's top sex symbols cold feet in the love department,' she later mused, 'and I am still laughing...whenever I see the Jones boy swivelling his hips and pretending to be the Great Lover!'

At the end of November, Diana signed a deal with Rediffusion for a television detective series entitled *The Unusual Miss Mulberry*. Her co-star was William Lucas, with shooting scheduled for early in 1965. The company, she said, were paying her £3,000 for each 60-minute episode. In the meantime, bidding a temporary but tearful farewell to Troy Dante, she flew to Los Angeles where she spent two weeks with Dickie Dawson and their sons. During the visit she refused to confirm whether the divorce was off or on, only that she would be reluctantly missing Christmas with her family this year because she was playing principal boy in *The Sleeping Beauty* in Bromley. What she did not add was that part of her contract insisted that Troy Dante should be her co-star.

When the pantomime closed in January 1965, Diana and Dante moved out of the Chelsea cottage and into a flat in King's Road where the neighbours were less fussy about the noise coming from their all-night parties. One of the first visitors here was Dante's wife, Barbara, who understandably wanted her man back. As had happened with Darryl Stewart, Diana denied knowing that he was married – that way, if the press began reporting unfavourably about their affair, she could plead ignorance and accuse him of leading her on, when in fact she had known the truth all along. According to her, Dante offered what he considered would prove the ideal solution to a tricky situation – Barbara could move into the flat, and everyone would live happily ever after as a *ménage à trois*! Almost certainly he never said anything of the sort, and Diana's feigned shock at such a suggestion may have helped convince herself – but few others, and certainly not her husband – that she had some principles, when truthfully she did not give two hoots what anyone thought of her. Indeed, since striding into the barracks at Swindon, 20 years earlier, she never had. Exactly what Diana said to Barbara Frederickson when they met is not on record – suffice to say, for the time being, Troy Dante's wife hastily retreated from the scene.

The Unusual Miss Mulberry had been devised by Rediffusion as a rival for the sci-spy series *The Avengers*, which had topped the ratings since 1961. Honor Blackman, Diana's catfight opponent in *Diamond City*, had recently left the show and been replaced by Diana Rigg. The producers of *Miss Mulberry* did not expect her to take – for no other reason than she was a brunette, whereas Blackman was a blonde, the theory being that blondes were more popular with male viewers (which Diana, along with Monroe and Bardot, had proved time and time again). She played Kay Mulberry, the daughter of a Scotland Yard detective who sets up her own agency and naturally never fails to solve a case. Rediffusion commissioned expensive hi-tech (for the day) sets, lots of gadgets and, of course, sexy outfits for the leading lady. In this respect, however, they appear to have come unstuck – for while Honor Blackman had kept her hourglass figure and would do so for many years to come, Diana had piled on a few pounds here and there. She was by no means overweight, not even 'cuddly' as she would be later on, but the slight addition to her girth showed up in her 'dominatrix' scenes. What is strange is that Rediffusion waited until six episodes had been canned before cancelling the series – stranger still, these episodes seem to have disappeared without ever being seen.

Feeling understandably despondent, Diana spent much of the rest of the year touring with her show. She was still living with Troy Dante, still deliberating over whether or not to divorce Dickie Dawson. In the autumn, she starred alongside Michael Bentine in *The Sandwich Man*– Bentine played a man with a sandwich board who wanders around London meeting all kinds of peculiar people, which just about sums up this too-daft-to-laugh-at farce. Despite being panned by the critics – though it was not her fault that the film was rubbish – and despite the rumour that Rediffusion had scrapped *Miss Mulberry* because they considered its star past her sell-by date – after a fallow 1966 'trawling' the clubs she so obviously detested, Diana took on her biggest challenge in years and the fulfilment of a dream – to work with one of her idols, the magnificent Joan Crawford.

'I've had a bloody good innings, and no doubt glamour *will* come back,' she had told Clive Hirschhorn of the *Sunday Express*.

Chapter Thirteen

There's a Lovely Lake in London!

Diana claimed that Barbara Frederickson's visit to the King's Road flat had robbed the place of its magic, and in the spring of 1967 she was on the move again – this time to a rented house in Berkshire. From here, she commuted to Shepperton Studios to shoot *Circus of Blood* (released in the United States as *Berserk!*) with Joan Crawford, and to make the final preparations for her divorce from Dickie Dawson. This time, there would be no going back.

Joan Crawford had especially asked for Diana, having admired her since seeing her in *Yield to the Night* – and also having some sympathy for the way she had been treated by the press, not unlike herself. In many ways, the two women were similar, particularly in their woeful experiences with the men in their lives. One of her husbands, Douglas Fairbanks Jr, had looked down his nose at her because she had come from the wrong side of the tracks, two others, Franchot Tone and Phillip Terry, had cheated on her with both men and women – though in this respect she had played them at their own game – but she had finally found happiness with husband number four, Pepsi Cola chairman Alfred Steele, only to have him die suddenly. As honorary chairwoman of Pepsi, Joan turned the set of her latest film into a massive advertising campaign for her favourite soft drink: crates of the stuff were everywhere, and on the first day of filming she sent notes to the cast and crew insisting that they help themselves – the only proviso being that they return the empty bottles, so she could report back to the company how popular 'her' product really was!

A particular thorn in Joan's side was her leading man, Ty

Hardin, a 36-year-old blond beefcake who had appeared in the television Western series, *Bronco*. Neither she nor Diana got along with him, and cracked up when they found out that his real name was Orison Whipple Hungerford Jr – behind his back, they called him 'Thigh Hard-On'. Hardin, despite spending much of his on-screen time baring his chest and flexing his muscles, was something of a religious zealot who quoted endlessly from the Bible, and frowned upon Diana and Joan's profane language and ribald anecdotes regarding 'fuck me' shoes (the ones with ankle straps which Joan made famous in the 1930s) and the many men in their lives. Diana told Joan the story (which may or may not have been true) about the time when, as Diana Fluck, she had been invited to open a garden party in Swindon and the vicar, terrified of getting her name wrong, had introduced her as Diana Clunt! Hardin does not, however, appear to have practised what he preached (albeit that he eventually became a self-styled Baptist minister) as in a colourful love-life he would go through no less than eight wives!

In the film, Joan played Monica Rivers, whose latest big-top tour is blighted by a series of gruesome murders. The first victim is a tightrope walker who plunges to his death when his wire is sabotaged. Monica tries to coerce her business partner (Michael Gough) into helping her cash in on the publicity: when he refuses, he too ends up dead. Next we have the replacement funambulist, Frank Hawkins (Hardin), whose speciality is performing his routine over a bed of spikes, without a safety net. Frank suspects that Monica may be the killer and confronts her: she is so besotted by him that, rather than deny this, she allows him to blackmail her into giving him a share of the business – we assume at this stage in the story because she is planning to bump *him* off too. Then her tearaway daughter Angela (Judy Geeson) arrives on the scene, having been expelled from school, and everything falls into place when Monica gives her the job of knife-thrower's assistant. Frank is high above the crowd when a dagger sails through the air and plunges between his shoulder blades, sending him plummeting to his death on the spikes below. And as Angela flees from the scene after unsuccessfully trying to murder her mother, she trips over a live cable and is electrocuted. Thrilling stuff!

Circus of Blood was hugely successful, almost solely on account of the pairing of Dors and Crawford, much as *What Ever Happened to Baby Jane?* had proved a smash when Joan had teamed up with her bitterest rival, Bette Davis. Joan, at 63, was old enough to be Diana's mother, yet in their scenes together she looks like a slightly older sister with, it has to be said, an even better figure. 'Her legs rival Dietrich's,' *Hollywood Screen Parade* enthused, 'and her tigress personality puts to shame most of the newest kittens who call themselves 1968-style actresses. She is a genuine movie star whose appeal never diminishes.' Diana did not in the least mind Joan getting all the plaudits: being given the opportunity to work with a star of such magnitude had been reward enough.

While shooting the film, Diana and Joan socialised together, and on the set Joan's bodyguards protected her new friend from reporters and marauding tax officials who hounded her while her divorce was going through. Some newspaper reports stated that she owed in excess of £50,000 in unpaid taxes – others that she had hardly ever paid any tax at all. The press wanted to know why she had given her Hollywood home to Dickie Dawson as part of their divorce settlement – more importantly, why was she not fighting him for custody of her children? She had, in fact, sacrificed the house on Angelo Drive to prevent this from being seized by the UK Inland Revenue. Had this happened, she said, her ex-husband and her sons would have had nowhere to live. As for Mark and Gary, Gary had been born in America: and they were both growing up as Americans and needed to stay in Hollywood so their education and social life would not be disrupted.

Dawson had of course been granted full custody because the courts had declared Diana to be an unsuitable mother, but had she *not* signed the house over to him, he would have managed perfectly well because an unexpected upward spiral in his career now saw him earning much more than she was. In 1963, Dawson had appeared in a sketch in *The Dick Van Dyke Show* and the following year had played a small part as a paratrooper in the closing scene of *King Rat*, starring George Segal. This had led to him being offered the part of Peter Newkirk, the wisecracking British corporal in CBS Television's long-running (168 episodes between 1965 and 1971) comedy series set in a POW camp during World War II, *Hogan's Heroes*.

When Diana's 'oppressors' failed to catch up with her at

Shepperton, they began camping outside her home to such an extent that she fled her rented house in the middle of the night, never to return. For several weeks her 'bolt hole' was another rented property, in Virginia Water, just down the road from her first home with Dickie Dawson. While here, the owner of the house she had just left served her with a £1,300 bill for unpaid rent and utility bills, and damage to the property – notably during one of Diana's parties, when Kim Waterfield had arrived in his helicopter and churned up the lawns. This had been a bash thrown in honour of dancer Rudolf Nureyev, who Diana said had swanned into the house looking like Marlene Dietrich in white leather, and sulked all evening because no one had treated him like he might have been her – finally exacting his revenge by urinating up against the helicopter.

To pay off this and her other debts, once *Circus of Blood* had finished shooting Diana hit the cabaret circuit once more, touring clubs mostly in the North of England – sometimes with Troy Dante, though she claimed that by now he was more interested in gambling than he was in her. She also appeared alongside Richard Johnson and Sylvia Syms in *Danger Route*. Directed by Seth Holt, who had famously made *The Nanny* (1965) with Bette Davis, this was a poor espionage thriller in which she played a rough-edged housekeeper.

Early in July, the Inland Revenue finally caught up with Diana and, joining forces with her other creditors, hit her with a preliminary administration order for a whopping £58,000. This, despite being plastered all over the press, she found far less humiliating than the incident which took place on 7 September in the foyer of London's Astoria Cinema, where she and Troy Dante were among the invited guests for the premiere of James Clavell's *To Sir with Love*, starring Sidney Poitier and Lulu. As flashbulbs popped and Diana paused to sign autographs, a private detective strode up to her and pushed a writ into her hand. Later, she claimed she had assumed the man to have been just another autograph hunter and that she had only realised it was a writ when she had opened the envelope once inside the auditorium. She knew, of course, exactly what the document was, otherwise she would have signed it along with the others. The writ was from a Devon club owner: she had failed to turn up for a cabaret engagement, or notify him that she was unable to perform that evening, as a result of which he had had to refund tickets for what had been a full house, ending up £2,000 out of pocket. Diana's excuse – that she had been suffering from another bout of pancreatitis – cut no ice with the court. This debt was added to the long list of others, and she was told that unless she settled with her creditors very soon, an application would be made for a bankruptcy receiving order.

And *still* Diana refused to draw in the reins! For a while now she had had her eye on Orchard Manor, a large mock-Tudor house set in three acres at Sunningdale in Berkshire. The asking price was £23,000, and despite being strapped for cash she bought it with money from her sons' trust funds. To her way of thinking, which it has to be said *was* a logical way of thinking, Dickie Dawson had taken Mark and Gary away from her, *he* owned the house which *she* had worked so hard to pay for at a time when he had been virtually unemployed, therefore now that he was earning more than she was, *he* should be responsible for their future! And in any case, she argued, if anything happened to her, Orchard House would be theirs. The papers were duly signed, and in April 1968 she and Troy Dante moved in.

Over the next few months, Diana worked nonstop in a desperate attempt to clear her debts. She turned down a lucrative tour of Australia, which might have taken her out of the red completely, because Dante did not wish to go there and she did not want to make the long flight alone. Between cabaret engagements she appeared in two films. *Hammerhead*, filmed on location in Portugal, was another spy thriller, only substantially better than the last one, with Vince Edwards, Peter Vaughan and Judy Geeson from *Circus of Horrors*. Diana made a play for the dashing Edwards (1928–96), the son of Italian immigrants who had hit the jackpot as television's sexiest medic in *Ben Casey*. He, however, like Scott Brady, was another gay actor she failed to seduce. *Baby Love*, on the other hand, is an oddity hardly likely to turn up in television retrospectives in today's paedophile-aware society. Diana, seen only in flashback scenes and with no dialogue, plays 'town mattress' Liz Thompson, who when the story opens has slashed her wrists in the bathtub. Her suicide is avenged by her 15-year-old nymphette daughter, Luci (Linda Hayden), who prostitutes herself to those she holds responsible for her mother's death: Liz's lover, his son *and* his wife. There is a nasty groping scene in a darkened cinema, and a brutal 'gang-banging' episode that does not make for pleasant viewing, particularly as Linda Hayden – who later starred in some of the *Confessions of...* sex comedies, was only 15 herself when these scenes were shot.

Diana's creditors, however, were baying for blood and on 31 May 1968 a bankruptcy order was filed against her, the terms of which dictated that she had until 5 July to come up with the £50,000-plus she owed. There was more drama when Dickie Dawson allowed her to spend some quality time with her sons. Accompanied by Amy Baker, Mark and Gary flew to England and for two weeks the visit appeared to be going well – until Diana suggested that maybe they should do this more frequently. The clearly psychotic nanny called Dawson and informed him that Diana was talking about keeping the boys at Orchard Manor, permanently against their will. The next day, Amy returned with her charges to Los Angeles, and Diana was contacted by Dawson's lawyer: Mark and Gary would never be permitted to visit her in England again.

Meanwhile, the July meeting with Diana's creditors reached a stalemate, and it was decided to hold a public enquiry early in October. For the second time, she was interviewed by Clive Hirschhorn of the *Sunday Express,* one of the few journalists to show her sympathy at this distressing time. In getting her point across, Diana certainly did not pull any punches:

> By rights, I should be dead by now. If I didn't have a sense of humour I'd have taken the proverbial overdose long ago, or become an alcoholic... All I can say is that I must have a hidden reserve of strength and resilience tucked away somewhere, and thank God for that! Whenever things seem absolutely hopeless, which is about fifty weeks out of fifty-two, I always seem to bounce back again. I've earned a million in my time...but to blow a million in ten years is just so damn ridiculous! And when I think of the number of people who've sponged off me, I could be sick with anger. It really is terrifying how gullible and naive I was, and still am. I was so unworldly. I fell for hard-luck stories the way boys fall for girls. And just to make things worse, I surrounded myself with gangsters, conmen and phoneys!

Diana had opened her heart and publicly acknowledged her greatest failing – always falling for the wrong man – yet within a week of her bankruptcy hearing she would do so again, albeit that the next man would be regarded as the greatest love of her life. Her case was heard by a stone-faced official receiver named Wilfred Whitehead, clearly not a Diana Dors fan. Whitehead had delved into her finances, going back to 1947 when she had been a Rank starlet. The fact that she had boasted to the press that she had earned a million pounds since then had set her up for a fall: once the figures were totted up, according to the documents requested by the court, she was seen to have earned one-tenth of this and Whitehead wanted to know what she had done with the rest. Shaking her head, Diana replied that she did not know, adding that she was the first to admit how foolish she had been not to have set any money aside to pay her taxes. When Whitehead asked her what she had done with the money she had earned so far *this* year, she confessed that every penny had gone on furnishing Orchard Manor. A list of these 'bits and bobs' was read out: a circular bed with faux leopardskin covers, crystal chandeliers, antiques and paintings, a heart-shaped shocking-pink bathtub, two-inch thick carpets, pure silk drapes, stained-glass windows and the obligatory swimming pool. An astonished Wilfred Whitehead adjourned the case until 5 December.

Diana meanwhile was offered a part in the curiously titled 'The Peeling of Sweet P. Lawrence', the pilot episode of London Weekend Television's *The Inquisitors*. This was promoted as a 'psychological detective series with gadgets', and producer Jim Goddard was hoping it would succeed where *The Unusual Miss Mulberry* had failed, in trouncing *The Avengers* in the ratings. Playing the leads were Tony Selby and Alan Lake, who Diana said she had seen in a television play, *The Thief*, that summer – and fancied. Whether she had or not is a matter for conjecture, for it had been aired while she had been singing at a club in the North. For her, the role was a return to type: that of a rough-and-ready stripper who refuses to give evidence after witnessing a murder, fearing that the killer will come after her. The first rehearsal took place in a warehouse off Bond Street on 10 October – a date which, exactly 16 years later, would strike a chill through the hearts of Diana Dors fans, as will be seen.

Diana claimed to have been excited at the prospect of working with Lake because his 'gypsy good looks' reminded her of on-his-way-out lover Troy Dante – while he initially confessed never to have seen any of her films, read anything about her in the newspapers, yet still was able to denounce her as 'Miss Tits and Lips' and 'not much of an actress' *before* they met! It was all hogwash, of course, but added to the publicity machine surrounding their whirlwind romance once they became an item.

Born in Stoke-on-Trent on 24 November 1940, Alan Lake typified the kind of man Diana felt most relaxed with: the archetypal rough diamond despite his Richard Burton-style mannerisms and deep, booming voice. Diana, of course, did not see him this way once Cupid's arrow had struck and, despite their ups and downs which rivalled any of the traumas she had gone through with Dennis Hamilton, would not have revised her opinion when she wrote about him in her memoirs many years later: 'He is a dark, handsome, brilliant actor with a singing voice that tops Tom Jones, a gift for writing poetry in the style of Dylan Thomas, and looks so pure Romany that he could be taken for any nationality.'

Lake had left school at 15, and tried his hand at any number of jobs – including working at local potteries – before enrolling with RADA. Like Diana, he had studied elocution to rid himself of his thick Midlands accent, and at the end of his first year had won an award for most promising newcomer. After completing his course he had stayed on at the academy to teach stagecraft and fencing – Lake was an expert swordsman, and performed all his own stunts in his 1965 television debut, *Hereward the Wake*, starring Alfred Lynch. From then on he was hardly off the screen, turning up in such top-rating series as *No Hiding Place, Dixon of Dock Green* and *The Saint*. Lake had also appeared in films, notably *Sky West and Crooked*, and *Charlie Bubbles* (1966/7). What Diana did not know at the time was that he had a three-year-old daughter, Katie, whom he had never seen, the result of a fling with a television producer.

During a break from their first rehearsal, Diana and Lake lunched together, and in the space of one hour had become sufficiently enamoured of each other to arrange a date for the next evening. One would hope this did not see him performing his 'party trick' – of seeing how many pints of beer he could line up on the bar and down before vomiting, the record, he later said, being 16! He took Diana to The Colony, a central London watering hole and a regular haunt of old flame Tommy Yeardye and some rather shady characters from the underworld. Here they stayed until the early hours of the morning. Lake could hardly stay on his feet, but he was sufficiently *compos mentis* to ask Diana to marry him, less than 48 hours after meeting her. She said yes, even though she was still living with Troy Dante.

The official announcement of their engagement was made on 29 October, when Lake presented Diana with an antique amethyst ring, a family heirloom. She took her time telling the world, she claimed, because this time she wanted to do things properly, which meant getting on the right side of her future in-laws – though Lake's parents, Cyril and Millicent, took to Diana at once, as did his older sister Vilma. Only then did Troy Dante learn – quite possibly by reading it in the press – that it was all over between them. He left Diana's home at once, and while most ousted lovers might have packed their belongings into a couple of suitcases, Diana provided this one with a car to pack them into, while to help with 'expenses' Dante took it upon himself to empty the slot machine she had bought for her children, to remind them of their indoor amusement arcade on Angelo Drive. 'Somehow, the picture of him, driving off in a second-hand Mini, with his pockets bulging with sixpences, sadly seemed to sum up our four years together,' she mused.

The media made much of the age gap, though there were only nine years between the couple, branding Lake a gold-digger when it was blatantly obvious by now that there was little if any gold to be dug for. 'It was love at first sight,' Diana told the *Daily Mirror*. 'I acted on impulse, but when were my instincts wrong?' When, one might equally have asked, had they ever been right?

Diana and Alan Lake were married at Caxton Hall on 23 November 1968 – in the very room where she had wed Dennis Hamilton 17 years earlier. Lake had wanted the ceremony to take place the next day, his 28th birthday, but there had been no vacant slot. Audaciously, perhaps, Diana had asked Dickie Dawson to bring their sons: not only did he ignore the request, he never told Mark and Gary about the wedding – they saw it on a news report.

The bride wore a short – very short – white dress, Lake a black crushed-velvet suit and white frilly highwayman shirt. The celebrity guests included Lionel Jeffries and John Walker of the Walker Brothers. The reception took place at the Astor Club: no expense was spared, and the party raged on for 36 hours.

Diana's wedding – or rather the cost of it – was the first item on the agenda one week later when she faced a second inquisition from official receiver Wilfred Whitehead at her rescheduled bankruptcy hearing. As a warning to other 'victims', she would later advise: 'The judge [sic] and prosecutors grill you like the Gestapo and do not feel that they have done their job correctly until they have finally reduced you to a quivering jelly...but the grand climax comes when they all get their emotional kicks as you stammer out that you have been a stupid fool, and promise to be very good and never do it again!' She claimed that the tab for the reception had been picked up by 'an anonymous benefactor who wishes to remain so', and refused to comment any further. When questioned about the hefty fees she had received for her cabaret work, she replied that it was frequently the custom of northern working men's clubs to pay the artiste at the end of the evening, cash-in-hand, and that on account of her hectic schedule she may occasionally have forgotten to declare this in her accounts: the court had contacted most of these clubs and knew exactly how much she had been paid, and how often she had 'forgotten' to pay this into her bank account, which had been almost every time! This led to Whitehead bringing up a much more serious charge – fraud, which would result in a minimum two-year prison sentence if the matter reached the high court and she was found guilty. Additionally, she was facing a charge of concealment of assets in that, in Whitehead's opinion, she had signed over her Los Angeles home to her ex-husband to prevent this from being repossessed and the money being placed in a kitty to pay off her creditors. Diana explained that she had only agreed to the 'donation' once a contract had been drawn up stating that the house would go to her sons, should Dawson predecease them, which was expected of any parent. Not only did she get away with this contract never being submitted as evidence, no questions were asked concerning her dipping into her sons' trust funds to purchase Orchard Manor.

Diana was extremely lucky not to be found guilty on both charges. Wilfred Whitehead subsequently issued instructions for an administration order to be set up so that she could pay a regular monthly sum to the court, which would be divided among her creditors. Outside the court, she let rip at those reporters she accused of only being there to gloat over her misfortune. When asked if she was flat broke, she shot back, 'You won't find *me* signing on at the labour exchange, if that's what you're hinting at!'

Only days after this hearing, Diana was in court once more, this time as a character witness for her husband, who was up on a drunk-driving charge, and one of disturbing the peace. Alan Lake had been sitting in her car outside a restaurant in Egham, Surrey – he claimed 'nodding off and minding his own business', while she had been inside dining – when a policeman had shone his torch through the window and ordered him to get out of the vehicle and take a breathalyser test. Lake did not drive, and the episode might have ended there had he not threatened to punch the young officer, who had subsequently arrested him, and caused more trouble at the police station. At the hearing, the judge dismissed the drunk-driving charge after Diana swore under oath that Lake had been sitting in the passenger seat at the time of the incident – how she could have known this when she was in the restaurant at the time was not challenged. Instead, he was fined for threatening behaviour and told that if he ever showed up in front of this particular judge again, he would receive considerably more than a fine. Diana defended him, declaring that he was 'gentle as a lamb', and that for the first and last time in his life, her husband had acted completely out of character. Yet, so far as Lake's violent streak was concerned, things would only get worse.

Chapter Fourteen

A Matter Of Faith

In February 1969, Diana announced that she was two months pregnant, news which coincided with London Weekend Television informing Alan Lake that they were dropping *The Inquisitors*. No excuse was given, though Diana suspected that the producer, Jim Goddard, had pulled the plug in the wake of the bad publicity generated by Lake's court appearance. For him – so far the only man in her life who Diana had not had to support – one rejection was more or less water off a duck's back. Though not the member of the acting fraternity's upper echelon she made him out to be, Lake was very much in demand for television roles and would never be short of work. Therefore, while he continued with his career, Diana had pondered over whether to keep the baby or not. 'Certainly, an addition to our family, although wonderful, would curtail the good times we were having,' she recalled, 'and I dearly wanted to continue these for a short while with my perfect husband.' Having children with Dickie Dawson, she said, had only made her miserable. She also believed that, at 37, she might have been too old to endure another pregnancy. Ultimately, she decided against a termination – there had been enough of these already – and set about finding a nanny who hopefully would not turn out like Amy Baker. Then, so she would not spend the next few months entirely idle, she accepted a modelling commission with Page Boy Maternity Wear. She had piled on the pounds somewhat, but she still looked stunning.

Diana's third son, Jason, was born in a London clinic on 11 September, and for a little while she took things easy. Despite vowing never to let his sons out of his sight again, Dickie Dawson allowed them to fly to England for the christening – chaperoned by Amy Baker, needless to say, and upon receipt of the money for their fares, in advance. Obviously, her ex-husband had forgotten Diana's generosity towards him when he had been strapped for cash. One of the godparents was Lionel Bart, who Diana recalled locking himself in her bathroom just as the cars pulled up to escort everyone to church. With difficulty, Diana managed to persuade him to come out, the front of his suit covered in what she believed was talcum powder. 'On the journey to the church he began to act very strangely, shouting the fact that he was an atheist and did not believe in God,' she recalled, adding how she had regretted asking him in the first place. The 'talcum powder' was of course cocaine, to which Bart was addicted, and which he had been snorting off the top of the toilet cistern!

Mark and Gary stayed on at Orchard Manor for Christmas and New Year, and got on famously with their stepfather, who is said to have been heartbroken when the time came for them to return home. Then it was back to work. Lake appeared in *There'll Be Some Changes Made* at the Fortune Theatre, and while there was offered one of the leads in Donald Howarth's comedy, *Three Months Gone*, scheduled to open at the Royal Court. He nurtured grandiose plans for himself and Diana, declaring that as they were already in their personal lives regarded as 'England's answer' to Richard Burton and Elizabeth Taylor then so professionally they would set up their own theatre company and become world renowned as the new Alfred Lunt and Lynn Fontanne – arguably America's most distinguished thespian couple. And this play, he concluded, would set that particular ball rolling. Initially, however, Diana flatly refused to play the role of sex-mad, menopausal, loud-mouthed, harridan housewife Mrs Hacker – until her husband convinced her that the role was very similar to that of the sexually repressed Martha in Burton and Taylor's acclaimed *Who's Afraid of Virginia Woolf?*

The play opened on 28 January 1970, the first time Diana had trod the boards in England for years, and the critics were there, to a man sharpening their quills in anticipation of watching her fall flat on her face. As such, they were in for a big disappointment – she threw every fibre of her being into every scene. Lunt and Fontanne they might not have been, but at the end of the evening she and Alan Lake were rewarded with a 10-minute standing ovation. 'Diana Dors may have been down,' she recalled, 'but she was most definitely not out!' Laurence Olivier, who had once wanted to work with her, rushed backstage to felicitate her on what he had considered a sterling performance. Praise indeed!

Three Months Gone subsequently transferred to the larger Duchess Theatre in the West End, where Diana was approached by another celebrity fan – Polish director Jerzy Skolimowski, who signed her to appear in *Deep End*. Diana's scene with John Moulder-Brown was completed in one day. Like *Baby Love*, the storyline involves underage sex, though attitudes towards the Skolimowsky film differed in that this was a 'lucky' 15-year-old boy (Moulder-Brown was 17 at the time) being molested by frustrated matrons as he fantasises over a slightly older girl played by Jane Asher. The film was BAFTA nominated, and one of the entries for that year's Venice Film Festival. Diana excelled as the sex-mad housewife who feigns having a fit of the vapours to get Mike (Moulder-Brown) into her cubicle, then fantasises aloud about George Best while grappling with him, flinging him around and finally grabbing him by the hair and forcing him to perform cunnilingus – perhaps one of the reasons why it has never been shown on mainstream television:

> Are *you* keen on football? It's always tackle, dribble-dribble, shoot! Why can't you look into my eyes? Stop staring at my tits! What position do you play in, boy? It doesn't matter. They're all playing all over the pitch, pushing hard…sliding in…shoot! Keep your head up, boy! [Forcing his head under her towel she has an orgasm and shoves him away.] Get out! I don't need you any more!

At around this time Diana also appeared in a cameo in Roy Boulting's film version of Terence Frisby's gentle sex comedy, *There's a Girl in My Soup*, starring Peter Sellers and Goldie Hawn – Jon Pertwee had starred in the London stage show, which had played to West End audiences for six years. She and Alan Lake had also been contracted by Yorkshire Television to appear in a sitcom – *Queenie's Castle* had been written especially for them by Keith Waterhouse and Willis Hall, and shooting was scheduled to begin in Leeds in the autumn. In the meantime, they flew to Sweden, where Diana made one of her most controversial films, *Swedish Wildcats*, a sexploitation flick from the then king of sleaze, New York-born Joe Sarno, some of whose titles – *Inside Little Oral Annie*, *A Tight Delight*, *Porked!* – say it all. In Britain and America – where they would allow it to be shown – it was released as *Every Afternoon*.

Setting what would be a precedent, Diana played a brothel madam, Margareta, who raises her two orphaned nieces to be ladies – and promptly puts them to work in her very posh whorehouse. This puts on nightly floorshows where the girls are painted like wild animals – zebras, snakes and panthers – so that the clients can 'hunt' them with oversized butterfly nets and have sex with them. 'I just *adore* mountain lions,' exclaims one old chap, a double entendre that even some Swedish viewers considered over the top. Elsewhere in the film there is a slave auction, and quite a lot of S&M, yet despite the intense sexual activity Diana is the one who walks away with the production. Alan Lake also had a small part, as one of the girls' bodyguards. Because the producer, an ebullient Swede named Vernon Becker, held them in such awe, he insisted that Diana, Lane and Urban Standar – a young actor ('Just about the most handsome young man I had ever seen!') playing Diana's Greek lover in the film, with whom she swore she would have had an affair had her husband not been there – assist him with casting the bit parts and extras. This involved visiting a club called *Le Sans-Morales*, where artistes of all ages, sizes and denomination performed sex acts live on the stage. Diana was no stranger to such events, having hosted the sex parties with Dennis Hamilton – and, according to her son Jason, as will be seen, also with Alan Lake – and later recalled how she had roared with laughter when the evening's 'humungous attraction' had found himself incapable of rising to the occasion. A few years later there would be a follow-up of sorts: *What The Swedish Butler Saw*. Featuring a mostly Scandinavian cast, this tells the story of a Victorian aristocrat who buys a former lunatic asylum and turns it into a bordello – with Diana playing the madam, naturally – unaware that it contains the secret lair of Jack the Ripper!

Diana and Lake appeared to be riding high on the crest of a wave. Then it all suddenly began collapsing about their ears when, for no apparent reason, he started drinking more heavily than usual and, following an argument with Diana which she claimed had been over some triviality, he took an overdose of barbiturates and was rushed to hospital.

Matters escalated just weeks later when, on Sunday 12 July 1970, Lake was arrested after an altercation at his local pub, the Red Lion. He and his best friend Lee Graham (who as Leapy Lea had recently had a chart hit with 'Little Arrows') had been drinking solidly all day, firstly in a lunchtime session at the pub – when astonishingly they had taken baby Jason with them – then, after downing a bottle of champagne at Orchard Manor, the pair returned to the Red Lion. Here, according to Lake, the relief manager, Anthony Stack, accused him of not paying for a drink during their earlier visit. Lake hit the roof at this, initially only swearing at Stack, but Graham went one step further and threw a pint pot at him. At this stage, two customers leaped to Stack's defence, whence the fight moved outside, others joined in, and there was an all-out brawl. Graham hit one man so hard that he broke his nose, and was himself brayed over the head with a beer-pump handle.

Almost certainly the fight would have ended there and then, had Lake not produced a flick-knife and passed this to his friend. Graham lunged at Stack, one assumes intending to stab him in the stomach, but Stack moved swiftly to one side and the blade slashed through his arm. In Diana's version of events the fight had taken place inside the Red Lion, and Graham had grabbed a *penknife* that just happened to be lying on the bar. As had happened with the earlier incident outside the restaurant, her 'evidence' was ignored by the police – quite simply, she had not been there. Some years later, writing in his column for *Euro Weekly News*, Graham explained what had really happened:

Punched and pummelled, I fell out of the door into the car park and was soon beaten to the ground. There I lay, curled up in the foetus position as the blows and kicks continued hard and fast. One of the mob had grabbed a large Martini umbrella and was stabbing and hitting me with it... Through all the chaos, numb and by now almost resigned to the amount of savagery raining down on me, suddenly sounding like the very devil himself I suddenly heard Lake's voice in my ear. 'Use this, Leapy,' it hissed, 'Use this!' I couldn't see him, but through my attackers' legs he managed to thrust the knife into my hand...

Lake and Graham were taken to Windsor police station and – astonishingly given the savagery of the brawl – held in custody for just two hours before being released on bail, pending a court hearing set for 2 September. The previous day, Diana had arranged with Dickie Dawson for Mark and Gary to spend time with her in England, solely on account of their fondness for Lake. No sooner had they arrived at Orchard Manor than Amy Baker was on the telephone to Dawson, who rather than instructing her to bring the boys home at once, agreed for them to stay with their mother until Lake's case was due to be heard in court. Diana had a better idea: *she* would accompany their sons back to Los Angeles, and Lake would travel with them so that Dawson would be able to see for himself that her new husband was not a hoodlum, but an otherwise gentle man whose only crime was having been in the wrong place at the wrong time. Just how Lake squared this two-week absence from the country with the authorities while on bail – if indeed they were even informed – is not known.

On 2 September, outside the Berkshire Assizes with Lake standing behind her and looking sheepish, Diana told reporters that she was hopeful of him getting off with a caution – he was not a violent man, she added, and this was his first offence, to which he would be pleading guilty *because* he was such an honourable man. The magistrate, however, Justice Eveleigh, did not think so and had every intention of making an example of the men in the dock. The fact that Anthony Stack had ducked to one side when Graham had gone for him with the knife had almost certainly saved his life – even so, the wound had necessitated 18 stitches. And Lake *had* passed him the knife and urged him to use it. Graham was sentenced to three years in prison for the attack, and Lake 18 months for accessory to malicious wounding. Both were told they were lucky not to be facing a murder charge, and given an additional nine months for damage to the Red Lion pub.

Outside the court, an irate Diana announced that there had been an inexcusable miscarriage of justice, and that her husband would be launching an appeal. Lake's lawyer advised him not to, declaring that, in view of the nature of the attack, he had got off lightly. Lake insisted on appealing, and the lawyer asked the court to take into consideration his client's 'ten-minute episode of befuddled judgement' and offer a reduction of sentence. Justice Phillimore did not mince his words: had *he* been the one presiding over the original trial, he declared, the sentences would have been much more severe – for Lake even more so, for in his opinion Lake was more culpable than Graham, who would not have thought of attacking his victim with a knife had not Lake passed this to him in the first place. Lake was subsequently transferred to Oxford Prison, while Graham was sent to Parkhurst. The next day, almost to a man, the tabloids made reference to Leapy Lea's one and only hit record – the fact that he would now have those famous 'little arrows' on his prison uniform.

Suffering from depression – hardly the ideal requirement for appearing in a sitcom – Diana drove up to Leeds to begin shooting *Queenie's Castle*. This was actually filmed in a real tower block (subsequently demolished) overlooking the city's open-air market – the spectacle of a miniskirted Diana strolling through this while shooting the opening sequence drew a huge crowd. Though it appears dated somewhat today – the early episodes are in monochrome – in the early 1970s it was ahead of its time regarding some of the topics which were discussed, and certainly with its then colourful language. Hylda Baker and Jimmy Jewel's *Nearest and Dearest* was criticised for extraneous use of the word *bloody*, but because this was a Diana Dors sitcom set in northern England, the scriptwriter threw in a liberal sprinkling of *pissing*, *bugger* and *bleeding*, and she was even able to get away with telling one character that when he had been born, the midwife had left the best part of him in the bottom of a tin bucket!

The series ran to three seasons, a total of 18 episodes, and aired between November 1970 and September 1972. Diana executed a perfect West Yorkshire accent and excelled as Queenie Shepherd, the domineering, 40-something matriarch of a dysfunctional family of three sons (Freddie Fletcher, Barrie Rutter, Brian Marshall) and a layabout brother-in-law (Tony Caunter, brought in at the last minute to replace Alan Lake) who is supposed to be looking after the clan while Queenie's husband is mysteriously absent. The show featured a host of future soap stars including

Roy Barraclough, Kathy Staff, Bryan Mosley and Lynne Perrie as the obnoxious neighbour and proprietress of the local cake shop, Mrs Petty. Some years later, *Queenie's Castle* would partly inspire the creators of Channel Four's cult (and much more explicit) drama series *Shameless*. Diana also appeared in a short-lived spin-off of sorts, as Di Dorkins, the manageress of a rowdy rugby team in *All Our Saturdays*, also starring Tony Caunter.

While working on the series, Diana zipped back and forth to Stoke-on-Trent to see Alan Lake's parents. When Lake was transferred to Verne Open Prison in Dorset, she also drove down there as often as visiting rules permitted, parking the Rolls in front of the building and never failing to cause a fuss when she mingled, albeit sincerely, with the other 'jailbird widows'. Her marriage, she said, had been reduced to a three-hour meeting once a month, sitting opposite each other at a Formica-topped table, next to a tea urn. Several times she launched a campaign to get him freed on 'compassionate' grounds, once aided by Laurence Olivier, who it must be said was taking a great risk to his career in wishing to have a man pardoned after being found guilty of such a violent crime. Needless to say, such pleas fell on deaf ears.

Diana had been contracted to play alcoholic, nymphomaniac single mother Helen in the television adaptation of Shelagh Delaney's *A Taste of Honey*, a role so memorably brought to the big screen by Dora Bryan. This was cancelled inexplicably – not that Diana was complaining, for rarely had she been so busy and over the next 12 months she was scarcely away from the set – whether this be the television studio or, in gaps between taping *Queenie's Castle*, on location. *The Pied Piper* was devised as a comeback vehicle for Scottish troubadour Donovan Leitch, whose career had suffered a slump in recent years. Directed by Jacques Demy of *Les Parapluies de Cherbourg* fame, this told the familiar tale of the young man who saved the people of Hamelin from the ravages of the Black Death during the 14th century. *Hannie Calder*, filmed on location in Spain and featuring Raquel Welch in the title role, was billed as a feminist Western – Welch played a grieving widow who learns how to shoot so she can get revenge on the men who killed her husband. The film finally saw her working with Ernest Borgnine, who she described as 'a darling', but she took an instant dislike to Welch, who she accused of spending too much time looking at herself in the mirror, rather than trying to improve her wooden acting. The film was released as part of a double-bill with *The Legend of Nigger Charley*, a title which did not go down well with some cinemas, who refused to show it.

Diana had just finished the second series of *Queenie's Castle* – ironically, an episode where the entire Shepherd clan end up in court on drunk-and-disorderly charges – when she received word that Alan Lake's sentence had been commuted to 12 months for good behaviour, and that he was about to be freed from prison. He was released at 7.30am on Saturday 16 October 1971, and to avoid turning the event into a media circus, Diana resisted meeting him at the gates. A number of reporters did turn up, and these were more interested in treating Lake like a returned prodigal than they were in why he had been sent to prison in the first place. How had life been for him on the inside, away from the woman he loved? He had coped, he replied, by putting on shows for the other prisoners. Had he been involved in any scrapes? Just the one, he said, when an inmate had made crude remarks about Diana and received a smack in the kisser. And what was he looking forward to most when he and Diana were reunited? 'What do *you* think?' he grinned, adding, 'And *after* I've held Diana in my arms, I need a good breakfast – and definitely no bloody porridge!'

From Verne, Lake was driven to a friend's house in Weymouth, where Diana joined him for the rest of the weekend. Here they were happy to pose for pictures with Jason, and for once she said very little save that this was the happiest day of her life. From here, the family travelled to Orchard Manor, where a 'Welcome Home Alan' banner had been draped across the gates, and where Diana laid on a sumptuous spread. Present were Lake's parents and sister, and for his first course Diana served him a soup dish filled with £6,000 in banknotes – despite her administration order and the fact that the taxman was keeping a watchful eye on her, she had put some of her undisclosed earnings to one side so that her husband would be able to treat himself to 'something nice' once he settled back into his routine.

Diana had also lined up a couple of other surprises. The first was another gift – a 17-hand grey mare named Sapphire, which caused him to burst into tears. The second was an appearance on Michael Parkinson's television chat show. This was taped and scheduled to be broadcast on 24 October, the day after Diana's 40th birthday. The BBC received a vast number of complaints when details were revealed before the broadcast, however, including an angry call from Michael Ramsey, Archbishop of Canterbury (his predecessor Geoffrey Fisher, who had denounced Diana as a wanton hussy, died just weeks before Lake was released from prison), who was perturbed that Parkinson had announced Lake as 'a rather amusing and likeable chap', and accused the BBC's head of light entertainment, Bill Cotton, of condoning criminal behaviour. Cotton therefore had no alternative but to replace the segment with a last-minute interview with actress Sarah Miles. There was to be some consolation, however, when a few days later Diana and Lake appeared together in an episode of *Dixon of Dock Green* – Lake playing a troublesome lodger and Diana his landlady.

Diana's next film was as evil housekeeper Mrs Wickens in *The Amazing Mr Blunden*, arguably her most unflattering role – fake warts and all – since that of the undertaker's servant in *Oliver Twist*. Directed by her friend Lionel Jeffries, hot on the heels of his hugely successful *The Railway Children*, and based on Antonia Barber's novel *The Ghosts*, this was promoted as a 'family horror-mystery'. It was filmed at Pinewood, and on location at Hetherden Hall, in the studio grounds (first used for *Chitty Chitty Bang Bang*, and since used many times for the *Carry On* films and *Midsomer Murders*). The action takes place during the last Christmas of World War I, and concerns a destitute war widow (Dorothy Alison) struggling to raise her three children in a tawdry Camden Town flat, who is visited by mysterious elderly solicitor Mr Blunden (Laurence Naismith), actually a time-travelling ghost, who informs her that she has inherited the 'housekeepership' of a derelict country mansion, a position she will retain until the rightful heir is traced. The house is of course haunted, and to divulge the plot from this point where the children encounter the ghosts of the long-dead former occupants, including Mrs Wickens, would only spoil the film for those who have not seen it.

Diana had almost completed the film, and Alan Lake was about to begin shooting *Innocent Bystanders* with Orson Welles, when, on 20 February 1972, he was badly injured in a riding accident. An experienced horseman, he was exercising Sapphire in Windsor

Great Park when he ducked to avoid hitting his head on a low-hanging tree branch: the horse panicked, reared up and crushed his spine against the branch before throwing him to the ground. The fact that two passers-by rushed to help only made matters worse: with no knowledge of first-aid techniques, they helped him to his feet, unaware that he had two fractured vertebrae, six broken ribs and a broken shoulder. Lake was admitted to Windsor Hospital, and later said that between bouts of consciousness, he had heard an unsympathetic doctor say, 'Put him in a side ward. Then when he pops off he won't disturb the other patients.' Certainly Diana was advised to prepare herself for the worst, and that the first 24 hours would prove crucial. She spent the whole of this period keeping a vigil next to his bed – which *was* in a side ward close to an entrance not far from the mortuary.

A few days later, Lake was transferred to Ashford Hospital, where he was put on traction. He was still in agony, and becoming addicted to the eight-times-daily morphine shots. Because he had not had a drink since the accident, he was also suffering from withdrawal symptoms. Diana could have helped him kick the habit: instead, along with the usual goodies, she brought him bottles of 'fruit juice' – effectively 10 per cent juice and 90 per cent vodka, a ritual which was continued by friends when she was working and unable to get to see him.

While hospitalised, Lake also received visitors who may not initially have been welcome, courtesy of the Lakes' new nanny, Gwen Daley, a recovering alcoholic and a devout Catholic involved with a religious order known as the Verona Fathers. Founded in 1867, they had always been heavily involved with missionary work, mostly in Central Africa, and in 1938 had established a student community (one of six in the UK) at Sunningdale, adjacent to Orchard Manor. Indeed, there was a small bridge at the bottom of Diana's garden connecting the two properties.

Diana had never liked the Verona Fathers: until 1972, she loathed Catholics, period, declaring that Catholicism was a religion of habit and fear – the fact that members of the faith had to attend Mass whether they wanted to or not, or risk eternal damnation. Her disapproval of the religion had intensified at the time of her affair with Rod Steiger, when she had found herself pilloried by Catholic groups in America. Catholics, she said then, were the world's biggest hypocrites – especially the women, who she had once publicly accused of going to church only to show off the latest acquisition to their wardrobe. 'I felt they were a sanctimonious lot who preached gloom, practised "confessing" their sins, but never did anything about putting them right,' she had added. Since arriving at Orchard Manor she had poked fun at her next-door neighbours, convinced that a group of young men living together as they did could only have been gay. Even in 1984, when her opinion of the Catholic Church had undergone a radical rehaul, she still sarcastically observed in her memoirs, under the heading FAIRIES, 'You know that saying about fairies at the bottom of the garden? I've certainly got two at the end of mine!'

The Verona Fathers always visited Lake when they knew Diana would not be around to send them packing. At first, he appears to have been as sceptical about them as she was, if not actually agnostic, but the fact that he had been brought back from the brink of death led him to believe that there really *was* a superior force out there who had wanted him to live. His friends, however, were of the opinion that the students had merely seized the opportunity to brainwash Lake when he had been at his most vulnerable – as his sister believed *he* subsequently tried to brainwash Diana and everyone else in his circle into converting to the religion. Vilma Lake is quoted (in Joan Flory and Damien Walne's *Only a Whisper Away*) as saying, 'Having accepted the faith himself, he wanted Diana, he wanted me, he wanted my mother, all of us to change. *He'd* discovered this faith, hadn't he? He went completely over the top, wanting us all to convert.'

Lake surprised everyone by recovering so quickly: just three weeks after the accident he was back at Orchard Manor and by July he was riding Sapphire again, rehearsing for his role in *The Swordsman*, in which he played the lead. After this wrapped in September, he and Diana flew to Venice for what they said was a belated honeymoon – some four years after their wedding. At the airport, Diana told reporters that this was to be a peaceful sojourn – no mink bikinis this time – during which they would discuss their new-found faith away from the media glare. Things did not turn out quite this way, however. Lake had started drinking again, so heavily this time that Diana claimed he had begun hallucinating. While in Italy the couple argued constantly though, unlike Dennis

Hamilton, this husband never raised his fist against her. One evening, as they were boarding a gondola to take a trip along the Grand Canal, a near-sozzled Lake slipped on the stone steps, banged his head on the side of the vessel and fell into the water. The gondolier managed to fish him out, covered in mud, cuts and bruises – and minus the £2,000 Cartier watch Diana had given him that morning.

The drama continued when the Lakes travelled down to Rome, where naturally they wanted to see the Vatican and imbibe the holy atmosphere of St Peter's. Hell-raiser actor Richard Harris was staying at their hotel – Diana later claimed they had bumped into him in St Peter's, which was not true – and the stunt the pair subsequently pulled hardly endeared them to the Vatican authorities or the Catholic Church. Harris, who was very rarely sober in those days, had made arrangements for a *Daily Express* photographer to snap him and Diana in the confessional – with him as the 'priest' absolving her of her sins. The fact that he used some not so very priestly language while doing so – with the doors to the confessional wide open so that passers-by could see Diana squatting in a short skirt, which was considered indecent – almost got them arrested. The pictures were wired back to the *Express* offices, but surprisingly were never published – though they have since resurfaced on various Internet websites.

Thankfully, so far as Diana's conversion was concerned, these 'offensive' images were not seen by any of the church authorities back home. Not that she had finally made up her mind to convert, until Father Teodoro Fontanari, one of the incumbents at Sunningdale, paid her a visit and suggested that the change of faith might help Alan Lake with his alcohol problem. Like her husband before her, she too was in a vulnerable state – recovering from a fall outside Wakefield Theatre Club in February 1973, when she had broken her ankle, necessitating an operation to insert a steel pin – and is believed by many to have capitulated only as a last resort to save her marriage, which had started to flounder. Immediately, Fontanari enrolled the couple for religious instruction with their local priest, Father Simon. The first to object to this was Michael Ramsey, Archbishop of Canterbury, who accused Diana of pulling yet another publicity stunt – as did senior members of the Catholic Church, who condemned her once more for the kind of life she had led: the very public shenanigans and sex parties with her first husband, the abortions, the messy divorce from her second, the criminal behaviour of her current one, the countless love affairs. She was, however, adamant that this time she had turned over a new leaf, and after a great deal of theological wrangling, in March 1974 she and Alan Lake were accepted into the Catholic faith by way of a private service at Sunningdale's Church of the Sacred Heart. Lionel Jeffries and his wife were godparents, and shortly afterwards the couple renewed their wedding vows. Diana later recalled how, when she had first entered the building, it was as if an angel had brushed by her cheek. Father Simon, not to be outdone, remembered the moment when the emotion had become too much for his celebrity recruit – how he had used Diana's hair to wipe away her tears, 'as Jesus did with Mary Magdalene'. This, many thought, was going a little *too* far.

Chapter Fifteen

Where Did They Go, All the Good Times?

For Diana, 'turning over a new leaf' while studying for and immediately after her conversion involved appearing in several (then) risqué films, including *The Amorous Milkman* (Tagline: 'He Gave 'Em Much More Than A Pinta!') and *Steptoe & Son Ride Again!* The former almost resulted in a lawsuit when soft-porn magazine *All-Colour Cockade* published a still from the film – a shot of a bare bottom that the editorial claimed was Diana's. She was outraged, or at least pretended to be, declaring that she had kept herself decent her whole life by steadfastly refusing to pose nude, and that this sort of thing was an affront to her religious integrity – obviously forgetting some of the other things she had got up to in her wilder days which might be deemed worse than taking her clothes off for a magazine. The publication subsequently launched an 'enquiry', and the owner of the much-discussed *derriere* was revealed as Jenny Westbrook, one of the bit-parts from the film.

Diana's excursions into schlock horror, which had first been tested with *Circus of Blood*, were considerably better. She worked with Peter Cushing in *From Beyond the Grave*, and with Jack Palance and Edith Evans in *The Infernal Doll*. In *Theatre of Blood*, Vincent Price played a hammy Shakespearean actor who takes revenge on those who failed to recognise his 'genius' – including Diana, a.k.a. Maisie Psaltery – by bumping them off the way the Bard did in his plays. In *Nothing but the Night*, filmed on location in Devon, she appeared alongside Christopher Lee.

At this time there was a hilarious episode when Diana made a guest appearance on Petula Clark's television show. The scenario called for her, Pet and Georgia Brown to perform 'Three Little Maids from School Are We' from Gilbert and Sullivan's *The Mikado*. Georgia's real name was Lillian Klot and, speaking of her own birth name, Diana asked the producer if their 'act' might be announced as 'The Flucking Klots'. Needless to say, the request was turned down.

Meanwhile, Alan Lake's drinking was getting steadily worse. Much as Dennis Hamilton had always craved Diana's forgiveness after each violent episode, so Lake swore to kick his habit once he had recovered from his latest bender – but never did. He was supposed to have been one of the guests alongside Dudley Moore and Zsa Zsa Gabor on the cleverly titled *Paws for Dors* – a pilot for what she hoped would be a regular chat show to rival the ones hosted by Michael Parkinson and Russell Harty – but, fearing problems, the producers brought in the Marquis of Bath at the last minute. The show fared well in the ratings, but for the time being there was no series – Diana had received a better, more challenging offer, that of Jocasta in Sophocles' controversial play, *Oedipus Tyrannus.*

The play was staged in June as part of the Chichester Festival: produced by the grandly named Hovannis Piliakin, it starred Australian actor and the festival's current artistic director, Keith Michell, in the title role and the supporting cast included Alfred Marks and Willoughby Goddard, famous for playing the villainous Gessler in the *William Tell* television series. Diana gave her all to play the part of the mythical queen who marries her own son after he murders his father – Oedipus has been at sea for many years and does not recognise her, and when the truth comes out she hangs herself, while he gouges his eyes out before wandering off into exile! It was an emotional piece, to say the least, not that this failed to prevent Diana and Michell from cracking up persistently during rehearsals. The critics who had already seen Diana in non-glamorous roles such as Mrs Wickens were enthusiastic, if not stunned that she could make herself look *so* grotesque, wearing garish make-up and a magenta wig; the ones who remembered her as 'the busty bird with the tits' – her words – from the 1950s were not. Even so, every performance was a sell-out.

Diana appeared just as unflattering in 'The Devil's Web', an episode of ITV's *Thriller* series which was filmed in October 1974 and broadcast in the New Year. She played Bessie Morne, a demented devil-worshipper hired to look after a paraplegic girl, and tries to initiate her into an evil cult. Diana later said that she had based her performance on Amy Baker, now seriously ill with lung cancer, though even the hated Amy had never been *this* bad!

Later, Diana would say that appearing in *Thriller* had put a jinx on her because, one morning en route to the studio, she had driven past a car crash and not given it much thought – only to learn that there had been a fatality. In the middle of November she began experiencing what her doctor initially suspected might have been migraines. Then on 24 November 1974 – Alan Lake's 34th birthday – she collapsed at home and, now suspecting something much worse, her doctor admitted her to London's National Hospital for Neurological Diseases. The doctor's fears were confirmed when she fell into a coma and specialists diagnosed meningitis. For 48 hours it really was touch and go. Lake, whose hand she had held all night long when told that he might die, now found their roles reversed and handled the situation badly – rushing out of the hospital to the nearest pub, and proceeding to get plastered until a pair of regulars returned him to his wife's bedside.

Over the next few days, as she slowly rallied, Diana received thousands of cards and messages from well-wishers from around the world. There were so many flowers that these flowed out into the corridor outside her room. One of the calls she received when she was well enough to sit up in bed was from Joan Crawford, but there was absolutely no word from her sons. Dickie Dawson had been informed that his ex-wife was possibly close to death, but had apparently declined to pass on the news to Mark and Gary. Later, Diana claimed she had not been surprised: she rarely if ever received birthday and Christmas cards from them, and they had never acknowledged the cards and gifts she had sent to them since divorcing their father. Gary subsequently told her how, since this time, Dawson had drilled it into the boys not to write, phone or even *think* about their mother. 'He kinda made out she was an evil woman,' he is quoted as saying in *Only a Whisper Away*. 'I just assumed, because I was anxious to see my father's point of view, that she didn't want us.' As for Diana's cards and gifts, it subsequently emerged these had been confiscated and destroyed by the jealous nanny, Amy Baker, to make it appear that Diana wanted nothing to do with them.

Diana was allowed home on 3 December, and over the next three months experienced hot flushes, dizzy spells and general weakness, which both she and her doctor initially attributed to an early menopause. In fact, she was pregnant. Since their conversion, and in any case believing herself at 43 to be beyond childbearing age, she and Alan Lake had obeyed the dictates of their new religion and refrained from using contraception. Now, in view of her frail health, she was advised to have a termination and her doctor booked her an appointment with a clinic in Brighton. Diana actually drove there, and at the last minute changed her mind. 'How could I, as a Catholic, go to mass, receive Holy Communion and pretend to be a Christian, and commit murder?' she recalled asking herself. 'I'd done that twice [sic] before in my life and still felt ashamed and guilty!'

The news was 'leaked' to the *Daily Mirror*'s agony aunt, Marjorie Proops, in May. Dismissing every aspect of her past as 'lurid and rotten', she added, 'I truly believe that for me, life is beginning at forty – well, at nearly forty-four to be exact!' Now that she had decided to proceed with the pregnancy, her doctor had advised complete rest, but she and Lake – who genuinely believed their Lunt and Fontanne moment was about to arrive – had been booked to appear in Janet Green's mystery play *Murder Mistaken* in Harrogate. Though the reviews were good and the critics appeared not to notice that there was something radically wrong with the leading man, each performance proved a triumph of mind over matter for Lake, who was suffering from the shakes. Then, on 28 August, Diana was admitted to the Westminster Hospital with dangerously high blood pressure, and doctors gave her the devastating news that she was carrying a dead child. The stillborn baby – a boy weighing just two pounds – was induced the next day. Lake suffered a temporary breakdown, which he again attempted to assuage by reaching for the bottle. Diana, though in tremendous shock, was more philosophical. This was God's will, she said, and the only way of getting over the tragedy for both of them would be to throw themselves into their work.

Diana took on the role of Mrs Bott, Violet Elizabeth's mother in the television adaptation of Richmal Crompton's *Just William* – Jason had a bit part. 'I've read all the books, and I found them absolutely delightful,' she said. In fact she had not read any of them, and hated the series. Alan Lake, meanwhile, appeared in several episodes of *Doctor Who*.

Sadly, now and over the next three years – while Alan Lake drifted from one bender to the next, and between repeated failed dry-outs at Northampton Hospital's Alcoholic Treatment Unit – the couple, singly or together, appeared in several of British cinema's most notorious turkeys: *Bedtime with Rosie, Keep It Up Downstairs, Adventures of a Taxi Driver* and *Adventures of a Private Eye* – the latter two bawdy comedies directed by Stanley Long, which led to her and Lake being approached by top-shelf mags supremo David Sullivan, who wanted them both to appear in *The Playbirds*, his soft-porn extravaganza showcasing the dubious talents of sex-queen Mary Millington. Besides a host of big-busted lovelies, the film boasted a stellar cast of British character actors including Kenny Lynch and Windsor Davies. Though Lake accepted his part, Diana refused, not wishing to be upstaged by Millington, who she initially disliked, though they would soon become close friends.

Mary Millington (1945–79) was at that time Britain's biggest female porn star, a career she had entered, having been discovered by David Sullivan, to earn money to care for her terminally ill mother. Her biggest film, *Come Play with Me*, released in 1977, also featured big British names such as Alfie Bass and Irene Handl. Later she would appear in *Eskimo Nell*, and bow out in the Sex Pistols' *Great Rock 'n' Roll Swindle*, which neither she nor Sid Vicious would live to see completed. When Diana learned that Mary had 'put her fanny to work' to pay her mother's medical bills she immediately warmed to her, and jumped at the chance to work with her when she and Lake were offered parts in Willie Roe's *Confessions from the David Galaxy Affair*, quite possibly the *worst* film Diana appeared in, which deserves no less than to be assigned to obscurity. It has Alan Lake as a sex-obsessed astronomer whose dialogue is so unbelievably cheesy that one imagines him the last 'stud' any woman would fall for – let alone Mary Millington's character who, having slept with thousands of lovers of both sexes, relies on him to give her her very first orgasm!

By now, Alan Lake's drinking was so out of control and his behaviour so obnoxious that he had started to become an embarrassment, resulting in several arrests for being drunk and disorderly. Sometimes, if not completely bladdered, he would bribe the landlord of whichever pub he was in to stage a lock-in, and afterwards forget where he was – sleeping off his excesses in someone's back garden or outbuilding, once in a ditch. Frequently, he made lewd remarks about the wives and girlfriends of complete strangers, just to start a fight. 'He always treated Diana kindly, while treating just about everybody else like shit,' Dorothy Squires said. Diana had booked him into rehab several times, but this time the treatment at Northampton Hospital, halfway through shooting *David Galaxy*, was much more horrendous than the usual drying out – locked in his room, Lake would be permitted to drink whatever he liked, and as much as he liked, then force-fed an emetic. For a little while, the cure worked, but as soon as shooting resumed on the film he found another way of getting his kicks – cocaine. Lake snorted so much of the stuff that he developed priapism, a condition where when he developed an erection it would not subside. For sex scenes in the film he was supposed to wear a 'modesty cover', but refused – necessitating in the director calling cut when he tried to actually penetrate Mary Millington in front of the entire set, and his being ordered into the bathroom to 'take care' of his problem.

Mary Millington was a profoundly disturbed woman. A self-professed 'one-quid whore' – in that each time she went to bed with a man, he had to pay her a token one pound in advance so that she thought herself at least worth something – she was also a serial kleptomaniac who frequently stole things she did not need just for the fun of it, and who was not averse to handing the items in before leaving the shop. On 18 August 1979, shortly after finishing her scenes in *The Great Rock 'n' Roll Swindle*, she was apprehended for stealing a necklace from a jeweller's shop in Barnstead, Surrey. The next day, rather than risk jail when her case came up in court – she had several other convictions waiting to be taken into consideration – she swallowed a fatal overdose of paracetamol.

The Lakes ignored friends who advised them not to attend Mary Millington's funeral, for fear that the Catholic Church might take exception to them hobnobbing with her porn-star colleagues and contacts from the London underworld. Lake was so drunk that he fell down several times during the ceremony, and Diana treated the event like she was guest of honour at some glitzy premiere – she later said because Millington would have wanted this. Three weeks later Gary Dawson, now 17 and almost six-feet tall, flew over from Los Angeles. Lake insisted on a 'best mates' weekend in Blackpool, with Diana staying home but insisting that they take Jason to see the town's famous illuminations. Leaving the boys in their suite at the plush Imperial Hotel, Lake headed for a North Shore nightclub, got into a fight and pulled a knife on bouncers who tried to eject him from the premises. He subsequently spent the night in a police cell, and was fined for possession of an offensive weapon. In view of the incident with Leapy Lea, he was lucky not to have been sent back to prison. Matters escalated so far as his drinking was concerned in January 1980 when his mother, to whom he had been very close, succumbed to cancer. His behaviour, exacerbated by intense grief, spiralled so out of control that Diana packed her bags and left him, taking Jason with her.

For a week, Diana stayed with friends in Brighton, and there was even talk of divorce until Alan Lake called her and promised to mend his ways. Once again he checked into a drying-out clinic. When asked by a local reporter why she was so insistent on staying with a man whose finger had been on the self-destruct button almost since she had first known him, she shrugged her shoulders and replied, 'Alan has to put up with *my* faults. The least I can do is put up with his!' So that Jason would be spared seeing his father at his very worst, however, he was sent off to boarding school. The press, who did not know the whole story, made much of this.

In the midst of this melee, Diana had begun writing her memoirs. In 1977 she had signed a contract with W.H. Allen, and adapting the *ABC* theme used by Marlene Dietrich for her 1961 autobiography, she had very quickly completed *For Adults Only*. Released on 14 February 1978 – Valentine's Day was, she said, her favourite day of the year, even more so than Christmas – within three months it had sold over 100,000 copies. The more raunchy, no-holds-barred *Behind Closed Dors* had followed in 1979 and now, with Jason away from home, she shut herself up in his room for seven weeks and slaved away at her autobiography *propre* (in that it was not another *ABC*), *Dors by Diana: An Intimate Self-Portrait*. She chose Jason's room, she said, because he was the one she loved the most at the time she was writing it – Mark and Gary she hardly ever saw (she once facetiously remarked that she doubted she would even recognise them if they passed her in the street), and her relationship with her husband was so strained, some days she could not stand being near him. To add to the atmosphere of the workplace, she covered the walls with hundreds of photographs of those she had loved and loathed over the years. So far as is known, she wrote every word herself and, unlike many celebrities, did not employ a ghostwriter.

While Diana was beavering away at her memoirs, her son Gary – something of a chip off the Dawson block who had worked a few of the smaller Los Angeles clubs, playing piano and doing impressions – relocated to England for a while and enrolled at the Guildford School of Music. To celebrate having him home – in what she regarded as a massive victory over Dickie Dawson – Diana bought Gary a Ford Granada. Only weeks after being handed the keys, he was arrested for failing to stop after an accident – he had clipped a stationary car, spun around in the road and careered into a telegraph pole. Not only this, the Granada was not insured, and he did not have a valid British licence. Diana accompanied him to the magistrates' court, where she argued on his behalf that he *did* own a US driver's licence which permitted him to drive there at the age of 16 – therefore he had assumed he would also be permitted to do so in England. Her pleas fell on deaf ears. Gary was fined £140, and banned from driving for three months.

In the hope that Gary might stick around – and that he and Jason, and Mark should he ever come over to England, might have their own place to entertain their friends and not disturb the 'adult goings-on' at Orchard Manor – Diana commissioned a lodge to be constructed just inside the gates of her home. For Alan Lake and herself, she planned a Romanesque-style swimming pool with underwater lighting – a structure so elaborate it would take over a year to complete. To help pay for it she appeared in any number of television chat and game shows, and in *Children of the Full Moon*, part of the *Hammer House of Horror* series.

Considering some of the dross she had been in recently, this made-for-television movie is possibly her finest work of the 1980s. A pair of newlyweds wander off into the woods after their car breaks down, and stumble upon an old mansion and its odd assortment of inhabitants: Mrs Ardoy – Diana, with a becoming West Country accent – and her brood of eight fostered werewolf children!

There was also another pilot for a chat show, *Open Dors*, which aired on Southern Television – Diana's first guest was a woman she could not stand, television clean-up campaigner Mary Whitehouse. This led to a seven-part series, still for the regional network, and featuring other 'reluctant celebrities' she disliked, just to give each show that extra edge of expectancy: she discussed pornography with anti-porn campaigner Lord Longford, nude revues with revue supremo Paul Raymond, and the royal family with anti-royalist MP Willie Hamilton – most of whom were not able to get a word in edgeways once Diana climbed on to her opinionated podium! She followed this series with a six-parter that *was* aired nationwide, during the then all-important lunchtime spot. Each episode of *The Diana Dors Show* was given a different theme: clairvoyance, clothes, food – and, of course, sex. This time the guests were 'eccentrics' like herself that she admired: Jeffrey Archer, Spike Milligan, Scottish journalist Fyfe Robertson, and fashion-guru-extraordinaire, Molly Parkin.

In 1981, Diana added another string to her multi-faceted bow when she appeared as the Fairy Godmother in the promotional video for Adam and the Ants' hit 'Prince Charming'. The record shot straight to Number 1 in the British charts in September 1981, where it remained for four weeks, but it was the video that was largely responsible for a bland, repetitive song selling millions of copies worldwide. Filmed at Shepperton Studios, a place which held fond memories for Diana, it starts off with Adam Ant, the Boy Cinders being bullied by his ugly sisters – and who of course gets to go the ball, once Diana has transformed his toy car into a pink Cadillac, and him into a rather fetching Regency figure. As midnight strikes, he does not turn back into the scullery boy but takes turns emulating Clint Eastwood (in *For a Few Dollars More*), Alice Cooper, Rudolf Valentino and Dick Turpin! Diana looks magnificent in a sparkly black dress, and had great fun learning and performing the cult 'cross-arm' dance with Ant, his musicians and the dozens of glamorous extras – not one of which even comes close to outshining her. 'Adam Ant is lovely, very professional and very intelligent – for a pop star,' she recalled. 'That is not to say that all pop stars are stupid, but he is very clever and knows exactly what he's doing and where he's going, so I have great respect for him.'

On 23 October, Diana celebrated her 50th birthday with a sumptuous bash thrown by her publishers at a private club in Kensington. Later in the evening this transferred to Skindles nightclub in Maidenhead, where Alan Lake presented her with a pink, heart-shaped cake decorated with huge breasts and a pair of oversized lips. The card read, 'Happy Birthday, Miss Tits & Lips'. Lake had wanted all three of Diana's sons to be present: Gary made his excuses, but Mark had not even responded to the invitation, or sent her a card. It was at this stage, allegedly, that she stopped caring about him. Time after time she had offered an olive branch to the Dawson boys – several times going to the trouble of flying to Los Angeles just for the weekend to see them, almost always to no avail where Mark was concerned.

Not long afterwards, as if they had glimpsed into the near future, Diana and Lake redrafted their wills. According to Dorothy Squires, Diana much admired Joan Crawford for having bequeathed 'not one cent' to her two eldest adopted children, Christopher and Christina – neither had treated her kindly, and shortly after Joan's death in 1977, Christina had begun penning her horrendous (many believed fabricated) kiss-and-tell, *Mommie Dearest*. 'Who knows, Diana may have been expecting her two older sons to do the dirty on her the way Crawford's daughter did,' Dorothy said, 'though God knows they wouldn't have been expecting her to die at fifty-two.' In the new will, Diana left her entire estate to Lake and vice versa, barring trust funds for Gary and Jason. Gary was further named as Jason's legal guardian, should anything happen to his parents. As for Mark, the son who had ignored her persistently since her split from Dickie Dawson – not least of all on her recent birthday, when everyone else had made such a fuss – not only did she bequeath him nothing, she actually disinherited him.

The birthday bash was to be the first party of many. Now that

Alan Lake had gained some control over his drinking, Diana began arranging 'soirées' at Orchard Manor that harked back to her hedonistic days with Dennis Hamilton. It was as if she was subconsciously aware that time might have been running out. Visitors to the house reported the couple growing their own cannabis, that this was Lake's only vice now that his drinking was restricted to fruit juice and mineral water. Whether Gary Dawson played any part in these get-togethers is not known, though the 'action' was witnessed by 12-year-old Jason when he came home from boarding school, as he recalled in an interview with the *Daily Mail*: 'My dad used to get drunk with Richard Harris and Oliver Reed. I'd come home from school and they'd all still be talking rubbish with the room smelling of cigarettes and alcohol. Lionel Bart had a cocaine habit, so he'd get trashed...Oliver Reed and Dad would have sword fights on the lawn.'

Jason elaborated on the hidden cameras in the bedrooms, and in the jacuzzi where the orgies and drugs binges could be watched on a giant screen in the sitting-room: 'It was a more up-to-date version of the two-way mirror. Some of the girls were wise to it. Mum and Dad just said, this is what happens, and I thought it was completely normal... It was definitely not how a child should be brought up. I don't think I should have been exposed to the things I saw.'

Though there were no new film roles in the offing, Diana busied herself with book promotions and cabaret appearances. She had added a new song to her repertoire, 'Where Did They Go?', which Harry Lloyd and Gloria Sklerov had written 10 years earlier for Peggy Lee. A portentous number of the same stamp as Peggy's earlier smash hit, 'Is That All There Is?' – which Diana had persuaded her friend Dorothy Squires to record – the lyrics suited her perfectly. The singer reflects on the positive aspects of her life – the lovers, the laughter, now gone forever – as she adds another candle to the cake. Sandie Shaw also recorded the song, but in view of the unforeseen tragedy waiting just around the corner, Diana's version is that much more poignant. Heartbreaking, even.

On the flipside of the record was a song called 'It's You Again', a meaningless ditty compared with the stupendous A-side, though it meant a lot to Diana because she duetted on it with Gary. If, however, she was hoping that singing with her son would keep him by her side just that little bit longer, she was mistaken. Not long after the record's release, Gary returned to his father's house in Los Angeles.

No sooner had Gary's plane taken off when, on 24 June 1982, Alan Lake found Diana in the garden at Orchard Manor, doubled up in pain. Her doctor admitted her at once to Windsor's Princess Margaret Hospital where surgeons performed what started out as a routine operation to remove an ovarian cyst – save that once this had been cut out, they discovered cancerous tissue which necessitated a hysterectomy.

Alan Lake tried to keep the news from Diana that she had cancer, but she learned the truth a few days later from her specialist. Devastated as she must have felt, once discharged from hospital she flung herself into her work as if nothing was untoward. She decided at once not to tell her sons – Gary and Mark would not care, she said, and she did not want Jason upsetting 'over nothing' because she truly believed that she would beat the disease. She was booked for a course of chemotherapy at Charing Cross Hospital – the sessions made her so ill she had to be kept in overnight after each one. Now that he had kicked the bottle and his own career was more or less back on track, Alan Lake was busier than ever but never once left her side. In her worst moments, Diana asked for Father Simon, the priest who had helped them with their conversion – the young man had left the priesthood, though, and no one knew how to find him. Despite feeling terribly weak on account of her treatment, when asked to stand in for an indisposed Gloria Hunniford, who then had an afternoon programme on Radio Two, she did not hesitate – her only stipulation was that she would not be expected to work the controls on her desk.

On 11 August, Diana and Alan Lake also surprised many people – not least of all the thousand mourners – by turning up at the funeral of Violet Kray, who had died of cancer the previous week. Wearing a black dress and sunglasses, she delivered a wreath – one of over 300 – to Violet's flat in Shoreditch, before heading for the church at Chingford. Later it emerged that Diana had known London's most notorious twins, currently serving life sentences for murder, for a number of years. Both Ronnie and Reggie Kray had attended Dennis Hamilton's parties at Woodhurst, when they had been starting out in their life of crime: Diana had visited

Reggie several times in the past year, since his transfer from Parkhurst to Broadmoor, and Violet had met up with Diana at Orchard Manor. She always believed that, despite their well-documented brutal gangland activities, the Krays' name should not have been synonymous with violence and evil – indeed, in her opinion they had been given a raw deal. 'It is easy to kick people when they are down, and much of the backbiting which goes on even now in the underworld where they once appeared, is jealousy on the part of their lesser contemporaries,' she observed, adding that the brothers had 'always remained totally within their own business' and that there were worse criminals around today – child-killers, for example – who were receiving far more lenient prison sentences than those which had been handed down to the Krays. She may have had a point. But would she have been of the same opinion if the judge who had sentenced Alan Lake to just 18 months had been less lenient towards him?

Diana's appearance at Violet Kray's funeral saw her being contacted by Don Boyd, with a view to Diana portraying her in a forthcoming biopic, *The Krays*. Diana declined for no other reason than she felt the chemotherapy sessions she was undergoing would affect her taking on a major challenge, though she would have been perfect in the role – one only has to study the famous photograph of Reggie and Ronnie, wearing boxing gloves and standing on either side of their mother, to see the uncanny resemblance between the two women. *The Krays*, starring former Spandau Ballet real-life twins Martin and Gary Kemp, would not see the light of day until 1990, when Violet was played by Billie Whitelaw.

Between hospital appointments, Diana spent much of the next few months resting at home. Only her closest friends knew the exact nature of her illness, and a sterling effort was made to keep the news from Jason. So far as is known, Gary and Mark – and the public at large – first found out on 7 October, when she was interviewed at Orchard Manor by breakfast televisions's Nick Owen. Looking radiant in a pale-blue kaftan, and seated next to her fabulous swimming pool, she tried to respond to Owen's questions honestly, the smile rarely fading from her face. Her expression clouded over, however, when he asked, 'Are you scared of cancer?' It was an insensitive if not stupid question, but she gave Owen her reply, 'Of *course* I'm scared. But I shall fight it all the way. It's chosen the wrong person in choosing *me*!'

Such bravado when facing the toughest fight of her life could only be admired. Just one week later, Eamonn Andrews 'nabbed' Diana for her second *This Is Your Life*. This time there were tributes from Liberace, who knew about her illness, and Bob Hope, who did not. The one which thrilled her the most, however, was the satellite-link message from Mark – she had not seen her eldest son for four years – and Gary, who told her, 'When you were taken ill, you really gave us a big scare, Mom. I've been thinking of all the things I kept meaning to put in all those letters I kept meaning to write!' And in time-honoured *This Is Your Life* fashion, this was the programme's big surprise – for the boys were not in Los Angeles, but right there in the studio, along with Mark's wife, Kathy. Hugging them all as the credits rolled, Diana burst into tears. 'It was all bullshit,' Dorothy Squires said. 'They didn't care about their mother at all. They'd just been told she had cancer and might not have long to live. They wanted to get her on side again, for obvious reasons!'

In May 1983, Diana joined TVam's *Good Morning* team for a weekly slot, *Diet with Diana*. She was paid £600 for each appearance, which – despite the TV company's policy on such matters – she demanded, and received, cash-in-hand. Recently there had been a change in the law resulting in a 10-year limit on bankruptcy, which meant that her debts had now been discharged, but Diana was still up to her tricks of not always declaring her earnings. Each week, along with 12 volunteers from the public, she was weighed live on air to see how many pounds she had lost since the previous show. She started off by tipping the scales at a staggering (for her) 200 pounds, and vowed to have reduced this to her regular weight of 140 pounds by the end of October – her 52nd birthday. Diana *did* lose weight, but tragically it was on account of her illness and not through dieting.

At around this time, Diana also 'made her peace' with Swindon – not that she had ever had anything to reproach herself for so far as the town of her birth was concerned. Indeed, some of its past dignitaries should have been asking her to forgive *them*. Now, the mayor, James Masters – himself recovering from a serious illness – saw her on television and invited her to the opening of the new

Vickers Airfield. She also officiated at the annual Trade Fair, where she spent most of her time helping out at the Cancer Research stall. Afterwards, in the mayor's car, she took a nostalgic trip around the town. Her old school, Selwood House, had been demolished but her childhood home on Marlborough Road was still there – after Bert Fluck's death it had been passed on to her mother's sister, Kit, then after her death it had been left to Diana, who had sold it. 'The place means nothing to me now,' she had said at the time. 'Why should I hang on to it?' During this final trip to Swindon, the establishment that interested her most was the hospice, where after speaking to several cancer patients she was shown the portrait of herself which had taken pride of place since the building had been erected. Diana would subsequently donate privately, and generously, towards its upkeep.

While appearing on TVam, Diana was offered the title role in the stage version of *What Ever Happened To Baby Jane?* scheduled to open in the West End in January 1984. She had marvelled at the film, starring long-time rivals Bette Davis and Joan Crawford, and while working with the latter had joked that if they ever decided upon a remake, she would make the perfect Jane! Bette Davis had of course turned the part of the unhinged ex-musical comedy star into her own personal monster. The Crawford part, that of Jane's long-suffering, wheelchair-bound sister, Blanche, was to have been played by former *Crossroads* star, Noele Gordon. When it was discovered that she too was undergoing treatment for cancer (she died in April 1985, 11 months after Diana) – and when on 3 September Diana was readmitted to Princess Margaret Hospital, the production was shelved.

Diana's cancer had returned with a vengeance and had now spread to her lower intestine. Alan Lake was in Greece, shooting an episode of *Hart to Hart*, and flew home at once to be told by surgeons that, following a four-hour emergency operation, Diana was lucky to still be alive. And yet she only remained in hospital for four days before discharging herself and – having missed just one *Diet with Diana* – returning to work. On 28 October, she stepped on to the scales to reveal that she had achieved her target by shedding 56 pounds. The public knew by now, however, that the loss had not come about by way of dieting.

Diana also had another dilemma to contend with: her husband's failure to cope with her illness. As her condition deteriorated, so he became increasingly paranoid about losing her – telling close friends that if she died, then he too would want to die. Lake went for days on end without sleeping, terrified that if he did, he would wake up and find her gone. When he stopped eating because much of the time Diana was too unwell to eat, and when he began hallucinating through lack of sleep, she realised that, despite how wretched she felt, desperate measures were called for regarding his health. Therefore, to afford them both a little respite, she persuaded him to enter the Cardinal Clinic, a unit specialising in psychiatric disorders. Lake stayed there for three weeks, until the beginning of December, when he discharged himself to tape a guest appearance with Diana in Cilla Black's television spectacular.

Diana continued working with TVam until early in the New Year, despite feeling so ill at times that it was an effort to get out of bed. Alan Lake begged her to reconsider when she was offered the part of Violet in the film adaptation of Nell Dunn's acclaimed stage play, *Steaming*. Dunn, famed for gritty dramas such as *Poor Cow* and *Up the Junction*, had set the piece – something of a precursor to television's later *Loose Women*, in the steam room at a bathhouse, where a group of very opinionated women let rip about the men in their lives. The film was directed by Joseph Losey, and appearing with Diana were Vanessa Redgrave, Sarah Miles, and Brenda Bruce. She was no longer undergoing chemotherapy treatment – her illness had progressed too far for this to have any effect – and she was taking 'cancer tablets' which were just helping control the pain. Even so, at times this was so bad that she had great difficulty walking. She had also virtually stopped eating, unable to keep anything down.

Diana managed to finish the film, but on 28 April she was readmitted to the Princess Margaret Hospital where, two days later, surgeons removed an intestinal blockage. By now the cancer had spread to her bone marrow and elsewhere, to such an extent that it would now prove inoperable. Alan Lake was given the news he had been dreading: Diana was dying.

There were radio news bulletins virtually every hour and it was impossible to open a newspaper without seeing Diana's photograph. Even the *Daily Express*'s frequently acid-tongued

Jean Rook confessed she had been walking around for days with a lump in her throat. On 2 May she wrote in her column:

> Di, a nation is praying for you. You're our solid 'Golden Oldie', the very best of unbeatable British. We love you and are proud of you for what you've been for fifty-two years. Our own! Bounce back, soon!

A priest was summoned, and Diana was given the last rites. Desperate to look her best, even as she approached the end, Diana asked Alan Lake to brush her hair and help her change out of the regulation hospital garb and into her favourite polka-dot nightdress. Around her neck she wore the gold DORS necklace he had given her some time ago – until her final operation, she had never once removed it, not even while sleeping. Lake was holding her hand when, during the early hours of 4 May 1984, she fell into a coma. At a little after nine that same evening, she quietly slipped away.

Epilogue

The next day, Diana's death made the headlines in every British newspaper. Alan Lake's statement to the press had been heartfelt, and to the point:

> I have lost my wife and soulmate. My son has lost a friend and mother, and the world has lost a legend.

Diana's funeral took place one week later at Sunningdale's Church of the Sacred Heart. Befitting the legend she had been for the past four decades, she was attired in a gold lamé gown and cape: the DORS necklace would be buried with her. Three Catholic priests officiated at the ceremony: Fathers O'Sullivan and Dominic, and, of course, Teodoro Fontanari.

Dozens of celebrities turned out to mourn her: Dorothy Squires, Lionel Blair, Freddie Starr, Barbara Windsor, Shirley Bassey, Danny La Rue (who had borrowed one of the Darnell gowns to impersonate her) and impressionist Faith Brown were but a few. A six-foot cross of pink rosebuds and white carnations from Alan Lake and Jason lay on top of the coffin. The card read, 'To my own sweet love. Only a whisper away. Love always.' The words 'Only A Whisper Away' would subsequently be inscribed on Diana's gravestone. A huge wreath had been sent by the Krays – Reggie had wanted to be released from prison to attend, but permission had been denied and the twins' elder brother, Charlie, came instead.

Right up to the very last minute, when the cortege was about to leave for the one-mile journey to the church, Alan Lake expected Gary and Mark to make an appearance. They did not, and were 'represented' by two single red roses – rumour had it that one of Diana's friends, perhaps Lionel Jeffries, had sent them so that her sons would not be made to look bad.

At a time when such things were rarely done, the requiem mass was relayed, via loudspeakers, to the hundreds of fans and locals standing outside the church. Patrick Holt recited Scott Holland's poem, 'Death Is Nothing At All'. Lionel Jeffries read from *Corinthians* and representing the people of Swindon was Mayor Jim Masters, who read a eulogy inside the church and at the graveside. The hymns included 'Morning Has Broken', 'Ave Maria', and 'Amazing Grace'. Soprano Wendy Kessack sang Handel's 'I Know That My Redeemer Liveth'. Alan Lake, holding on to Jason, plucked a rose from the cross he had sent and dropped it into the grave as the coffin was being lowered.

Few of Alan Lake's friends expected him to cope well – if at all – without his beloved wife. Shortly after Diana's death, he burned most of her clothes, including the fabulous Darnell gowns. She had been so beautiful and unique, he said – he certainly was not wrong there – that absolutely no one else would have been worthy of wearing them.

Half-heartedly, Lake continued working, among other things appearing in the police drama *Juliet Bravo* and an episode of *Hammer House of Horror*. He organised a memorial service, which was held on 24 July in the crypt of Westminster Cathedral – a surprisingly small turnout in comparison with Diana's funeral. When not working, he spent much of the time lounging on their bed, watching videos of her old films – not drinking, but high on drugs, anything to dull the pain he was feeling. He is known to have made at least one suicide attempt – swallowing pills and vomiting them back.

October and November were the months Lake was least looking forward to: Diana's birthday, their wedding anniversary, and his 44th birthday, the first he would be celebrating without her. Friends prepared to rally around him when the time came: in the meantime they thought it best to let him grieve and spend some quality time with Jason. None of those close to him even thought about another important date – 10 October, what would have been 16 years to the day since they first met.

Unable to keep the place going now there was no money coming in from Diana, and in any case no longer wishing to live there now she was gone, Alan Lake had put Orchard Manor on the open market. The asking price was a whopping £325,000, still less than its actual value in the hope of a quick sale. On 10 October, he drove Jason to the local railway station where he caught the train to London – now a budding actor, the 15-year-old had a small part in Stephen Poliakoff's *Breaking the Silence*, soon to open at the Barbican. His father, Jason later said, had seemed a little morose, but no more so than he had been since losing Diana.

Later in the day, Lake was due to show a prospective buyer around the property. At 12.45pm, he was interviewed on the telephone by Jean Rook – she was writing about the house in her *Daily Express* column. According to Rook, Lake's closing words to her were, 'It's a bad day today, the day I met her. It's bedlam.' Exactly one hour later, Lake walked into Jason's room, pushed the barrel of a shotgun into his mouth, and pulled the trigger. His housekeeper, Honor Webb, was downstairs when she heard the explosion. It was she who found him and called the emergency services.

There was no suicide note – perhaps no need for one. In spite of their ups and downs, after a lifetime of men, most of whom had alternated between using her as a meal ticket and a punchbag, Diana had truly found the love of her life with this man, and he had already confided in friends that he intended to remain celibate for the rest of his life because women of her quality came around only once in every lifetime. Death had therefore been preferable to his hell on earth.

Jason was contacted at once. 'I didn't cry,' he recalled. 'I was afraid that if I began, I'd open the floodgates and never stop.' Twenty years after the event, he would remain unjudgemental when speaking of his father:

He tried his best but he couldn't face life without my mother. When you're as depressed as he was, you don't think of the consequences. You just want the pain to go away, although part of me thought, 'You shouldn't have left me.' Killing himself was the bravest thing my dad could have done.

One week later, Lake's daughter Katie and Jason, along with many of the friends and celebrities who had flocked to Sunningdale earlier that summer, turned up again to say goodbye. One of the greatest (albeit at times traumatic) love stories of the 20th century was laid to rest in a little Berkshire cemetery.

Perhaps the last word should be left to former lover Rod Steiger, who, reluctantly acknowledging the tiresome 'British Monroe' tag which had got in the way of her achieving the same greatness as a Dietrich or a Garbo, could not have summed her up more perfectly:

> She was instinctively intelligent, which is the most important kind of intelligence as far as I'm concerned. She was a splendid woman, but behind it all, her talent was swamped by an image. *That* was Diana's greatest tragedy, that many people never saw past the blonde hair and the fabulous figure.

Bibliography

Anon: 'Diana Dors' Hottest Love Affair', *Suppressed*, 1957

Anon: 'Diana Manages a Pop Group', *Melody Maker* 1964

Anon: 'Joe Has the Eye of the Tiger', *The Visitor* (Morecambe), 2004

Balfour, John: 'Are British Films Going Too Far?', *Daily Sketch*, 1955

Bret, David: Interviews with Dorothy Squires

Bret, David: *Rock Hudson*, Robson Books, 2004

'Candidus': 'Close That Dors!', *Daily Sketch*, 1956

Chatfield, Phillips: 'What Diana Dors Never Knew About Her Ever Lovin' Hubby', *Confidential*, 1957

Connolly, Mike: 'Up The Hammer & Sickle, Girl!', *Hollywood Reporter*, 1956

Dors, Diana: 'Intimately Yours!', *Titbits*, 1953

Dors, Diana: 'My Wonderful Guy', *Picturegoer*, 1956

Dors, Diana: 'Nobody Knows What I've Been Through', *Woman*, 1981

Dors, Diana: 'Where I Went Wrong', *Woman's Own*, 1974

Dors, Diana: *Behind Closed Dors*, W.H. Allen, 1979

Dors, Diana: *For Adults Only*, W.H. Allen, 1978

Flory, Joan & Walne, Damien: *Diana Dors: Only a Whisper Away*, Lennard, 1987

Franklin, Olga: 'The Amazing Miss Fluck', *Daily Sketch*, 1956

Graham, Lee: 'The Red Lion Incident', *Euro Weekly News*, 2007

Hirschhorn, Clive: 'Diana Dors: A Boadicea for the 20th Century', *Sunday Times*, 1982

Hirschhorn, Clive: 'Diana Dors: I'm Out in the Cold, Now!', 'Diana Dors: I'm Trouble Prone!', *Sunday Express*, 1966

Hirschhorn, Clive: 'Diana Dors: Men Were My Downfall', *Sunday Express*, 1978

Hopper, Hedda: *The Whole Truth & Nothing But*, Doubleday, 1963

Iddon, Don: 'The Girl from Swindon Goes Hunting for a House', *Daily Mirror*, 1956

Lake, Jason: 'Diana's Demons', *Daily Mail*, 2004

Macnab, Geoffrey: *J. Arthur Rank & the British Film Industry*, Routledge, 1993

Muller, Robert: 'Diana, Queen of Cannes', *Picturegoer*, 1956

Muller, Robert: 'The Trials of Diana Dors', *Picturegoer*, 1955

Parsons, Louella: *Tell It to Louella*, Putnam, 1961

Pugh, Marshall: 'Hamilton Regrets the End of the Dors Romance', *Daily Mirror*, 1956

Quinlan, David: *Quinlan's Film Stars/ Quinlan's Illustrated Directory of Film Character Actors*, Batsford, 1981 & 1986

Roen, Paul: *High Camp: A Gay Guide to Camp & Cult Films Vol. 1*: Leyland, 1994

Rook, Jean: 'Di, the nation is praying for you...', *Daily Express*, 1984

Rook, Jean: 'Diana Dors, the Great Survivor', *Daily Express*, 1983

Tynan, Kenneth: 'The Siren From Swindon', *Picturegoer*, 1955

Winncroft, Eileen: 'The Only English Femme Fatale', *Picturegoer* 1956

Wise, Damon: *Come By Sunday: The Fabulous, Ruined Life of Diana Dors*, Sedgwick & Jackson, 1998

Wiseman, Thomas: 'The Far from Shocking News about Diana Dors', *London Evening Standard*, 1960

Zec, Donald: 'Why Diana Thinks the World of Miss Dors', *Daily Mirror*, 1956

Other sources are acknowledged within the text.

Appendix 9

Diana Dors: Filmography

THE SHOP AT SLY CORNER
George King Productions   1946
Director: George King. Script: Edmund Percy, Reginald Long, Katherine Strueby. Photography: Hone Glendinning. Music: George Melachrino. With Oskar Homolka, Derek Farr, Muriel Pavlow, Kenneth Griffith, Irene Handle. Diana (unbilled) played Mildred. Also known as 'Code of Scotland Yard'. 91 mins.

HOLIDAY CAMP
Gainsborough Pictures   1947
Director: Ken Annakin. Script: Godfrey Winn, Sydney and Muriel Box, Peter Rogers. Photography: Jack E. Cox. Music: Bob Busby. With Flora Robson, Jack Warner, Kathleen Harrison. Diana (unbilled) played a jitterbug dancer. 97 mins.

DANCING WITH CRIME
Coronet Films   1947
Director: John Paddy Carstairs. Script: Peter Fraser, Brock Williams. Photography: Richard H. Wyer. Music: Benjamin Frankel. With Richard Attenborough, Sheila Sim, Garry Marsh, Bill Owens, Dirk Bogarde. Diana (unbilled) played Annette. 83 mins.

STREETS PAVED WITH WATER
Gainsborough Pictures   1947
Directors/Script: Joe Mendoza, Anthony Skene. Photography: Stephen Dade. With Maxwell Reed, Jane Hylton, Andrew Crawford. Diana was 4th billing. The film was abandoned.

MY SISTER AND I
Rank   1948
Director: Harold Huth. Script: Emery Bonnet, Michael Medwin. Photography: Harry Waxman. With Sally Ann Howes, Dermot

Walsh, Martita Hunt, Barbara Mullen. Diana, at the end of credits, was billed as 'Dreary Girl'. 97 mins.

PENNY AND THE POWNALL CASE
Rank   1948
Director: Slim Hand. Script: W.E. Fairchild. Photography: Walter J. Harver. With Ralph Michael, Peggy Evans, Christopher Lee. Diana (4th billing) played Molly James. 47 mins.

THE CALENDAR
Rank   1948
Director: Arthur Crabtree. Script: Edgar Wallace, Geoffrey Kerr. Photography: Cyril J. Knowles, Reginald H. Wyer. With Greta Gynt, John McCallum, Raymond Lovell, Sonia Holm. Diana, in a bit part, played Hawkins. 79 mins.

HERE COME THE HUGGETTS
Rank   1948
Director: Ken Annakin. Script: Sydney and Muriel Box. Photography: Reginald H. Wyer. With Jack Warner, Kathleen Harrison, Jane Hylton, Petula Clark, Susan Shaw. Diana (8th billing) played Diana Hopkins. 93 mins.

VOTE FOR HUGGETT!
Rank   1949
Director: Ken Annakin. Script: Denis and Mable Constanduras. Photography: Reginald H. Wyer. With Jack Warner, Kathleen Harrison, Petula Clark, Jane Hylton, Susan Shaw. Diana (6th billing) played Diana Gowan. 84 mins.

IT'S NOT CRICKET
Rank   1949
Directors: Roy Rich, Alfred Roome. Script: Gerard Bryant, Lyn Lockwood. Photography: Gordon Lang. With Basil Radford, Naunton Wayne, Susan Shaw, Alan Wheatley. Diana, in a bit part, played 'Blonde'. 77 mins.

A BOY, A GIRL AND A BIKE
Rank   1949
Director: Ralph Smart. Script: Ralph Keene, John Sommerfield. Photography: Ray Elton, Phil Grindrod. With John McCallum,

Honor Blackman, Patrick Holt, Anthony Newley. Diana (4th billing) played Ada Foster. 92 mins.

DIAMOND CITY
Rank   1950
Director: David MacDonald. Script: Roger Bray, Roland Pertwee. Photography: Reginald H. Wyer. With David Farrar, Honor Blackman, Andrew Crawford, Mervyn Johns. Diana (3rd billing) played Dora Bracken. 93 mins.

GOOD TIME GIRL
Rank   1950*
Director: David MacDonald. Script: Sydney and Muriel Box. Photography: Stephen Dade. With Jean Kent, Dennis Price, Herbert Lom, Flora Robson. Diana, in a bit part, played Lyla Lawrence. 93 mins. (*completed 1947)

DANCE HALL
Rank   1950
Director: Charles Crichton. Script: E.V.H. Emmett, Alexander Mackendrick. Photography: Douglas Slocombe. With Donald Houston, Bonar Colleano, Petula Clark. Diana (6th billing) played Carole. 80 mins.

WORM'S EYE VIEW
Henry Halstead Productions   1951
Director: Jack Raymond. Script: R.F. Delderfield. Photography: James Wilson. With Ronald Shiner, Garry Marsh. Diana (3rd billing) played Thelma. 77 mins.

LADY GODIVA RIDES AGAIN
London Film Productions   1951
Director: Frank Launder. Script: Frank Launder, Val Valentine. Photography: Wilkie Cooper. Music: Muir Matheson. With Dennis Price, John McCallum, Stanley Holloway, Pauline Stroud, Joan Collins, Ruth Ellis. Diana (3rd billing) played Dolores August (a.k.a. Bikini Baby, the film's US title). 90 mins.

THE LAST PAGE / MAN BAIT
Hammer Films   1952
Director: Terence Fisher. Script: James Hadley Chase, Frederick

Knott. Photography: Walter Harvey. With George Brent, Marguerite Chapman, Raymond Huntley, Eleanor Summerfield. Diana (8th billing) played Ruby. 84 mins.

MY WIFE'S LODGER
David Dent Productions   1952
Director: Maurice Elvey. Script: Stafford Dickens, Dominic Roche. Photography: Phil Grindrod, Len Harris. With Dominic Roche, Olive Sloane, Alan Sedgwick, Leslie Dwyer. Diana (3rd billing) played Eunice Higginbottom. 80 mins.

THE GREAT GAME
David Dent Productions   1953
Director: Maurice Elvey. Script: Basil Thomas, Wolfgang Wilhelm. Photography: Phil Grindrod. With James Hayter, Thora Hird, John Laurie. Diana (3rd billing) played Lulu Smith. 80 mins.

THE SAINT'S RETURN
Hammer Films   1953
Director: Seymour Friedman. Script: Leslie Charteris, Allan MacKinnon. Photography: Walter J. Harvey. With Louis Hayward, Naomi Chance, Sydney Tafley. Diana (making a guest appearance) played 'The blonde in Lennar's apartment'. 73 mins.

IS YOUR HONEYMOON REALLY NECESSARY?
David Dent Productions   1953
Director: Maurice Elvey. Script: Vivian Tidmarsh. Photography: Phil Grindrod. With David Tomlinson, Bonar Colleano, Sid James. Diana (2nd billing) played Candy Markham. 80 mins.

IT'S A GRAND LIFE!
Mancunian Films   1953
Director: John Blakeley. Script: Frank Randle, H.F. Maltby. Photography: Ernest Palmer. With Frank Randle, Dan Young, Michael Brennan, Jennifer Jayne. Diana (2nd billing) played Cpl Paula Clements. 102 mins.

THE WEAK AND THE WICKED
Marble Arch Productions   1954
Director: J. Lee Thompson. Script: Joan Henry, Anne Burnaby, J. Lee Thompson. Photography: Gilbert Taylor. With Glynis Johns,

John Gregson, Olive Sloane, Rachel Roberts. Diana (2nd billing) played Betty Brown. 72 mins.

AS LONG AS THEY'RE HAPPY
Group Films   1955
Director: J. Lee Thompson. Script: Alan Melville, Vernon Sylvaine. Photography: Gilbert Taylor. Music: Stanley Black. With Jack Buchanan, Janette Scott, Jeannie Carson. Diana (cameo) played Pearl Delaney. 91 mins.

MISS TULIP STAYS THE NIGHT / DEAD BY MORNING
Jaywell Films   1955
Director: Leslie Arliss. Script: John O. Douglas, Jack Hulbert. Photography: Kenneth Talbot. With Patrick Holt, Jack Hulbert, Cicely Courtneidge. Diana (top billing) played Kate Dax. 68 mins.

A KID FOR TWO FARTHINGS
London Films   1955
Director: Carol Reed. Script: Wolf Mankowitz. Photography: Edward Scaife. With Celia Johnson, David Kossoff, Joe Robinson, Primo Carnera, Sid James, Irene Handl. Diana (2nd billing) played Sonia. 96 mins.

VALUE FOR MONEY
Group Films   1955
Director: Ken Annakin. Script: Derek Boothroyd, R.F. Delderfield. Photography: Geoffrey Unsworth. Music: Malcolm Arnold. With John Gregson, Susan Stephen, Derek Farr, Frank Pettingell. Diana (2nd billing) played Ruthine West. 90 mins.

AN ALLIGATOR NAMED DAISY
Rank   1955
Director: J. Lee Thompson. Script: Jack Davies, Charles Terrot. Photography: Reginald H. Wyer. Music: Stanley Black. With Donald Sinden, Jeannie Carson, James Robertson Justice, Stanley Holloway, Stephen Boyd, Jimmy Edwards, Gilbert Harding. Diana (4th billing) played Vanessa Colebrook. 88 mins.

YIELD TO THE NIGHT / THE BLONDE SINNER
Kenwood Productions   1956
Director: J. Lee Thompson. Script: Joan Henry, John Cresswell.

Photography: Gilbert Taylor. Music: Ray Martin. With Yvonne Mitchell, Michael Craig, Olga Lindo, Marie Nye. Diana (top billing) played Mary Hilton. 99 mins.

THE UNHOLY WIFE / THE LADY AND THE PROWLER
RKO/John Farrow Productions   1957
Director: John Farrow. Script: William Durkee, Jonathan Latimer. Photography: Lucien Ballard. With Rod Steiger, Tom Tryon, Beulah Bondi, Marie Windsor. Diana (top billing) played Phyllis Hochen. 94 mins.

THE LONG HAUL
Marksman Productions   1957
Director: Ken Hughes. Script: Ken Hughes, Mervyn Mills. Photography: Basil Emmott. With Victor Mature, Gene Anderson, Patrick Allen, Liam Redmond. Diana (4th billing) played Lynn. 100 mins.

I MARRIED A WOMAN
Gomalco Productions   1958 *
Director: Hal Kanter. Script: Goodman Ace. Photography: Lucien Ballard. Music: Cyril J. Mockridge. With George Gobel, Adolphe Menjou, Jessie Royce Landis, Angie Dickinson, John Wayne (uncredited). Diana (2nd billing) played Janice Blake Briggs. 85 mins. (* completed 1956, distribution withheld until 1958)

LA RAGAZZA DEL PALIO / THE LOVE SPECIALIST
Cité Films   1958
Director: Luigi Zampa. Script: Ennio De Concini, Liana Ferri. Photography: Giuseppe Rotunno. With Vittorio Gassman, Franca Valeri, Bruce Cabot, Teresa Pellati. Diana (top billing) played Diana Dixon. 102 mins.

TREAD SOFTLY STRANGER
George Minter Productions   1958
Director: George Parry. Script: George Minter, Denis O'Dell. Photography: Douglas Slocombe. Music: Tristram Cary. With George Baker, Terence Morgan, Patrick Allen, Jane Griffiths. Diana (top billing) played Calico. 90 mins.

PASSPORT TO SHAME / ROOM 43
United Co-Productions   1959
Director: Alvin Rakoff. Script: Patrick Alexander. Photography: Jack Asher. With Herbert Lom, Eddie Constantine, Odile Versois, Brenda De Banzie, Jackie Collins, Joan Sims, Michael Caine (uncredited). Diana (top billing) played Vicki. 86 mins.

SCENT OF MYSTERY / HOLIDAY IN SPAIN
Mike Todd Jr Productions   1960
Director: Jack Cardiff. Script: Gerard Kersh, Kelley Roos. Photography: John von Kotze. With Denholm Elliott, Peter Lorre, Paul Lukas, Leo McKern, Elizabeth Taylor. Diana (8th billing) played Winifred Jordan. 125 mins.

ON THE DOUBLE
Dena Productions   1961
Director: Melville Shavelson. Script: Melville Shavelson, Jack Rose. Photography: Harry Stradling, Geoffrey Unsworth. With Danny Kaye, Dana Wynter, Wilfrid Hyde-White, Margaret Rutherford. Diana (5th billing) played Sergeant Bridget Stanhope. 92 mins.

KING OF THE ROARING TWENTIES
Bischoff-Diamond Films   1961
Director: Joseph M. Newman. Script: Leo Katcher, Jo Swerling. Photography: Carl E. Guthrie. With David Janssen, Dianne Foster, Mickey Rooney, Jack Carson. Diana (5th billing) played Madge. 106 mins.

ENCONTRA A MALLORCA   1962
Director: José Maria Ochoa
No other details. Abandoned due to lack of finances.

MRS GIBBONS' BOYS
Halstead Productions   1962
Director: Max Varnel. Script: Peter Blackmore, Will Glickman. Photography: Stanley Pavey. With Kathleen Harrison, Lionel Jeffries, John Le Mesurier, Dick Emery. Diana (3rd billing) played Myra. 82 minutes.

WEST 11
Angel Productions   1963
Director: Michael Winner. Script: Willis Hall, Keith Waterhouse.

Photography: Otto Heller. Music: Stanley Black. With Alfred Lynch, Kathleen Breck, Eric Portman, Kathleen Harrison, Freda Jackson. Diana (4th billing) played Georgia. 93 mins.

ALLEZ FRANCE!
CICC Productions   1964
Director & Script: Robert Dhéry. Photography: Jean Tournier. With Pierre Doris, Pierre Dac, Jean Richard, Mark Lester, Arthur Mullard. Diana (cameo) played herself. 90 mins.

THE SANDWICH MAN
Titan International   1966
Director: Robert Hartford-Davis. Script: Michael Bentine. Photography: Peter Newbrook. With Michael Bentine, Norman Wisdom, Bernard Cribbins, Dora Bryan, Harry H. Corbett. Diana (cameo) played 'The First Billingsgate Lady'. 95 mins.

BERSERK! / CIRCUS OF BLOOD
Herman Cohen Productions   1967
Director: Jim O'Connolly. Script: Herman Cohen, Aben Kandel. Photography: Desmond Dickinson. With Joan Crawford, Ty Hardin, Michael Gough, Judy Geeson. Diana (3rd billing) played Matilda. 96 mins.

DANGER ROUTE
Amicus Productions   1967
Director: Seth Holt. Script: Meade Roberts, Robert Stewart. Photography: Harry Waxman. With Richard Johnson, Carol Lynley, Barbara Bouchet, Sylvia Syms. Diana (6th billing) played Rhoda Gooderich. 92 mins.

HAMMERHEAD
Irving Allen Productions   1968
Director: David Miller. Script: Herbert Baker, William Bast. Photography: Wilkie Cooper, Kenneth Talbot. With Vince Edwards, Peter Vaughan, Judy Geeson, Patrick Holt. Diana (4th billing) played Kit. 100 mins.

BABY LOVE
Avton Films   1968
Director: Alastair Read. Script: Tina Chad Christian, Guido Coen.

Photography: Desmond Dickinson. With Ann Lynn, Keith Barron, Linda Hayden, Dick Emery, Troy Dante. Diana (4th billing) played Liz Thompson. 93 mins.

THERE'S A GIRL IN MY SOUP
Charter Film Productions 1970
Director: Roy Boulter. Script: Terence Frisby. Photography: Harry Waxman. Music: Mike d'Abo. With Peter Sellers, Goldie Hawn, Tony Britton, Nicky Henson. Diana (5th billing) played 'John's Wife'. 95 mins.

DEEP END
Bavaria Atelier Films 1970
Director: Jerzy Skolimowski. Script: Jerzy Skolimowski, Boleslaw Sulits. Photography: Charly Steinberger. With John Moulder-Brown, Jane Asher, Karl Michael Vogler, Christopher Sandford. Diana (5th billing) played 'Mike's 1 Lady Client'. 90 mins.

HANNIE CALDER
Cutwel Productions 1971
Director: Burt Kennedy. Script: Burt Kennedy, Peter Cooper. Photography: Edward Scaife. With Raquel Welch, Robert Culp, Ernest Borgnine, Christopher Lee. Diana (7th billing) played 'The Madame'. 85 mins.

THE PIED PIPER
Sagittarius Productions 1972
Director & Script: Jacques Demy, Andrew Birkin. Photography: Andrew Birkin. Photography: Peter Suschitsky. Music: Donovan Leitch. With Donovan Leitch, John Hurt, Donald Pleasence, Jack Wild. Diana (3rd billing) played Frau Poppendick. 90 mins.

SWEDISH WILDCATS/ EVERY AFTERNOON
Unicorn Enterprises 1972
Director: Joe Sarno. Script: Joe Sarno, Vernon Becker. Photography: Lasse Bjorne. With Cia Lowgren, Soveig Andersson, Peter Kinberg, Urban Standar, Alan Lake. Diana (top billing) played Margareta. 92 mins.

THE AMAZING MR BLUNDEN
Helmdale Films 1972
Director: Lionel Jeffries. Script: Lionel Jeffries, Antonia Barber.

Music: Elmer Bernstein. Photography: Gerry Fisher. With Laurence Naismith, Lynne Frederick, Garry Miller, Rosalyn Lander. Diana (6th billing) played Mrs Wickens. 99 mins.

STEPTOE & SON RIDE AGAIN!
Associated London Films   1973
Director: Peter Sykes. Script: Ray Galton, Alan Simpson. Photography: Ernest Steward. With Wilfrid Brambell, Harry H. Corbett, Milo O'Shea, Neil McCarthy. Diana (3rd billing) played 'Woman in Flat'. 95 mins.

THEATRE OF BLOOD
Cinema Productions   1973
Director: Douglas Hickox. Script: Anthony Greville-Bell, Stanley Mann. Photography: Wolfgang Suschitsky. With Vincent Price, Diana Rigg, Ian Hendry, Coral Brown. Diana (cameo) played Maisie Paltry. 104 mins.

NOTHING BUT THE NIGHT
Charlemagne Productions   1973
Director: Peter Sasdy. Script: John Blackburn, Brian Hayles. Photography: Ken Talbot. With Christopher Lee, Peter Cushing, Georgia Brown, Keith Barron. Diana (3rd billing) played Anna Harb. 90 mins.

FROM BEYOND THE GRAVE
Amicus Productions   1974
Director: Kevin Connor. Script: R. Chetwynd-Hayes, Ray Christodoulou, Photography: Alan Hume. With Ian Bannen, Ian Carmichael, Peter Cushing, Margaret Leighton. Diana (4th billing) played Mabel Lowe. 94 mins.

THE INFERNAL DOLL
Harbour Productions   1974
Director: Freddie Francis. Script: Herman Cohen. Photographer: John Wilcox. With Jack Palance, Edith Evans, Julie Ege, Trevor Howard. Diana (2nd billing) played Dolly. 96 mins.

THE AMOROUS MILKMAN
Twickenham Films   1975
Director & Script: Derren Nesbitt. Photography: Jim Allen. With

Julie Ege, Brendan Price, Donna Reading. Diana (2nd billing) played Rita. 86 mins.

WHAT THE SWEDISH BUTLER SAW
Films AB Robur   1975
Director: Vernon Becker. Script: Vernon Becker, Barry Downs. Photography: Tony Forsberg. With Ole Soltoft, Sue Longhurst, Charlie Elvegard, Malou Cartwright. Diana (7th billing) played Madame Helena. 93 mins.

BEDTIME WITH ROSIE
London International Films   1975
Director: Wolf Rilla. Script: Ivor Burgoyne. Photography: Mark McDonald. With Una Stubbs, Ivor Burgoyne, Johnny Briggs, Nicky Henson. Diana (3rd billing) played Aunty Annie. 76 mins.

THREE FOR ALL
Dejanus Films   1975
Director: Martin Campbell. Script: Tudor Gates, Harold Shampan. Photography: Ian Wilson. With Adrienne Posta, Lesley North, Cheryll Hall, George Baker. Diana (cameo) played Mrs Hall. 90 mins.

ADVENTURES OF A TAXI DRIVER
Salon Productions   1976
Director: Stanley Long. Script: Stanley Long, Suzanne Mercer. Photography: Peter Sinclair. With Barry Evans, Adrienne Posta, Judy Geeson, Liz Fraser. Diana (4th billing) played Mrs North. 89 mins.

KEEP IT DOWNSTAIRS
Pyramid Pictures   1976
Director: Robert Young. Script: Hazel Adair. Photography: Alan Pudney. Music: Michael Nyman. With Jack Wild, William Rushton, Carmen Silvera, Aimi McDonald, Mary Millington. Diana (top billing) played Daisy Dureneck. 94 mins.

ADVENTURES OF A PRIVATE EYE
Salon Productions   1977
Director: Stanley Long. Script: Michael Armstrong. Photography: Peter Sinclair. With Christopher Neil, Suzy Kendall, Harry H.

Corbett, Fred Emney. Diana (4th billing) played Mrs Home. 96 mins.

CONFESSIONS FROM THE DAVID GALAXY AFFAIR
Roldvale Productions   1979
Director: Willy Roe. Script: George Evans. Photography: Douglas Hill. With Alan Lake, Glynn Edwards, Anthony Booth, Mary Millington, John Moulder-Brown. Diana (4th billing) played Jenny Stride. 97 mins.

STEAMING
Worldfilm Series   1985
Director: Joseph Losey. Script: Robin Bexter, Nell Dunn. Photography: Chris Challis. Music: Richard Harvey. With Vanessa Redgrave, Sarah Miles, Patti Love, Brenda Bruce. Diana (3rd billing) played Violet. 102 mins.

Appendix II

Diana Dors: Selected Television Dramas

THE LOVELY PLACE
Douglas Fairbanks Presents   1954
Director: Leslie Arliss. Script: Gabrielle Upton. With Douglas Fairbanks Jr (host), Ron Randell, Angela O'Farrell. Diana played Angie.

THE INNOCENT
Armchair Theatre   1960
Director: Charles Jarrott. Script: Bob Kester. With Patrick Macnee, Ian Hunter, Basil Dignam. Diana played Jane Francis. Songs: 'The Point of No Return', 'Tired of Love'.

THE SORCERER'S APPRENTICE
Alfred Hitchcock Presents   1962*
Director: Joseph Letjes. Script: Robert Bloch. With Alfred Hitchcock (host), Brandon De Wilde, David J. Stewart, Larry Kert. Diana played Irene Sandini. (*The play was banned from broadcast at the time and surfaced many years later)

RUN FOR DOOM!
Alfred Hitchcock Presents   1963
Director: Bernard Girard. Script: James Bridges, Henry Kane. With John Gavin, Scott Brady, Carl Benton Reid. Diana played Nickie Carole.

A NICE LITTLE BUSINESS
Armchair Theatre   1964
Director: Guy Verney. Script: Marc Brandell. With William Franklyn, Anthony Bate, Arthur Lowe. Diana played Grace Maxwell.

WHERE HAVE ALL THE GHOSTS GONE?
Boy Meets Girl   1968
Directors: Naomi Capon, Alan Gibson. Script: David Compton, Terence Dudley. With Ray Brooks, Marty Cruikshank, Robert James. Diana played Megan Norton-Grey.

QUEENIE'S CASTLE
Yorkshire Television –18 episodes in three series   1970–72
Producers: John Duncan, Ian Davidson. Script: Keith Waterhouse, Willis Hall. With Tony Caunter (replacing Alan Lake), Freddie Fletcher, Barry Rutter, Brian Marshall, Lynn Perrie, Bryan Mosley. Diana played Queenie Shepherd.

ALL OUR SATURDAYS
Yorkshire Television   – 6 episodes   1973
Producer: Ian Davidson. Script: Stuart Harris (two episodes, the rest unknown). With Tony Caunter, Norman Jones, Anthony Jackson, Doug Fisher. Diana played Di Dorkins.

THE DEVIL'S WEB
Thriller   1975
Director: Shaun O'Riordan. Script: Brian Clemens. With Andrea Marcovicci, Cec Linder, Ed Bishop. Diana played Bessy Morne.

CHILDREN OF THE FULL MOON
Hammer House of Horror   1980
Director: Tom Clegg. Script: Murray Smith. Photography: Frank Watts. With Christopher Cazenove, Celia Gregory, Robert Urquart, Jacob Witkin, Victoria Wood. Diana (3rd billing) played Mrs Ardoy.

Appendix 999

Diana Dors: Vinyl Discography

'A Kiss and a Cuddle' / 'I Feel So Mmm'
(1954) No other details

Swingin' Dors: 'The Point of No Return'; 'That's How It Is'; 'Let There Be Love'; 'Namely You'; 'Imagination'; 'Roller Coaster Blues'; 'The Gentleman Is a Dope'; 'April Heart'; 'I'm in Love for the Very First Time'; 'Crazy He Calls Me'; 'Come By Sunday'; 'Tired of Love'
(1960) Pye NPL 18044

'April Heart'/ 'Point of No Return'
(1960) Pye 7N 15242

'So Little Time' / 'It's Too Late'
(1960) Fontana

'Security' / 'Gary'
(1966) Polydor

'Passing By' / 'It's a Small World'
(1977) EMI

'Where Did They Go?' / 'It's You Again' (with Gary Dawson)
(1982) Nomis NOM 1

Va-Va-Voom! Screen Sirens Sing
Also featuring Sophia Loren, Mamie Van Doren, Jane Russell, Jayne Mansfield, Elke Sommer, Marilyn Monroe, Ann-Margret.

Diana sings: 'So Little Time'; 'Come By Sunday'; 'Crazy He Calls Me'

Me; It's Too Late.
(1985) Rhino RNTA 1999

Index